TINKERTOWN

TINKERTOWN

*A Wheatfield, an
Airbase, and Us:
The Story of Midwest
City & Tinker AFB*

JIM WILLIS

*Foreword by General Roger Brady USAF
(ret.)*

ArtStrings, LLC

Copyright Page

Library of Congress Cataloging-in-Publication Data
Names: Willis, Jim, 1946 – author. I Brady, Roger, 1946 – foreword.
Title: Tinkertown: A wheatfield, an airbase, and us
Description: Winchester, Kentucky : ArtStrings, LLC. (2024)
Identifiers: ISBN 979-8-218-38536-1 (paperback)

Cover design by Jim Willis
Cover photo by Sarah Richter/Pixabay

Epigraph

"Life can only be understood backwards,
But it must be lived forwards."
... Soren Kierkegaard

Midwest City .... Then & Now

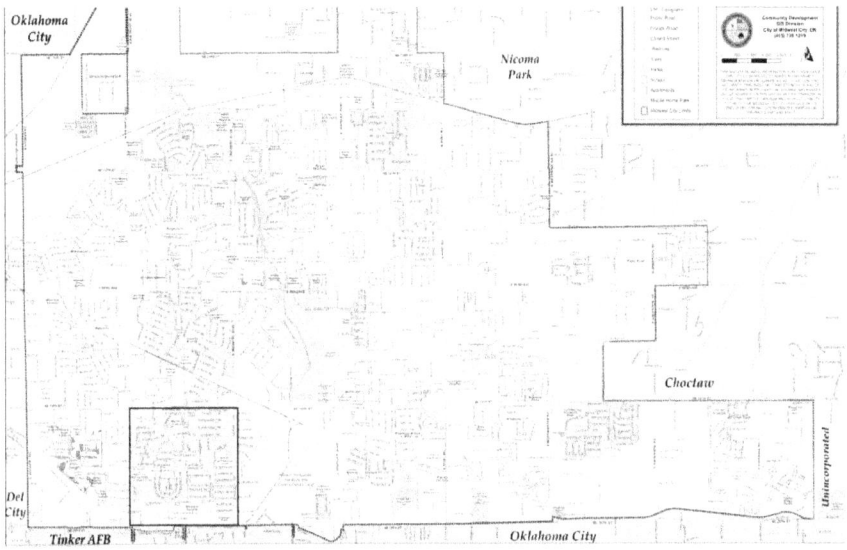

Map of Midwest City today. The "Original Mile" is the boxed square on the lower left. Tinker
AFB sits on the south side of Southeast 29th Street along the bottom.

Community Development Division, Midwest City, Oklahoma

Dedication

To the people of Midwest City and Tinker AFB and to those great Shetland ponies

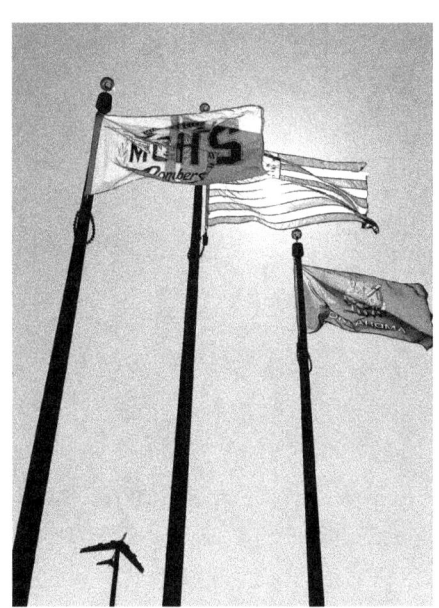

The MCHS, American, and Oklahoma flags and a replica of a B-52 Bomber fly over the MCHS Vietnam Memorial Plaza and History Center.
(Photo by Jim Willis)

Other Books by This Author

https://scribblerjim.wixsite.com/jim-willis-web-site

The 1960s on Film (with Mark Miller)
Daily Life in the 1960s Counterculture
Tweeting to Freedom
Documents Decoded: 1960s Counterculture
From Twitter to Tahrir Square: Ethics of Social and New Media Communications (Vols. 1 & 2) (Bala Musa & Jim Willis)
Daily Life Behind the Iron Curtain
100 Media Moments that changed America
The Mind of a Journalist
The Media Effect: How the News Influences Politics and Government
The Human Journalist
Prelude to Greatness: Sooner Football in the 1990s
(with Jay Smith)
Images of Germany in the American Media
Reporting on Risks (with Albert Adelowo Okunade)
The Age of Multimedia and Turbonews
The Shadow World
Journalism: State of the Art
Surviving in the Newspaper Business

Acknowledgements

"It takes a village," is a saying that applies to both the theme of this book as well as its factual and contextual content. Although, as the author, I lived this life growing up in Midwest City, Oklahoma, across from Tinker Air Force Base, I have remained unaware of much of this area's history until I began researching my hometown. And that research came to involve a lot of human and archival sources and artifacts.

As for the latter, one is the town statue of the town's founder, W.P. "Bill" Atkinson, standing by one of his prized Shetland ponies in the plaza commemorating the town's "Original Mile." As I got to know the story of Midwest City and Tinker Air Force Base, I came to realize how much that statue signifies about both places that merged into this *Tinkertown* of which I write.

As for the people whose stories and written works I plumbed for facts and anecdotes, there are many. I should start with Bill Atkinson's granddaughter, Cindy Mikeman, who was my first interview. She greeted me at the Atkinson pony farm estate in his spacious home that is now owned and curated by Rose State College, of which Cindy is a vice president.

Of immense help were my former MCHS classmates and friends Bob Osmond and Marty Thompson, joint curators of the Midwest City High School History Center. These two have volunteered endless hours in keeping the history of the school and town alive, taking over for its founding curator, Shirley Nicholson, who played a key role in the development of the Mid-Del School District, as Oscar Rose's administrative assistant. Bob and Marty have hosted me at the history center and have provided me a lot of detailed information over the past several months. Donations to the work of the MCHS History Center can be made by addressing them to Midwest City History Center, P.O. Box 30793, Midwest City, OK 73140.

Another important source is Barbara Sessions, a career professional communicator who is heavily involved in chronicling the history of the Mid-Del School District. Barbara, who is also a former classmate, has been very helpful in my research.

For his expertise on Air Force matters, I talked a lot to Gen. Roger A. Brady (Ret.), who is a classmate from MCHS and who has become a good friend over the years. Roger was gracious enough to write the Foreword for this book.

Chad Williams, research director for the Oklahoma Historical Society, was also helpful as he guided me to the society's online Gateway that produced a myriad of original documents and news stories. Turns out that Chad himself is a Midwest City High School graduate. Another online database that proved helpful was the archive collection of stories from *The Daily Oklahoman* and *Oklahoma City Times*, which morphed years ago into the present-day newspaper, *The Oklahoman*.

I had a very good conversation with Dr. Rachel Hopkins, who produced a wonderful podcast focusing on the ponies of early Midwest City for KGOU Radio in Norman, Oklahoma.

Five Oklahomans who produced a great deal of written history about Midwest City and Tinker are Susan Moeri Lee, Scarlett J. Bowman, James L. Crowder, Hugh E. Cosby, and Lily Boettcher, and you will see several references to their work.

Of key interest was a "Reconnaissance Level Architectural/Historical Survey of the Original Mile of Midwest City, Oklahoma," done by Meacham & Associates of Norman, Oklahoma.

Added to these are the interviews did with many others who grew up in Midwest City like Ken Brust, son of the town's first mayor Royal Brust; Morri Rose, grandson of the legendary founder of the school district, Oscar V. Rose; Pam Olson Boettcher, Mary Clem Good Morris, Steve Vargo, Ralph Lantz, Mary Kay Havens, and my own sister, C.J. Powell, who lived the pioneering story of Midwest City alongside me.

Added to these memories were the information and stories provided me by friends like Chaniece Kennedy, Jane Vickers Bogan, Linda Stell Smith, Rusty Weller, Michael Hawk, Betsy Bray Baustert, John Carpenter, Cindy Jo Lopez, and the many other MCHS graduates who responded to my queries in social media seeking anecdotes and memories. Included in that list were some former aviation maintainers and relatives who talked about the stress and experiences of working at Tinker.

Especially helpful for these latter comments were the Facebook pages of Midwest City High School History Center, Midwest City, Oklahoma: History & Memories; Friends of Midwest City, Midwest City Memories and Midwest City Memories II, Midwest City Bomber Alumni Memorial Page, and the MCHS Class of 1964.

A special thanks goes to my longtime friend and publishing advisor, Joe Hight, owner of *Best of Books*, a large independent bookstore in Edmond, Oklahoma, and former managing editor for features for *The Oklahoman*. Joe is still educating young people about journalism as the Edith Gaylord Chair of Journalism Ethics at the University of Central Oklahoma. Joe is also an author and his book, *Unnecessary Sorrow*, is a poignant but tragic story of his brother's life and death.

I also want to thank members of my writer's group here in new hometown of Winchester, Kentucky. John and Julie Maruskin, Marie Parsons, Bill McCann, and Jeanne Grant Lister have all listened to anecdotes from this manuscript and have lent their advice and support over the year. It means a lot to me.

The photos in the book are ones that I've shot myself, along with several photos from the royalty-free site of Pixabay.com, and their talented contributors. The silhouetted plane in the hangar in Chapter 10 is by a photographer who lists themselves on Pixabay only as member No. 12019. The retired B-52 in the Foreword is by Pixabay's "Nightowl." The sonic boom jet on the Chapter 5 page is by member No. 12012.

The kite flyer on Chapter 4 is by a photographer who lists themselves as Shlomaster. The "Berlin Train" photo on Chapter 1 is by Pixabay contributor Tobias Rhebein. The closeup of the Shetland ponies face in Chapter 4 is by Sarah Richter, while the Rose State photo in Chapter 12 is from the college's public information department. The "Save Tinker" photo in Chapter 11 is from the Tinker public affairs office/history center, as are two other photos of aircraft in hangars. The appearance of U.S. Department of Defense (DoD) visual information does not imply or constitute DoD endorsement. The photo of the white puzzle pieces in Chapter 9 is from Public Domain Pictures. The Chapter 13 photo of me on the beach is by Anne Willis.

Speaking of her, I want to thank my lovely and talented wife Annie who is the one really responsible for my starting this book in the first place. Over the years I've told her many stories about Midwest City in the early years, and she has been so patient in listening. It was she who encouraged me to put these stories into a book, which is exactly what I did. Thanks, Annie!

I am indebted to all these people and the others with whom I've been chatting about our hometown for the past year. As I said in the opening, *"It takes a village."*

Foreword: The Tinkertown Partnership

By Roger Brady, MCHS '64

Editor's Note: Roger Brady is a retired four-star general in the Air Force, having served 41 years of active duty. He is a command pilot with more than 3,900 hours in tanker, airlift, and training aircraft. His final assignment was as Commander, U.S. Air Forces in Europe. He and his wife Litha are graduates of MCHS, University of Oklahoma, and Colorado State University. Roger also holds an M.A. from Southeastern Baptist Theological Seminary. The couple have three children, Caroline, Andrew, and Lincoln, an almost-Labrador Retriever of uncertain provenance.

A tale of a town and an adjacent military base that benefit from each other's existence is not unique, but the histories of Midwest City and Tinker Air Force Base are intertwined in ways that affect the generations that spend their formative years there and are forever impacted by the experience. *Tinkertown* is one man's story of his hometown, but everyone and every hometown has a story. Readers of this book will react differently, depending on their own personal experiences, but there are aspects to this story that resonate beyond the facts of the story itself, beyond Midwest City and beyond Oklahoma.

The story of Midwest City and Tinker Air Force Base is one that has much larger implications than just a town and a military base who flourish together economically, though being the largest employer in the state with a $3.5 billion impact is, as they say, nothing to be sneezed at. But the deeper meaning of the relationship is not as obvious unless one has experienced it. It is a story about community and, I believe, a story of important relationships and the development and sustainment of culture that do not receive sufficient consideration in today's busier lives. There are some aspects of this community that are like none other, and the reader has been given a peek inside this community from the personal experiences of a master teller of stories. This is Jim's story.

Roger and Jim, MCHS Seniors 1964
Bomber Yearbook

While we all have stories of our hometown and its impact on us, few of us will preserve them in writing. Jim Willis has been writing about the society around him for several decades, but *Tinkertown* may be his most impactful and certainly the most personal effort to date. Unlike Jim, who spent almost his entire growing-up years in Midwest City, I was a latecomer to the community. My father had retired from teaching and coaching high school football and moved the family to Midwest City for my junior year to be closer to his new employer, and so I could play football at one of the best programs in the state.

Jim and I became acquainted playing football but were not especially close in those years. We hung out in different but overlapping social circles in what was a rather large high school. Being of the Vietnam generation when we headed off to college, we were both in ROTC, which was mandatory when we first entered. He was Navy, and I was Air Force. We bumped into each other occasionally during our time at the University of Oklahoma, but our chosen paths would take us in different directions. Our next encounter after college would come almost fifty years later. Jim saw some picture online from the fiftieth reunion of our 1964 class and reached out, beginning a close relationship that continues to this day. We bonded over faith, politics, writing and the ups and downs of Sooner football. We also talk about Midwest City, our classmates, and the impact of those years of our lives. Jim has honored me with the opportunity to provide a Foreword to this very interesting story.

I have written a lot over the years, but I've not had an assignment like this one. As Jim shared his experiences in Midwest City, my own memories kicked in and it became personal for me as well. My association with Midwest City has been two-fold, but as you'll see I find they are inextricably linked.

As Jim has described, Tinker AFB is an important part of what a writer once described as the "arsenal of democracy." Both the B-52 Stratofortress bomber and the KC-135 Stratotanker are maintained there. Those two aircraft alone make it possible for the USAF to literally range the world with Air Power, both for humanitarian purposes and to wage devastating warfare. They alone make the USAF quantitatively and qualitatively the most feared and respected force in the world, but they are only a part of the story. Virtually every aircraft engine in the USAF inventory is maintained at Tinker, and as Jim explains, multiple operational units have called the base home over the years. Bill Atkinson had the rare foresight to purchase the land, plan a city to support and be supported by the base that was to be built, and the generations that followed have maintained the vitality of this partnership. I was never assigned to Tinker AFB during my very long career, but my professional and personal connections grew, nonetheless. As a young aircraft commander, I flew a KC-135A from my home base in Columbus, Ohio, to Tinker to be inducted into the repair line and flew a newly refurbished one home. That has been happening for decades at Tinker, as that aircraft (still in service for over 75 years), as well as B-52s, have received depot-level, periodic overhauls over their service lives.

Over more than 40 years, more than a half dozen of my fellow Airmen, good friends I served with around the Air Force, would command Tinker AFB. Some of them made their retirement home in the area, and all of them feel a special attachment to the community. Installation commanders have a unique relationship with their adjoining communities, and as Jim mentions, their cooperation is vital to the health and welfare of both institutions. Commanders obviously have the needs of their mission and their obligations to the Constitution as their overriding priority, but even when the interests of the two do not perfectly align they must cooperate for both to flourish.

Of the various civil-military relationships in American society, none is more fraught with political intrigue than those associated with a major repair depot. The financial impact to the community is enormous, and an ever-present reality to the commander, town officials and, of course, the congressional delegation. Threats of base closure, which Jim describes so well, are never far from the minds of local officials. The cost of maintaining excess bases is enormous for military services, but the impact on communities and the risk to the tenure of congregational delegations who allow a base to be closed make further reduction of military bases less likely and, frankly, a toxic subject to broach in Washington, DC.

The fact that Tinker has survived multiple threats of base closure is not insignificant. Among the factors affecting such decisions are the cost of moving the mission, the quality of life provided to military families, the economic impact on the region, and the strength of relationship with the local community. Tinker remains the largest of the three remaining air depots, and its future certainly seems secure.

Do the military-civil relationships really matter beyond the obvious economic ramifications? I believe they do. They matter in ways that cannot be reduced to a financial spreadsheet. The military services are, by design, values-driven organizations. Since the inception of the all-volunteer force following the Vietnam conflict, every member serves because they chose to. They pledge an oath of allegiance, not to a government or a leader or a political party, but to the Constitution of the United States. For whatever their period of service, they pick up their families, household goods, vehicles, dogs, and cats and go wherever the service needs them, whenever it requires that they do so.

Not surprisingly, military bases tend to thrive in areas where the residents have similar values. The military tends to mirror the society it serves, and all political views can be found there, but the foundational ethos is one of service. It is obviously rather traditional. One's worth is measured by what one contributes to the whole rather than what is achieved for self.

I found Midwest City to be that way, also. People were committed to something outside themselves, whether it was the mission of Tinker or making the Midwest City Bombers a better team. While we had our "stars," the focus was the team. The productivity of a workforce is always a key component of evaluating the value of a base like an air depot that has a huge civilian workforce. It involves the relationship between the leadership and the workforce, and whether the workforce can deliver quality work on an established schedule. The synergy of the people of central Oklahoma and the military was and is a key factor in the success of the base and the well-being of the community.

Oklahoma is a place where extreme weather and sometimes marginal soil makes farming a difficult, season-to-season struggle, and extraordinary effort to produce results is the ordinary demand farmers face there. The sustainment of engines and aircraft that are growing older by the day and are flown by young men and women whose grandparents flew the same airframes, requires the same consistent dedication and unwavering tenacity required by Oklahoma, making success all the more meaningful and appreciated.

Military families, transient by nature, must make the best of every place they land. They involve themselves in PTA, teach school, coach youth teams, and volunteer in scouts, churches, and school support groups. The military and civilian communities become a single, hand-in-glove fit. They have certainly been that in Midwest City, Oklahoma.

As a 15-year-old junior, I found Midwest City a place to grow and learn. I also found a wife and we married at the Tinker AFB chapel. Her father was a colonel at the base starting an organization that developed new ways to take care of aging aircraft, the same thing Tinker is doing today. Midwest City focused my path in every aspect of life. It was a somewhat sheltered life, however, in an almost exclusively white town. That reality would require considerable growth and maturity as we ventured into a world where others had more or less than we did and did not look, or sound like us. It required soul-searching and self-examination, but it was necessary to become who we should be.

When I read Jim's book, my thoughts went to the novel, *You Can't go Home Again,* by Thomas Wolfe, and it made me wonder. *Can* you go home again? Actually, we cannot go home again, and we probably do not really want to. We are different people. I once heard a psychologist give a lecture in which he said, "We are all

General Roger A. Brady (ret.)
U.S. Air Force photo

trying to either live up to who we were in high school, or we're trying to live it down." That's a clever statement with some truth to it, but the reality is that we at least need to know where we have come from and learn from whatever the impact of that experience was. Did we learn from it what we should have learned?

I believe what we see and what some of us experienced in *Tinkertown* can be viewed in two ways. Lots of what we experience in our youth and regard as important is ephemeral and will be cast aside as we live and mature. However, what we learn about the value of looking outward from ourselves to the betterment and service of others is transcendent and worth our attention.

Hard data tells us that Americans have a lower propensity to serve in uniform than ever before in our history. This means that, over time, Americans become less connected to or even aware of the community that is the guarantor of protection of their way of life. Every sociological study tells us that Americans have become more individualistic and less agreed on common values (or that objective values even exist!) than ever before. I suggest that communities like *Tinkertown* give us models that provide hope for preserving an important heritage.

The B-52 Stratofortress Bomber in its Mojave Desert retirement. It's replacement is the B-52H.

Photo by "Nightowl"/Pixabay

Prologue: Blending History and Memoir

This book chronicles the blended history of two places in Oklahoma, each made unique because they both came into existence at the same time, not all that long ago, right across the street from each other, in the shadow of the state's capital city. These places have always been joined at the hip, a case study in symbiosis. One would likely not have lasted long without the other, and neither would have experienced the growth it did by itself.

Together, Tinker Field, which began life in 1942 under a quick succession of names (Midwest Air Depot, Oklahoma City Air Depot, and Tinker Field), and Midwest City have influenced each other physically, socially, and culturally since their founders' first shovels went into the ground in 1942.

Today, that air depot is Tinker Air Force Base, and it is the largest Air Force maintenance installation for aircraft in the world and is also the largest single-site employer for Oklahoma producing an economic imprint of $3.51 billion. As for Midwest City, it arose from cropland to become the eighth largest city in the state with a population of more than 65,000 at its height.

C.J. and me looking for mischief.
(Photo by Hazel M. Willis)

And, as each of these influenced the other, the *people* of Midwest City and Tinker influenced both. I'm sure a similar set of dynamics has been experienced by other military towns and their installations. Yet the dynamics here bear striking differences. For one thing, most of the employees at Tinker Air Force Base are not military, but civilians who work for the government in civil service jobs and as civilian contractors. That has always made this Air Force base seem just as much like a civilian industrial plant as a military base.

Midwest City began as a working-class community of people who got their first real job there after the state's infamous Dust Bowl era. A large portion of its population still fits that blue-collar demographic, although many who were educated in Midwest City's excellent school system have advanced into stellar professional careers. Another difference is that the town was built from the ground up out of farmland specifically to service the workers at Tinker. So, the town and the base formed a partnership from the very beginning.

Throughout the book, I've been asking myself the question, "How much of me comes from this hometown and why?" Looked at another way, "Is where I'm from, who I am?" I would suggest readers of this book ask yourselves the same question, because the answer may be as surprising for you as it was for me. I have come to realize that growing up in a town means more than it was your address when you were young. It means you didn't just grow up in a specific zip code; you grew up in a specific culture. And it's more than probable that this culture rubbed off on you and stayed with you for many years, if not your whole life. Yes, we grow and change to greater or lesser degrees, but that hometown baseline of values, hopes, fears, likes and dislikes probably remains.

Examples of the *Tinkertown* symbiosis abound, and it's why I give the book this name. The most obvious example is the ways in which Midwest City – a blueprinted and planned community before the first house was ever built – was created to serve the needs of those carrying out the mission of Tinker field: its thousands of employees and service members.

It is noteworthy that the urban designer who developed the Midwest City plan patterned it after the plan of Washington D.C. Midwest City's founder, W.P. "Bill" Atkinson, was introduced to this planner by Pentagon officials, and Atkinson made good on his promise to develop such a full-service town. Many years later, when Tinker faced the real threat of a closure by the Defense Department in 1993 and again in 1995, the people of Midwest City, Tinker, and Oklahoma City worked together in protesting and ensuring that the base stay open. As a result, Tinker AFB was removed from the government's base closure list.

Since I was one of the young people to experience the early decades of Tinker and Midwest City, much of this story of **Tinkertown** is told through my eyes, my memories and experiences, and those of my friends who were part of the fabric of the story. To all this is, I've interviewed others, plumbed them for memories, and combed through the largesse of documents, photographs, films, and other artifacts about Midwest City and Tinker. I was especially pleased when my friend and high school classmate, Air Force General Roger A. Brady, agreed to do the Foreword describing the importance of Tinker to both the Air Force mission and to America itself. Having a four-star general, who also lived in Midwest City and quarterbacked the high school football team, offer his insight into the story is a great asset to the book.

As to who I am, you could call me a material witness to this story, I am a journalist who is a product of the Tinkertown social and cultural chemistry, even though I wasn't born there. Although I like to think I began life as an Oklahoma Sooner, such was not the case. I drew my first breath in the Buckeye state of Ohio, in its capital city of Columbus. The year was 1946, the month was March, and the War in the Pacific had been over six months and fourteen days. The dropping of the two atomic bombs on Japan had brought the entirety of World War II to an end. Of course, I knew nothing of this on that March 19 morning when I first opened my eyes to this earthly life.

As is the case with newborn infants, about the only things I did know was how to eat and how to cry when I wasn't eating. I also knew how to sleep, albeit in shorter spurts than my mom and dad would have liked. For some time, my world seemed populated by only three people, other than me: my mother, my father, and my big sister C.J. (short for Cecelia Jane), already more worldly than me at age 2. Of course, there were others around, in the form of teddy bears, a dog and cat, but I hadn't figured out yet that these were not of the same species as Mommy, Daddy, and C.J. I have absolutely no complaints about these initial two or three years, partly because I remember only a fraction of 1 percent about them. But I don't ever remember feeling insecure or unloved, and what more can a little kid ask for? Not that I didn't try, of course.

I have only a couple indelible memories of my first three years in Columbus. The most vivid one – probably because it was a regular oc-currence – was watching the big trains out back that would chug past our apartment complex several times every day. C.J. and I would sit out back of our apartment and stare up the grade as each train would approach, pass by, and then head off to their destinations. We'd wave at the engineer who was at the throttle of the beast's engine, and he would often be wearing one of those striped railroad caps from bygone days. A cigarette might be dangling from his lips that would break into a broad smile as he saw us kids. Sometimes, he would reach above him and a yank on the whistle cord. The train was saying hello as we waved good-bye.

There was a long and rich history of railroading in Ohio, which was a crossroads state for national train service. It has been said that Ohio is stitched together in steel, and Columbus was the hub of the state.

The New York-Chicago and New York-St. Louis routes here crossed tracks with Pocahontas coal roads making a beeline to Lake Erie and the railroad gateways of Norfolk & Western, and the Chesapeake & Ohio. In fact, by 1946, Ohio ranked sixth among U.S. states in rail mileage as trains traveled 8,416 route-miles among 35 roads. But to C.J. and me, this was the most impressive part of the industry: just watching these massive train engines and cars roll past our apartment with such regularity.

So, while other kids might listen to the Green Hornet on radio or go to the movies with their parents for entertainment, C.J. and I probably spent more of our free time out back watching the trains take people and goods on down the track. And it's not a stretch to think that this experience is where wanderlust first entered my soul. In a very short time, however, I would be adding a lust for airplane travel onto my passion for moving trains. That would happen when my family moved to a town in Oklahoma right across the street from a huge Air Force base named Tinker Field.

In whatever form of transport, I fell in love with the idea of going to new and exciting places (the adjectives meant the same thing to me). This wanderlust would be my companion and motivator for the rest of my life as I traversed the country and the globe. The imagineering I did as a young child, wondering what adventures these train and plane passengers were taking, would be the same kind of wonderment I would have as an adult as I imagined what it would be like to live over the next hill, or the ones beyond that. And, many times, I would just pack up and go see for myself.

Later in life I remember seeing the Steve Martin/John Candy film, *Planes, Trains, and Automobiles,* and thinking how much of my life has been spent happily traveling in all three. I could even add boats to that list because, perhaps ironically for a guy who grew up in an Air Force town, I chose the Navy in college and spent some time on a destroyer in the Pacific as a midshipman.

The other Columbus memory that stands out is of C.J. chasing me around the front yard trying to hug me and give me wet, sloppy kisses on my cheek. I actually have a picture or two of that lying around. Although she and I would have our normal brother/sister flare-ups as we grew up, we always had an unusually close relationship. And, like my wanderlust, that would remain a constant throughout my life. C.J. has always been there to support me and put a positive spin on whatever bonehead mistake I would make in life. That would prove true time and again for the rest of my growing-up years which would be spent in the state of Oklahoma.

Beyond these memories, the rest of my toddler Columbus experience is forever hidden from my view. I don't even have a memory of our move from Ohio to Oklahoma, which we did in 1949 when my dad got a job in advertising at an Oklahoma City television station. Dad had been out of the Navy for a couple years and had moved to Columbus to do promotional artwork for a savings and loan there. He had always had a talent for sketching, and it served him well as he transitioned into ad design and later, in ad sales and management.

The Dust Bowl days of Oklahoma were only a few years removed from our arrival there.
(Photo by Pixabay photographers)

Dad was part of a new breed of *Madmen,* albeit in Oklahoma City and not New York. In fact, he would become president of the Oklahoma Ad Club. He had a brother in Oklahoma, and I always assumed that was part of the reason we moved there. His name was LeRoy but we all called him Doc because he was a dentist. In fact, he was the first dentist in a brand-new town just southeast of Oklahoma City, called Midwest City. More on this place and its bland name later. Doc was already successful in his practice and had friends in high places in the Oklahoma City area. One was a man named Ken Wright, who was a local celebrity organist (a big deal then) with the NBC-TV affiliate in Oklahoma City, WKY-TV. I've always felt it was connections like this that helped Dad land his job at WKY in advertising or – as it was called then in TV land – "selling time."

The upshot was we were leaving Columbus and heading to Oklahoma and this new suburb of Midwest City. It was fine with C.J. and me (what do you know at ages 3 and 5?), and I know Mom saw the necessity in it, although Oklahoma would become a reluctantly acquired taste for a woman who had known some finer things in life in her native Pennsylvania. Oklahoma, on the other hand, was only a decade removed from the "Dust Bowl "days, and John Steinbeck's classic book about it *(The Grapes of Wrath).*

The film version of the book, starring Henry Fonda, had premiered a few years earlier in 1940. Most of the nation still identified Oklahoma with poverty and saw it as the state that people were leaving; not flocking to. So, as I would learn over the next few years, Mom struggled with the plains culture she was headed into. All, in all, though she handled it very well.

One thing would prove true, however: our Oklahoma home in this new town called Midwest City, alongside this big Air Force base called Tinker, would be an adventure worthy of a young boy who was already captivated by the novelties of life. The same would wind up true for my future friends, many of whose parents worked at Tinker Field either as military or civilian personnel.

What follows is the story lived by all of us. But first, the stories of the founding of Tinker Field and Midwest City need telling, along with the key role an amazing Oklahoma entrepreneur played in the success of both.

-- Jim Willis, 2024

Contents

I

The Coming War and the Need for Tinker

Tinker Air Force Base, which began life officially as the Midwest Air Depot and then, for three months, as the Oklahoma City Air Depot, would likely not have come into existence in April 1941 as such a vital facility without World War II. Even if it had, it is doubtful it would have become the huge air maintenance base it became. Nor would it have survived at least two attempts by the Defense Department to close it down in later years. But it did, and today Tinker Air Force Base is one of the biggest and most vital military installations in America. It is located directly across Southeast 29th Street from Midwest City, Oklahoma, which likely wouldn't be there without it.

Both Tinker and the city are nine miles southeast of downtown Oklahoma City. A bitter feud would erupt between civic leaders in Oklahoma City and the young, upstart Midwest City when the state's capital city could not officially lay claim to being the host city for Tinker. In actuality, the base was federal property, belonging neither in Midwest City nor Oklahoma City limits until Oklahoma City finally annexed it 1959. Still, both cities wanted to proclaim themselves as host cities, and only one could accurately say so. After all, the sprawling base sits right across Southeast 29th Street from Midwest City. You could throw a rock from one side and hit the other.

The Oklahoma City Chamber of Commerce had not foreseen a young real estate developer from Texas discovering where the base would be built and buying up all the land adjacent to it, creating another host town entirely. But that's a story found in the next chapter.

Today's Tinker Air Force Base covers more than 5,000 acres of land, and services aircraft takeoffs and landings with two 10,000-foot runways. Some 7,000 military personnel, including a Naval unit, work there along with more than 15,000 civil service employees and contractors. Tinker is the home to the Oklahoma City Air Logistics Center, the 552nd Air Control Wing, the 507th Refueling Wing, 513th Air Control Group, Navy Strategic Communications Wing One, Defense Logistics Agency's Defense Distribution Depot for Oklahoma City, Third Combat Communications Group, Thirty-eighth Engineering Installation Group, and Defense Megacenter of Oklahoma City. (1)

Maj. Gen. Clarence L. Tinker
(U.S. Air Force Photo)

But in its earliest year, the air base was called the Midwest Air Depot until October 14, 1942, when it was renamed (for three months) as the Oklahoma City Air Depot, and then for Maj. Gen. Clarence L. Tinker, born part Osage in Pawhuska, Oklahoma, who lost his life in the Pacific. Tinker was commanding a flight of LB-30 aircraft on a bombing run against the Japanese in Wake Island in June1942. One of the many things about the air base that neither I nor most of my friends knew, was just who this Tinker was or why he deserved to have a base named for him. Had we known, we would have been impressed to have our town's air base named for him. The veterans-run military website, *We are the Mighty*, has labeled Maj. Gen. Tinker a "total badass" who was a perfect fit for the tough jobs that needed doing in fighting the war in the Pacific. This was one of those men whose life seemed stranger than fiction. Tinker was born on Osage Nation land in 1887 Oklahoma, was raised an Osage, attended federally funded schools for Native Americans and loved to hear stories from the old west about Osage warriors and Osage scouts who rode with American calvary units. (2) He attended the Wentworth

Military academy in Missouri, where his military career began, and was 21 when the mass murders of Osage Indians began occurring back in his native Pawhuska, Oklahoma, over the fight for oil in that state. That was the focus of David Grann's book, *Killers of the Flower Moon*, and Tinker's family lived through it.

Tinker received his commission in the U.S. Army Infantry in 1912, started taking flying lessons, and transferred to the Army's Air Service in 1922. He was sent to England as Assistant Military Attache' and his aircraft developed engine problems while flying near some cliffs. The plane crashed and was engulfed in flames, but Tinker managed to escape from the fiery wreckage, only to realize his co-pilot was still inside. Ignoring his own safety, he ran back into the burning aircraft and rescued the unconscious aviator from the fuselage, suffering serious burns in doing so. (3)

Tinker later became the commandant of the Air Corps Flying School in Texas, was promoted to Brigadier General (the first Native

American to reach that rank) and was sent by the Army to command the 7th Air Force in Hawaii to organize defenses there after the Pearl Harbor attack. It was in the Pacific that he lost his life in the battle for Wake Island. He was the first general officer to die in the war. In a tribute to Maj. Gen. Tinker, one veteran noted, "Clarence L. Tinker was not always an airman, but he was always a warrior." (4) Now, just several weeks later, this new air base in my newly adopted hometown was named for him.

Yet just 14 months before the general lost his life, there was no military air depot at all in Oklahoma. The site where Tinker Field would sit was nothing but wheat fields for as far as the eye could see. Then, in the wink of an eye, the War Department announced on April 8, 1941, that the Oklahoma City area would be the site for this important base. Construction began soon after that announcement.

The urgency for the new air depot was blown in by the winds of war in Europe. With Hitler advancing in Europe and overrunning other nations, the United States War Department (today the Department of Defense) had realized by 1940 that it was only a matter of time before America would be drawn into the war, either as an arms supplier to the Allies or as a direct combatant, or both. When that happened, the U.S. military would be confronting the German Air Force, or Luftwaffe, which was the best in the world in 1939. Its aircraft were much better than nearly all types of Allied planes in the air. The Luftwaffe was a ground-cooperation force created to support the German Army, and Germany had been going through a four-year period in which they rebuilt their military might. Each year more and more aircraft came off production lines.

The Luftwaffe had been officially created in May 1935, after the passage of the "Law for the Reconstruction of the National Defense Forces." More informally, that had become known worldwide as the German rearmament program, of which the Luftwaffe was a central piece. This law and program brought back into existence an army, navy, and air force for Germany, which had all been essentially banned by the Treaty of Versailles following Germany's defeat in World War I. In reality, the country had been building pieces of its air defense system since Day One of the treaty's signing. There were "Freikorps" air units, then glider and sailplane formations, and a secret training facility in the Soviet Union. (5)

With the rearmament program, however, new combat aircraft were built, and existing ones were armed and ready for battle. By 1939, Germany had 4,733 war planes ready for combat, plus another 3,562 aircraft that could be pressed into service for support duty. The Luftwaffe had standardized its planes' airframes and engines, making it more efficient to repair them and giving them an operational force of 1,050 bombers and 1,000 fighters by that year. Even though the Allied nations had as many or more aircraft then, this number included many different types of planes and some of those were obsolete and didn't fare well against the Luftwaffe in battle.

Great Britain had experienced setbacks in its rearmament program and was building only one modern fighter in 1939. It was called the Hawker Hurricane, a single-seater monoplane fighter that saw heavy service in World War II and accounted for 60 percent of all British air victories in the famed Battle of Britain. (6) It would be joined in the skies by a fellow fighter that became a legend, the Spitfire, also called the Submarine Spitfire. But that plane didn't make its appearance until 1940. Still, it was built in time for the Battle of Britain and England built more of these fighters than any others during the war. Alongside the Hurricane, the Spitfire helped save Britain from German takeover. (7)

Inside the mammoth Douglas Building, aircraft were built and maintained for World War II
and into the 21st Century and beyond.
(U.S. Air Force photo)

France found itself lagging in effective combat planes in 1939, as most of its bombers and 20 percent of its fighters were obsolete. As a result, France was trying hard to purchase better combat planes in America in 1939, at the same time that the U.S. War Department began seeing the need to restock its own supply of combat aircraft.

The U.S. Army Air Corps (which would become the U.S. Army Air Forces in 1941 and the U.S. Air Force in 1947) had a total strength of 1,401 aircraft then, but only 800 of them were combat types and some of those were obsolete.(8) Fortunately, the Navy had seen a great need for more Naval planes in 1938 and had already begun working on building 3,000 new aircraft. But the Air Corps inventory of planes was in critical need of improvement.

Therefore, on April 3, 1939, President Franklin Delano Roosevelt signed the National Defense Act of 1940 that authorized a $300 million budget and the construction of 6,000 airplanes for the Army Air Corps. The act also boosted the number of Air Corps personnel to 48,203, consisting of 3,203 officers (most of whom were to be pilots) and 45,000 enlisted troops who would serve to maintain the aircraft or take crew positions, largely as gunners. (9)

But weapons of war were only one piece of the puzzle that the Defense Department needed to assemble in 1940-41. The second piece was raising and training the professional troops and crews needed to build, maintain, and fly these aircraft once they were built. To ensure that this task was completed, President Roosevelt signed into law what would be America's first peacetime military draft in September 1940, fifteen months before the Japanese attacked Pearl Harbor in the Pacific on December 7, 1941. (10) The draft would draw 151,883 young Oklahoma men into service, and on one day alone – October 16, 1940, -- 28,510 young men signed up for the draft. That was the largest single-day draft registration in Oklahoma's short history. Altogether, throughout World War II, more Sooners were drafted into service than either its much larger border state of Texas or the state of Arkansas. (11)

That draft came just in time because, by the time of that attack, America's military strength had increased to nearly 2.2 million military troops in uniform. Millions more would follow during the early war years, many of whom entered as volunteers, although most of the recruits – about 10 million in fact, entered through the draft. The lion's share of them were assigned to the Army (infantry, artillery, and air corps), because the other branches were better staffed with volunteers. As the war went on, though, those branches were also assigned more draftees.

The third piece of the puzzle facing the Defense Department was production. That's where The Midwest Air Depot came in. A great need existed to ramp up the building of military aircraft, and to do it quickly. Production miracles would be needed to build the needed aircraft, especially after Roosevelt proposed boldly that America build 50,000 aircraft annually. Few believed it would be possible to actually produce that many airplanes in such a small window of time, but they would be proven wrong.

For all these reasons, the Midwest Air Depot first began taking shape southeast of Oklahoma City the summer of 1941, several months before the first home was built in what would become Midwest City. The first earth was turned for the Air Force facility on July 30, less than five months before the December 6 attack on Pearl Harbor.

Helping to preside over the groundbreaking, the president of the Oklahoma City Chamber of Commerce delivered his remarks from the seat of a large bulldozer in 104-degree heat. His name was W.E. Hightower, and he told the assembled crowd that building an 1,820-acre air depot was too huge of a project to start with a hand spade or shovel. "This is a mechanized age," he said. "I think this tractor is the least we should use for an affair symbolizing a project of such magnitude." (12)

When Hightower and other civil leaders had begun promoting Oklahoma City as the site of the needed airfield, they envisioned only a military depot that would serve the defense needs of the country but, just as importantly, provide great economic relief needed in a state that had just come out of the Dust Bowl years. Poverty was rampant; jobs were few. The new air depot looked like a gold-plated solution. Little did they know that a simple air depot would soon become a permanent aircraft repair facility for all kinds of air transports.

"In the decade prior to the historic event, the continuing drain of population sapped the spirit of Oklahoma's economy," wrote Tinker historian James L. Crowder. "By all judgments, the depression of the Dust Bowl Thirties was as great in the young Sooner State as anywhere in the country. The damage to the triad of industry, land, and people was devastating as each part seemed to crumple with the strain from the other two. At times, only hope and vision remained." (13)

And that vision would grow and grow from the initial point in 1940 when R.A. Singletary, who managed government relations for the Oklahoma City Chamber of Commerce, was told by Defense Department officials that the United States Army had decided to build an air depot to build bombers and train pilots. Initially, the plan was to site the facility at what was then the Oklahoma City Municipal Airport (which later became Will Rogers World Airport).

The new air depot would require the city to earmark 60 acres for its site, although an adjacent piece of land might be needed for expansion.

The original military unit assigned to the base would amount to 2,200 troops, 200 of which would be officers and the remainder would be enlisted troops. This facility was to be called the Oklahoma City Air Depot. At that time, the Army was the home of the Air Corps, which would become the Air Force branch of service following the war. One million dollars would be needed to construct base facilities and services such as mess halls, barracks, and recreation areas. (14)

Singletary immediately passed on his good news to Oklahoma City civic leaders who met in executive session to discuss the proposed expansion of the municipal airport, located on the city's south side.

As committee chair E.K. Gaylord, who would also the founding publisher of *The Daily Oklahoman* newspaper, said later, "This is the greatest opportunity has come before Oklahoma City in many years. In fact, the only visible expansion we can take hold of at the present time that amounts to a great deal." (15)

In no time, city leaders created a foundation and convinced 127 local businessmen to pledge a total of $137,000 to fund the purchase of the needed land for the Army training depot. Soon afterwards, the news was made public in Gaylord's newspaper, and area residents heard for the first time that the city had secured options for 1,219 acres of land to expand the existing Oklahoma City airport to accommodate bomber construction, landing, and pilot training. Plans also were calling for a new municipal airport on the northwest side of Oklahoma City. (16)

But plans were about to change. While civic leaders were focused on this expansion project, word came from another city businessman, Fred Jones, who was a presidential appointee on the country's War Production Board. While sitting on that board, Jones learned of yet another government plan to site and construct a huge air depot somewhere between Dallas-Fort Worth and Kansas City. Another Oklahoma City civic leader, Stanley Draper had already gotten wind of the proposed air depot through Singletary who was working his contacts in Washington. In fact, Singletary had already been briefed on what needs the new air depot would meet and what the site requirements for such a facility would need to be. When Singletary learned the impact such a base would have, he realized the enormous potential for the state of Oklahoma if the site could be located near its capital city. Facts which he learned were the following:

- The depot would be constructed as a permanent facility that would employ as many as 2,500 people during peace time, and more during war time.
- The depot would require 900 acres of land, and two-thirds of that must be flat topography.
- The costs to build the depot was estimated at $10-$15 million.
- The site would probably only serve as an air depot and not a factory. Those functions would be split between different Army installations. Oklahoma City should lobby for one or the other; not both. (17)

Oklahoma City decided to bid for the depot, which meant holding off on their plans to buy land for a bomber factory. Singletary reported back to Washington, and the site where Tinker AFB now sits – on Southeast 29th street, 9 miles from downtown Oklahoma City – was proposed.

The July 1940, groundbreaking was thus the culmination of more than a year's worth of decisions by the War Department of where to locate the air depot and what its functions would be. The Oklahoma City-area site met all the qualifications, and the facility would translate into thousands of jobs that were badly needed in a state that was still reeling from the poverty years. Unemployment had been running very high in Oklahoma, and the construction of the Midwest Air Depot would mean instant work for so many who were jobless. The economic benefits to the area, both during and after construction, were enormous.

Oklahoma City civic leader Frank Buttram said the new air depot would be more valuable to Oklahoma City than its oil fields. (18) What he didn't know at the time, was that – contrary to what Singletary had been told by the Defense Department – this new facility would, in fact, serve as *both* an air depot maintenance facility *and* an aircraft factory building needed planes. The positive economic impact to Oklahoma would be even greater than Buttram had predicted.

As 1941 ended, the Air Force appointed Lt. Col. William R. Turnbull to become the first base commander of the Midwest Air Depot. One of the streets in Midwest City's "Original Mile" would be named for him. Although the base had not yet been built, operations started on January 15, 1942, five weeks after America's entry into World War II began. Colonel Turnbull set up his 8x10-foot office on the second.

floor of the Commerce Exchange Building in downtown Oklahoma City, some 10 miles from the new base he was commanding. He began working immediately with Ted Wheaton, who was a civil service employee from San Antonio's Duncan Field, to create the Office of Civilian Personnel. The two of them started hiring the civil service workers who would form a huge component to the personnel roster of the air depot. By July of 1942, some 2,800 new employees were hired and sent to the San Antonia air base for training. (19)

A few months later, shipments of air material arrived and were stored in temporary warehouses at the air depot where construction was underway at a fast pace, 24/7. Personnel hiring continued at warp speed as well, and in one six-hour period some 500 job applications for civil service jobs were processed. The first troops began arriving for duty at the base but had to be bivouacked in tent barracks at Will Rogers Airfield, Oklahoma City's civilian airport, several miles southwest of the new Midwest Air Depot, now under construction. These troops were bussed daily to the base and assisted in building the barracks they would be housed in permanently. Meanwhile, the first official military unit was created at the depot, and it was the 17th Mobile Air Depot Group. It was commanded by Capt. Sylvester Morrison.

U.S. Army Air corps policy was that only recognized, credible aircraft companies could work on the final assembly of military airplanes, although many parts could be built by companies not in the aviation business. Automobile assembly plants, for instance, were used as subcontractors for aircraft parts. This partnership between the military and private industry proved very successful in America's efforts to win World War II. But to do so, production facilities would have to be established in the interior of the country as well as on the coasts. As Thomas A. Wikle wrote, "Before the war, Douglas Aircraft was among the largest aircraft manufactures in the United States, employing about seven thousand US workers, the majority in California. When the War Department announced that new defense plants would be located in the central United States, industry leaders such as Donald Douglas voiced concern over finding enough workers far away from established sources of labor on the East and West Coasts.

Another skeptic was William Knudsen, chairman of the Office of Production Management, who told Army Chief of Staff George C. Marshall, "We can't move Detroit." (20) So, the Douglas Aircraft Company was asked to build and produce planes at the Midwest Air Depot. A second Douglas production plan would be built in Tulsa. That plant would produce B-24 bombers, also called the Liberator and the "Flying Boxcar." That plant would also produce the A-24 Banshee, a modified version of the Navy's Dauntless Dive Bomber and the A-26 Invader, made to attack troop convoys and trains. The Midwest Air Depot would produce the C-47 transport planes known as the "Skytrain," and later, the A-20 Havoc medium-range bomber, and A-26 Invader.

The Midwest Air Depot began with the runways, hangars, and barracks housing officers and airmen of the Air Force, followed shortly by the groundbreaking of a three-quarter-mile brick building to be known as the Douglas Building. It was paid for by the Douglas Aircraft Co., which would build the aircraft known as the Skytrains and Havocs and maintain all military airplanes coming to the depot for service and repairs.

Formal groundbreaking for the Douglas plant was staged on Independence Day (July 4) 1942, although actual construction had started more than three months earlier, on March 23. The Douglas Building would become – and remain -- the largest structure at Tinker. It measured three-quarters of a mile long, nearly 1,000 feet wide, was made of red brick, and was windowless, mostly because of needed blackout conditions at night. The completed cost of the massive building was $24 million, the equivalent of $4.8 billion in 2023 dollars. Despite the huge size, the plant was finished a year later, on March 26, 1943. And, as if it weren't already big enough, another 270 acres was added to the building on which was built a $5 million-dollar aircraft modification annex. (21)

It was there that Tinker modified C-47 Skytrains to the Army's specifications. The plant built 5,347 Skytrains from 1943-1945 and was turning out 13 of them every day for a time. But that wasn't the only thing built there. Douglas workers produced spare parts for the Skytrains, nicknamed the "Gooney Birds," and for C-54 Skymaster Big Brother military transport planes and 900 A-26 Invader attack bombers. Upwards to 38,000 Sooners worked at the Douglas plant, and more than half of them were women. (22)

The Skytrain (which is what Midwest City's first movie theater would be called) was an unsung hero of World War II and a real workhorse of a transport plane. So much so that Gen. Dwight D. Eisenhower named the Skytrain when asked to list the most important weapons that resulted in Allied victory in the war. He cited its carrying capacity that allowed it to haul huge loads of war materiel, Jeeps, and soldiers, along with food and ammunition. It became affectionately known as the "Gooney Bird" because its big, lumbering image mirrored that of the giant albatross birds found on the Pacific's Midway Island. (23)

Before WWII began, most military airplanes were produced in groups, as the technicians moved from aircraft to aircraft. But that was too slow of a process for Defense Department needs, and the engineers at Douglas started borrowing and adapting mass production processes already in place at automotive plants, innovated by Ford Motor Company. And, instead of custom parts built by skilled craftsmen, Douglas began using interchangeable parts. To cover any cost overruns coming from the new production system, the government changed from using fixed-price contracts to manufacturer cost plus a fixed fee. (24)

The base had begun taking shape by the summer of 1942, although boardwalks had to serve as sidewalks around the depot which would remain a work in progress for some time. Nevertheless, myriad construction crews began finishing aircraft hangars and other permanent buildings, and by the end of the summer 129 men of the 22nd Air Depot Squadron became the first military residents to move into the first two barracks on base. In another few weeks, crews started paving roads in the depot and completed work on the base's large Headquarters Building 460, comprising 50,000 square feet in size. When it was done, Turnbull and the base leadership moved in, along with the personnel office. (25)

The need for civilian workers at the depot was constant at this stage, and it is impossible to overstate how important these thousands of jobs were for a city and state that was still climbing out of the dustbowl that had caused employment in Oklahoma to plummet during the 1930s and into the start of the 1940s. It was this swift need for workers that necessitated a town be built to house and accommodate them. That town would be Midwest City, and it would be located on the north side of 29th Street. That story, itself a phenomenon, unfolds in Chapter 2.

Tinker was to become the largest American military aircraft maintenance installation in the world, and its very first scheduled project in 1942 was installing low-target bomb releases on 40 BT-13s. The BT-13 Valiant was the basic trainer most widely used by the U.S. Army Air Corps (which became the United States Air Force in 1947). Pilots flew the Valiants during the second stage of their three-stage flight training.

The sum of all the activity at Tinker proved to be the first of several miracles performed to get the military up to speed in a hurry. This depot's initial construction, together with the base's initial operations, unfolded at the very same time. Col. Turnbull and his crews had helped greatly to close the gap between unpreparedness and preparedness for America's participation in World War II. Work continued through the war at an unrelenting speed at Tinker and all other air bases around the country. By 1944, aircraft plants built nearly 100,000 in a year. Ford Motor Company's huge Willow Run bomber factory in Michigan wound up building nearly one plane every hour.

But Tinker was also churning out an inordinate share of aircraft.

As the war went on, thousands of Sooners, both civilians and military, showed what this new air base could do as a permanent repair depot and maintenance facility. Tinker's reputation for excellence grew quickly, and its fame spread.

In 1943, only a year after construction had begun. Some 13,500 people were employed at the air base itself, while another 23,000 worked for Douglas Aircraft at the new Douglas plant just completed east of Tinker's runways. Almost half of all the workers at Douglas were women, and they came to illustrate the famed "Rosie the Riveter" images of female aircraft workers that the country began promoting back in World War I. All anyone had to do was walk into the Douglas Plant at Tinker to see that these "Rosies" were much more than an image. They were the real deal and contributed mightily to the Allied success in World War II.

"Interest in women was driven, in part, by their performance in positions that required dexterity or speed," wrote historian Thomas A. Wilke. "Under an accelerated training schedule, the depot plant added new employees at a rate of 200 per day ... As the number of female workers with families grew, childcare became an issue, prompting the government to open daycare facilities at schools. Concerned about the potential for sabotage and espionage, Douglas employees were urged not to talk about specific aspects of their jobs. Douglas employees in Tulsa and Midwest City participated in a wide variety of company-sponsored activities such as men's and women's softball leagues.53 In 1944 the Skytrain Theater opened in Midwest City, showing newsreels and feature-length films." (26)

A Tinker Air Force history document states that, while there were many women who worked in traditional occupations at the time for women such as clerical or janitorial positions, "most of them held production jobs such as aircraft and engine mechanics, welders, electricians, sheet metal workers, instrument repair technicians, quality control inspectors, equipment operators, security guards, warehouse workers, etc. Tinker women workers performed maintenance on such aircraft as the B-17, B-24, and B-29, and engines such as the R1820,

R2600, and R3350. To the east across the north/south runway, women made up 50.6 percent of the workforce in the Douglas Plant, now Building 3001, and they built half of all C-47 Skytrains produced for the Allied war effort. After the war, a significant number of them asked to stay on at Tinker in various positions and had long careers there." (27)

The air base newspaper honored several of these women workers in a December 23, 1942, story, about the winner and runners-up of a contest they called the "Typical Woman War Worker." The contest was won by Hazel N. Vickers and the story said, "Referred to her by her co-workers as efficient, cheerful and vitally interested in her job, Mrs. Vickers is employed as an aircraft dispatcher in Operations, a responsible job which she holds down very capably." (28) Runners-up were Anne Clark, Martha Webb, and Ollie Ball.

Work continued 24/7 at Tinker during the war, as three shifts were created, and activity never lagged through day or night. To accommodate workers on odd working hours, leisure and recreational activities were available 24-hours a day, and bowling leagues were established during the hours of 2 a.m. and 4 a.m. (29)

In addition to the thousands of C-47 Skytrains, Tinker also built the A-20 Havoc medium-range bomber, night fighter, and reconnaissance aircraft. (30) At the same time, the "Tinker toilers" (as the maintenance crews were called) repaired, maintained, and modified B-17, B-24, and B-29 bombers. A key assignment for them was to modify the B-29 Superfortress bombers that allowed them to be used in the Pacific theater for high-altitude, precision bombing campaigns.

Such an aircraft production agenda did not come cheaply, however, and Congress found it necessary to authorize massive defense budgets and spending hikes that went from $1.5 billion in 1940 to $81.5 billion in 1945. By the fourth year of the war, America was the world's leader in arms production, and the country was producing even more than would be needed to win that war. Tinker Air Force Base proved to be a vital part of that success story. (31)

Another way in which Tinker would contribute to the country's defense was in the arena of civilian defense. Volunteers trained in aircraft spotting, first aid, firefighting, and even bomb removal (although, fortunately, the latter

would not be needed in the states). They served as air raid wardens, organized and supervised practice drills, including blackouts. Some 10 million Americans had volunteered for civil defense service by the second year of World War II, and some of those served at Tinker. (32)

Tinker also has hosted the Flying Castle Composite Squadron of the Civil Air Patrol, another nationwide volunteer program that lasted long after the war and is still active today. The membership focus is on cadet, cadet sponsor, and active senior members. Weekly meetings are mainly aimed at advancing young cadets through the CAP Cadet Program. Separate meetings are held for active senior members.

The origins of the CAP go back to 1936 as Hitler was planning his advances into other European countries. A veteran aviator from World War I, Gill Rob Wilson, returned from a trip to Germany convinced the United States was headed for war at some future point. His vision was to mobilize civilian aviators and young pilot trainees to serve in a civilian defense corps to monitor and patrol the skies over The U.S. Departments of Commerce, Navy, and War approved his proposal for a Civilian Air Patrol and the CAP national headquarters opened on December 1, 1936. By 1942,

German and Japanese submarines began appearing off the east and west coasts of America and in the Gulf of Mexico. By June of 1942, enemy attacks by German submarines attacked and destroyed almost 400 merchant vessels and oil tankers off the U.S. Atlantic coastline, often within sight of the country's shoreline. It became part of the CAP function to monitor such activity and report any sightings to the War Department, Navy, and Air Force. (33)

The CAP was created as an auxiliary to the Armed Forces, which were short-handed when the war began. The planes used were privately owned, modified to carry light bombs if needed. The CAP pilots and ground crews became the eyes of the home skies, and these pilots patrolled the skies for nearly 250,000 total hours. They served a great need in adding to the safe transport of the weapons of war to the battlefields of Europe and the Pacific. Today, the CAP is tasked with supporting American towns and cities with emergency response, a variety of aviation and ground services, youth development and promoting air, space, and cyber power. (34)

In my own personal experience, when I reached my teen years in Midwest City, I became aware of the CAP and its popularity with young men and women who were interested in aviation careers. Many wanted to become pilots, and the CAP offered training for that. Some of my friends became Air Force pilots because of the influence of the Civilian Air Patrol.

Following the war, operations at the Douglas Plant ceased briefly, and the fear grew that Tinker might close down as well. That fear was unfounded, though, and in 1945 it was announced that *Tinker* would actually expand its operations and take control of the Douglas Plant, making it a permanent facility. Then, in February 1946, Tinker employees began modification of the B-29 bombers, gearing them up for atomic bomb testing close to the bikini Atoll. The most historic plane to pay a visit to Tinker then was the *Enola Gay*, when it came to the base for overhaul. (34)

Other name changes would come soon. In 1946, the maintenance and supply operations would become the Oklahoma City Air Materiel Area (OCAMA), and in 1948 the Tinker Air Depot became Tinker Air Force Base, following the creation of the Department of the Air Force in 1947.

The next year, 1948, Tinker took the direct hit of a tornado on March 20. Some 100 aircraft were either damaged or destroyed, eight people were injured, and overall damages totaled $10 million. Then, just five days later, a second tornado hit the base causing another $6 million in damages, with 119 planes damaged or destroyed. Only one injury was reported. Miraculously, there were no deaths reported from either twister.

The next year, 1949, my family and I moved to our Midwest City home, three blocks from Tinker's main entrance. The base had transitioned to peacetime operations, but its future was just beginning, as was the 6-year-old town. I was a wide-eyed boy of 3 who would be growing up in a young town, next to a young Air Force base, and the adventures were just beginning.

A 1944 promotional publication proclaims the new Midwest City as
"The City of Tomorrow" that starts life as a totally planned
community, built primarily to serve the needs of Tinker Field
families.
MCHS History Center

2

A Very Thematic Man and his City of Tomorrow

![The Atkinson home in Midwest City]

The Atkinson home in Midwest City
Photo by Jim Willis

"Midwest City is rightly called the 'City of Tomorrow.' More than that, it is the city of a bright tomorrow, standing on the horizon of a new day. Begun with the coming of the war which insured for its people life and liberty, Midwest City looks forward, at the conclusion of that war, to the pursuit of happiness, providing for its residents all of the facilities necessary to insure an era of genuine progress in time of peace. It is an adventure in living, and a blueprint for the better life."

• Midwest City promotional brochure, 1944

An energetic and outgoing Cindy Mikeman sits at a dining table in the most historic home in Midwest City, Oklahoma. It is a sprawling ranch home on a spacious, green estate, near a long red stable of stall after stall that used to house the highly popular Shetland ponies in town. The stable is impeccable in appearance, the grounds and riding arena both well-manicured. The home belonged to Cindy's grandfather, whose legendary name was W.P. "Bill" Atkinson, the undisputed founder of Midwest City.

His estate is now the Atkinson Heritage Center & Museum, and it belongs to Rose State College, the successful community college of Midwest City with an annual enrollment of several thousand students on its 116-acre campus. Cindy is vice-president for the college's foundation and resource development.

I had seen Cindy talk about Bill Atkinson on Midwest City's 75th anniversary video in 2018. I grew up in Midwest City, having arrived at age 3 with my family in 1949, and I was back in my hometown researching this book. I had returned after many years to discover what the man, Bill Atkinson, was really like. I had only known him from a distance as a child and teen, and most of what I knew came from overhearing stories about him from my parents or from townspeople over the drug store counter or, the diner, or at the gas station. I was impressed with what Cindy said on that video, and she obviously has great affection for her late "granddaddy." In her role at Rose State, she oversees the Heritage Center, now used as an event center by the college and various civic groups in Midwest City and Tinker.

She is a talented, self-made businesswoman with degrees from Rose State College, Oklahoma State University, and the University of Central Oklahoma. "Many people don't even know I'm an Atkinson," she says. "My mother was Granddaddy's daughter Eugenia, and her married name was Davis. So, Atkinson is not in my name, and that's fine with me because it has enabled me to just be myself; one of the people of Midwest City." (1)

Cindy sits for my interview at the same dinner table she frequented for meals in her younger years with her Atkinson family. She speaks admiringly of the Atkinson family's patriarch.

"Granddaddy worked here, lived here, played here," she says with a smile. "He loved his family, and he loved this community of Midwest City. He was so connected to it. He was such a good man who welcomed everyone out to his "red barn," pony farm and even into this home. Granddaddy had this barn built just outside to house different kinds of farm animals," she recalls. "The only requirement was they had to all be red or reddish in color. He even had red chickens! He loved animals, and he knew others did, too, so he would invite families from Tinker and Midwest City out to see his red barn on Sunday afternoons and mix with the red animals. He was a family man and wanted to create a community of families and offer them fun things to do." (2)

A large stable for the ponies is still there. Atkinson's love for ponies caused him to build it and purchase them. Then he opened the stable up to Midwest Cityans and Tinker families on Sunday afternoon and invited families out to let their children ride his ponies around the outdoor arena. It became hugely popular, and the Shetland Pony became a trademark of Atkinson and his Midwest City.

Cindy pauses and adds another descriptor of him which seems spot-on when thinking about this totally planned community he developed.

"Granddaddy was also a very *thematic man*. He saw a theme in things he created and knew how the different parts of the whole could work together and complement each other. And that was right down to the color of his tie matching his suit and the event he was attending." (3) He would sometimes even select the colors in a new house from his necktie.

In Midwest City, which Atkinson founded in 1942, he envisioned a *thematic town* which would soon become a city; a full-service community that would meet all the needs of the thousands of new military troops and civilian workers that were about to pour into the brand-new Midwest Air Depot (renamed Tinker Field in 1942) right across Southeast 29th Street from the 320 acres of wheatfields he had just purchased. Although he didn't know it at the time, the one *"Original Mile "*of town he created would snowball into 24 square miles comprising a city of 60,000 people. But whether it remained small or grew, Atkinson saw a city that would be a safe, family-oriented community, one that would be self-contained even though it sat less than 10 miles from downtown Oklahoma City. And its fortunes would be tied undeniably to how well it serviced the people of Tinker Field.

Not that there weren't white settlers here before Atkinson began building Midwest City. In fact, they were settlers from Europe. In the late 19th century, after much of the indigenous population was resettled in "Indian Territory," railroad bosses pressured President Benjamin Harrison to open Oklahoma's "Unassigned Lands." In 1889, these Europeans were part of the thousands who streamed in on the great land run on April 22. They came from Germany, Czechoslovakia, Moravia, and Bohemia and staked their claims in the rural area that would become Midwest City just over a half-century later.

As a 1992 historical survey pointed out, "The community formed from the Germans and Czechoslovakians south and east of present-day Midwest City became known as the *Mishak* Community. Mishak had a church, a cemetery, two stores, a barn, a cotton gin, blacksmith shop, two-dance halls, a post office, and later, a gas station. The community eventually was bought by the government with the arrival of the Midwest [Air] Depot. The area including and surrounding Midwest City was used solely for agricultural purposes until the land for the Midwest Air

Depot was purchased. It was within several months that the land adjacent to the north side of the depot was purchased from several farmers by Bill Atkinson, and Midwest City was born." (4)

W.P. Bill Atkinson

The fact that Bill Atkinson managed to accomplish this feat of turning wheat into a thriving town, just as World War II was beginning, is the stuff of legend; only *this* legend is true. And the fact that he had arisen from impoverished beginnings as a child who lost his mother at age 9, make his accomplishments even more remarkable. Yet, in the way that young "Willie," as he was known, reacted to the death of his mother and the personal struggles of his father, one can find the spirit and determination that drove this man to visualize and realize his dream of building a city. And to me, as a resident of his town, it always seemed that some of his can-do spirit and grit wore off on us Midwest Cityans in the process.

I recently read an opinion which seems true when I think of how this city influenced me and my friends. "Even if you don't seem to feel an outward connection to your hometown, think about this: one of the first questions people tend to ask is, '*Where are you from?*' They say that home is where the heart is, and for most people, their hometowns are an important and integral part of their very persona. Whether they stir fond memories or sad ones, and whether you plan to return someday or not, your hometown played an important role in helping you become the person you are today." (5)

Many might be surprised to find that the man who came to care so deeply about the state of Oklahoma was not actually born there at all. William Paul Atkinson was born in the East Texas town of Carthage, on November 9, 1906. His father, Paul, was a carpenter and young Willie admired his skills. It would seem he was the recipient of those builder's skills, and they emerged when the adult Bill began building homes later.

But historian Scarlett J. Bowman also notes his father was also burdened by alcohol and was unable to recover from that enough to care for the family as he wanted to do. Such would *not* be the case with Bill himself. As he grew to a man, he avoided liquor, served buttermilk at all his social gatherings, and was a family man through and through.

But, as a child, "Willie" witnessed the job of caring for his family fall to his beloved mother, Maggie Tiller Atkinson. Hers was an arduous mission as mother since she had four children altogether to take care of. Still, she took her responsibility seriously and found ways to bring money in, chiefly as a seamstress, to feed and clothe her children. Atkinson would later describe her as the most dominant influence in his young life, and he loved her dearly. He even supported her home businesses – and learned skills as a salesman, too – by promoting her seamstress skills to neighbors around town and soliciting business for her.

Tragically, Maggie Atkinson succumbed to pneumonia when Bill was only 9, and she passed away on the ninth day of her illness. Before she died, however, she told her son, "Always be nice and good to people, and you can't help but succeed." She also asked him to get a college education and work hard all his life at whatever profession he chose. (6) Bill Atkinson made that promise to his mother and fulfilled it during his lifetime. He took his mother's parting request to heart, and it helped make him the success that he became just a few years later.

Young Bill Atkinson developed an interest in journalism and went to work as a "printer's devil," doing manual labor around the Carthage weekly newspaper and gaining useful knowledge about how a newspaper was run and printed. When the weekly folded, Bill found work on other small papers until he graduated from high school in 1924. He was a good student, and his motivation to succeed was apparent even in his teen years. He applied and was accepted at Lon Morris Junior College in nearby Jacksonville, Texas, and two years later transferred to Texas Christian University (TCU) in Fort Worth. There he became business manager of the TCU newspaper, *The Skiff*, and worked out an agreement with its editor Amos Melton (a fellow student) where they could both profit from revenue generated by the newspaper. The university approved of the arrangement, and Atkinson had found a useful revenue stream for himself and Melton.

This was one example of how enterprising the young Atkinson was, and he built his entrepreneurial philosophy upon a win-win foundation, finding ways to help others and making money out of doing it. Another illustration of this is told by his granddaughter Cindy who called it "the yellow raincoat incident."

While a student at TCU, Atkinson proposed an unusual advertising scheme to area merchants that could increase their exposure to students on campus, while being less expensive than media advertising. Atkinson owned a long yellow raincoat that stood out whenever he wore it. So, he created graphic advertisements for clients which he would attach to his raincoat and take long walks around campus in it, drawing attention to the ads adorning it. (7)

Atkinson used the money from his early enterprises to pay off his tuition bills and had $4,000 left over when he graduated in 1928. And, in the process, he graduated Magna Cum Laude and completed a double major in both journalism and business. (8) He married his high school sweetheart, Rubye Eugenia Beauchamp two months after graduation, and went to work for an ecumenical publication serving churches called the All-Church Press. The general manager, Douglas Tomlinson, agreed to let Atkinson go to Oklahoma City to start a new publication there, affiliated with the All-Church Press, called *The Oklahoma City Star*.

That was Atkinson's introduction to the Sooner State and to the amazing career that awaited him there.

In Oklahoma City, Atkinson secured contracts to print and publish newspapers and newsletters for many of the bigger Oklahoma City-area churches. Along with that success came a promotion to district manager of the All-Church Press. His hard work was noticed by others, including Edward K. Gaylord, the most powerful man in Oklahoma, who was also the founding owner and publisher of *The Oklahoman and Times* newspapers, the flagship enterprises of the Oklahoma Publishing Company.

Gaylord brought Atkinson into the inner circle of the Oklahoma City Chamber of Commerce, and people often referred to Atkinson as one of Gaylord's trusted "fair-haired boys." (9) At age 28, Atkinson was recruited by Oklahoma City University to join its Journalism Department faculty, and he quickly became chair of that department.

As Bill and Rubye Atkinson saw their family grow, he began planning a larger home for them in Oklahoma City. Perhaps calling on the memories of his own father's carpentry skills, Atkinson took a central role in designing and supervising the building of the home. In fact, it is said that his knowledge of construction impressed the actual homebuilder, E. C. Stanfield, so much that Stanfield employed Atkinson to market and sell his other homes.

Atkinson liked the job so much and was so good at it, that he decided to leave journalism and his teaching post at OCU and put his second TCU major to use in the real estate business. In fact, in 1940, he bought Stanfield's homebuilding company entirely and became a builder and developer himself. The next year, when Atkinson was only 35 years old, his new company built and sold more homes in Oklahoma City than any other real estate company in the whole state. (10)

Eugenia Atkinson Davis remembers her father as a man who delighted in home construction but was just – if not more – passionate about building family-oriented communities where residents would feel safe and enjoy the experience of living there.

"The original square mile was arranged as a family-friendly community, complete with shopping center, churches, parks and schools," she said. "He wanted Midwest City to be a community where families could enjoy a good life, all the while supporting the ongoing work at the base (Tinker Field)." (11)

The story of how Midwest City came into existence, and the central role played by Atkinson in building it, reads like a novel. It is, as has been said, intimately connected with the beginnings of Tinker Field, which are detailed in Chapter 1. Bill Atkinson's story dovetails seamlessly with the founding of Tinker.

The location was kept secret from the public to discourage land speculation and inflated land prices, but nearly every land developer in Oklahoma City was intent on finding out where the base was going to be built. Bill Atkinson was the only developer who found out, and it didn't hurt that he had been trained as a journalist and worked as one for several years. It also didn't hurt that E.K. Gaylord had brought him into the executive body of the Oklahoma City Chamber of Commerce, which had led the effort to get the air depot located there. In that group, he overheard tidbits of information about the base, and then on Feb. 7, 1941, Gaylord's newspaper *The Daily Oklahoman*, published site requirements for the new base. Among those requirements were the following:

- The land had to be 9-10 miles from an urban city.
- It had to be serviceable with water.
- It had to be serviceable by railroad.
- It had to be flat.
- It had to be at least 3 miles from the nearest oil drilling fields.
- There had to be a lot of it. The projected base could encompass some 1,500 acres. (12)

As a real estate developer in Oklahoma City, Atkinson knew the territory and its topography like the back of his hand. So, using his maps and knowledge of the area, coupled with the interviewing techniques he acquired as a reporter, he determined the best location was southeast of Oklahoma City along Southeast 29th Street. So, he climbed in his car and began driving east along that road where there was nothing but wheat fields and farms cultivating grain. Glancing in his rearview mirror at the Oklahoma City skyline, he determined he was about 10 miles from it.

He decided to find some farmers and start asking if their land was for sale. He discovered that no land was for sale on the south side of 29th Street, but there was plenty for sale on the *north side* of the street. He grew more curious. He spoke with one southside farmer who said he had no land to sell now, but he might have some in six weeks if Atkinson wanted to check back. Asked what the price might be, the farmer said about $150 per acre. (13)

So now Atkinson knew how long he had before the deal was sealed for the air base, and how much the land in the area was going for. Here is how Cindy Mikeman summarizes the way Atkinson used his ingenuity and skills from that point on:

"He was such a great communicator with people," she said. "He was a true visionary and a businessman 24/7. He was always creating, and he was a master at asking questions. All of the answers to the questions he was asking, would be answers that would help him in the future. So he got out of his car and went up to a home, and the lady of the home -- who lived on the south side of 29th Street – greeted him at the door. And he said, 'It's very interesting, because none of the farmers on the south side of 29th want to sell their property. And I know that you are not supposed to say anything, but if you wouldn't mind to just *wink an eye* if I'm asking you the right question.' And the question was, 'Has anyone spoken to you all about purchasing your property? 'She winked her eye. That's the beginning of the city." (14)

Atkinson knew he had the right spot, and he immediately started talking to farmers north of 29th Street. Here he found willing sellers, and the first man to sell him land was Frank Trosper, one of the original settlers who joined in the great land run of 1889 when the unassigned lands in Oklahoma territory were opened to the public. It is said that Trosper, in this year of 1941, still owned the mule that he used in that run and that this mule was still alive.

Trosper composed his own contract for the land on his old typewriter and sold Atkinson the first 160 acres that would soon become the original part of Midwest City. Then he made Atkinson a gift of his mule's saddle, and that saddle still hangs in the pony barn on the Atkinson Heritage Center and Museum. Trosper agreed to keep the land sale secret, and Atkinson delayed filing a deed to the property until he was able to purchase enough more to start his planned community. He soon purchased another 160 acres from Trosper's fellow farmer and friend, Joe Chesser. (15)

Now Bill Atkinson had 320 acres for what would become half of the original mile of Midwest City, a town he would name after the Midwest Air Depot, which was to be built right across the street. Atkinson must have cringed when the Gaylord and the Oklahoma City Chamber of Commerce convinced the War Department to change the name of the Midwest Air Depot to Tinker Field, since he had already named his town Midwest City, but he had confidence the town didn't need to carry the actual name of the air base to prosper.

As for the reasons the chamber of commerce pressed for the name change, that remains an open question: was it really to honor Gen. Clarence Tinker, or was it to keep Atkinson's Midwest City from sharing the base's name? Or both?

Atkinson would soon double his acreage to 640, and that tract is what is now called the "OM" for Original Mile. It was bounded on the south side by 29th Street, on the west by a street to appropriately be called Air Depot, on the east by the equally appropriately named Midwest Boulevard, and on the north by 15th Street.

Atkinson himself looked back on his founding of Midwest City in a 1993 interview KOCO-TV interview with reporter Ronny Kaye in Oklahoma City. He called the story of that founding, "the most misunderstood thing that has occurred, probably in the state of Oklahoma."

He explained, "I had become the leading home builder and developer at that particular time. One day Mr. Gaylord came out with a front-page story ... and he didn't know it yet, but he literally told me where Tinker would be located."

Atkinson said he knew the metro area better than anyone else, so he was able to match the site to the land requirements that Gaylord had posted for the proposed air depot.

About the feud that developed between the two men later, Atkinson said, "Mr. Gaylord and I were close personal friends. He wanted what was best for Oklahoma City, and I wanted what was best, too. I really loved the man."

While many developers might say they had reached their goal in simply identifying the base location and buying up the adjacent land for housing, Atkinson knew he had more work to do. He was thinking beyond the streets and houses that needed to be built, and he understood that unless he built an entire town that could service all the needs of the people of the air depot, then he might lose the whole project.

After all, it would have been in the rights of the War Department to snatch up that land for a greater purpose in building a community to support the air depot. So, Atkinson made the first of many flights to Washington, D.C., to inform military leaders about his purchase of the land and to *ask them* what kind of a town they would like to see built there.

They were impressed with this young developer and his candor, coupled with his desire to serve the needs of those who would work at the depot. So, they endorsed his land purchase and put him in touch with an expert urban planner, Seward Mott, who drew up what would be the award-winning plan for the original mile of Midwest City. Mott was excited about the opportunity to design an entire community and told Atkinson, "If this thing develops, it will be the first in my long career in planning that I have had the opportunity to take a large piece of raw ground, with no obstructions, and plan a complete city, the way one should be planned." (16)

Three years later, in 1944, Mott would stand before the National

Association of Real Estate Boards in Chicago and speak about his designed city. "Midwest City, a successful experiment in cooperative community building ... I think Midwest City is the answer for home builders and also for the city planner in securing the development of self-contained neighborhoods, rather than the construction of isolated little groups of homes." (17)

Heaping more accolades on the new city, the *Christian Science Monitor* wrote on September 5, 1944, that this was one of the first towns in America "to be completely blueprinted before construction was begun." (18)

As it turns out, Mott's design "was an indirect influence of Thomas Jefferson, an architect in his own right," according to architectural writer Marcus Whiffen. "The relationship between the Original Mile of Midwest City and Jefferson can be found in the design of the streets. Jefferson assisted with the task of street planning in Washington D.C., and Mott in Midwest City." (19)

The design consisted of curvilinear streets and cul-de-sacs which would keep motorists at safe speeds. The idea was to prevent auto accidents as much as possible in town, with few long straight streets and as few intersections as possible. The street design, in fact was credited with preventing any traffic fatalities at all during Midwest City's first eighteen years of existence. The design also kept children safer playing in their yards, not having to worry about speeding motorists.

The winding streets would also allow for the creation of different size lots and allowed each architect to put the best suitable house on the lot. And, as for the names of the streets, they also fit Atkinson's thematic approach, with the theme here being none other than the newly renamed Tinker Field. Therefore, streets carried the names of aircraft companies (Lockheed, Aeronica, Boeing, Curtis, and Douglas, for example) or were named for Army Air Corps officers like General William Senter, or Col. Wallace Turnbull. The latter was the first base commander at Tinker.

The main entry into Midwest City came north off Southeast 29th Street on a street named Mid-American Boulevard. It was at this intersection that Atkinson placed the town's first shopping center, Atkinson Plaza, built in two long halves and divided by this street. Whether intended or not by Atkinson, many residents believed an aerial view of this shopping center evoked the image of an airplane, with Mid-America Boulevard being the fuselage and the east and west halves of the shopping center its wings.

Mid-America Boulevard ran north for a city block and then split east and west around the city hall plaza that contained not only City Hall, but the fire and police stations, the public library, and a large water tower built over the main city well.

For many years this water tower would be a landmark painted in a red-and-white checkerboard pattern before it was converted to black and gold, the colors of Midwest City High School. The two forks of Mid-America then continued north in a curved pattern and dead-ended into East and West Lockheed Drives. In fact, the home I grew up in was at 301 East Lockheed, and it put me in walking distance of nearly every place in town. Other streets in town followed similar curvilinear patterns.

Bill Atkinson broke ground on the first of his five original houses on Turnbull Drive on April 4, 1942, eleven months before Midwest City received its charter and was incorporated as a town. From that point on, the building boom was in full swing when Atkinson wound up receiving all 700 building permits handed out in the Oklahoma City area due to wartime restrictions on building supplies.

Feeling the protest of other area homebuilders who were left out, and realizing he couldn't build all these homes himself, the city's founder began selling lots and giving permits to 15 prominent builders, headed by Atkinson, who began constructing hundreds of homes and a few apartment buildings. This group was named the Allied Home Builders and included John W. Lyon, Sylvanus G. Felix, Steve Pennington, Amos Bouse, H.B. Atkinson, Manly M. Moore, Russell Showalter, C.E. Fuffner, N.D. Woods, Ed Jensen, Curtis

The original builders, surrounding Bill Atkinson, seated in center.
"City of Tomorrow" promotional brochure

L. Smith, Ben C. Wileman, Cord Wilson, and Roger Givens.

These builders worked out a plan to split the area to be built, each building his own preferred type of home, which produced overall architectural variety, while offering similar housing styles in each builder's area. The shopping center and business district was built by Atkinson himself, along with many of the homes in areas he called "Veterans Village," and (the only other time I've ever seen this name used,) "Tinker Town," on the eastern edge of the air depot. That area, however, would be subsumed in the base expansion.

All homes built in Midwest City had to adhere to Federal Housing Administration (FHA) guidelines, and the FHA then provided low-interest loans for the working-class homeowners who bought them. The FHA had been created in 1934 by President Roosevelt to provide relief for the homebuilding industry by insuring mortgages for homebuyers. The country's construction boom had come to an abrupt halt with the stock market crash of 1929. Homebuilding in America was suspended as a result, and would-be homebuyers were forced into rental units.

To resolve the impasse, Congress passed the Federal Housing Act in 1934, which created the Federal Housing Administration to over-see FHA-backed homes. The FHA lowered interest rates on mortgages, improved home appraisal methods, and developed strategies and standards for city planning, land planning, and home construction. In order to qualify for FHA-backed mortgages, homes had to align with the administration's specifications.

The creation of the FHA did the trick, and homebuilding began booming again. Whereas homebuyers had only been able to borrow up to 80 percent of the cost of a home and have only 20 years to pay it off, now they could borrow up to 90 percent and repay it over 30 years. It is doubtful Midwest City would have developed into the city it became without the Federal Housing Authority.

For one thing, Seward Mott – the man who designed the plan for the Original Mile of the city, also served as the director of land planning for the FHA. By following his design for the homes, streets, and sub-divisions of Midwest City, Atkinson knew the homes Mott suggested would conform to FHA guidelines, and those families who bought them would benefit from the low-cost FHA financing.

The homes were simple, mostly around 900 square feet in size, with 2 or 3 bedrooms and one bath. To simplify the building process and get the neighborhoods built as quickly as possible, only a few designs and elevations were used, and some streets consisted of nearly identical homes. These original homes sold for prices between $2,000 and $4,000, and rents ran between $35-$50 per month.

A few months after home construction began in the spring of 1942, few people would have looked at this building scene in the middle of a large wheatfield and considered it an ideal place to live. Housing neighborhoods went up faster than the streets could be paved, and there was mud everywhere when it rained. For a time, in fact, these pioneering homebuyers referred to Midwest City as "*Mudwest* City." Looking back on 1943 (the first operational year for Midwest City School), principal James E. Sutton recalled, "The winter was bad, and there was much rain and mud.

The raw pioneering proved too difficult for a few teachers, parents and children, and they left for more settled situations. But the majority of teachers and students alike treated their experience as one great adventure, and they rose to whatever heights – or depths – that came. I don't believe I have ever seen so much mud. It was difficult to keep streets up with the building of houses; therefore, some streets were unpaved long after the houses were built. We waded in mud to school; we waded in mud to the restrooms, and we waded in mud to class-rooms." (20)

Nevertheless, home construction went quickly in the original mile plat, and by the end of 1944, Midwest City contained 1,466 single-family homes were completed, along with a shopping center (Atkinson Plaza), a single school housing K-12, a municipal building, and five churches.

According to a 1992 State Historical Society review of Midwest City's first 50 years, "This phenomenon, in a wartime economy, in-trigued several architectural engineers." (21) And a historical survey would later say of the city's Original Mile, "It serves as an excellent ex-ample of the type of neighborhood which was supported by the Federal Housing Administration. The architecture, which includes war housing and postwar housing, is also significant as an excellent example of this period." (22)

Two early houses of the early 1950s in Midwest City
"City of Tomorrow" promotional brochure

Matthew Pearce of the Oklahoma Historical Society noted of the homes, "They have been often referred to as the little house that could.

You could put them up cheaply, and they did the job for the families that lived in them." (23)

And, since there were multiple other builders who purchased lots from Atkinson in the original square mile, there was variation in the elevations of many homes. "You're not going to see two houses that are the same," said Mikeman. (24) Even so, many of the original homes on an original given street like Lockheed Drive did appear to have come out of the same mold. It was only when the other builders started construction on later streets did the designs begin to vary in the way Mikeman noted.

One thing did prove true to predictions, though: Midwest City seemed to be a *family town* from the start. Some have even asked, "Could you buy a house if you were not a family?" Mikeman's answer to that was, "I'm sure you could, but I don't know of any single individuals who bought one of these original houses. But we did have an apartment complex [the Fleetwood Apartments only a block from Tinker). That's where a lot of the single individuals would live." (25)

If there was one structure in the Atkinson Plaza Shopping Center that depicted the welding of Midwest City to Tinker Field it was the center's 1,100-seat movie theater, the only indoor one in town. As were all the building in the shopping center, it was a cream-colored brick structure with a tall vertical sign that read, "SKYTRAIN." It was the most visible building in the downtown area, and it was a name that most of us kids took for granted without knowing what it signified other than some kind of air ship. As noted in Chapter 1, the Skytrain was the workhorse C-47 transport plane of World War II's Army Air Corps, and the air base right across 29th Street – Tinker Field – had built more than 5,000 of them, or over half of all those planes used during the war. They were a backbone of America's war effort, and now the Skytrain Theater was the cornerstone of Midwest City's entertainment effort.

But the Skytrain wasn't to be the only movie theater in town with Air Force related names. Soon, drive-in movies were added, and the first two were the *Tinker* and *Bomber* drive-ins. Atkinson was always thinking about complementary parts to the whole in Midwest City, and they had to support his theme of a full-service town that owed its existence to Tinker Field.

One other downtown business deserves singling out as an example of how Atkinson responded to the needs of the city's earliest residents. As families began pouring into town, they realized there was no supermarket there, and the nearest one was eight miles west on 29th Street in the Capitol Hill section of Oklahoma City. Many voiced their desire for their own downtown supermarket to Atkinson, and he began looking for a grocer to start one. He discovered, however, that companies were leery of building in a military town, fearful that the base would close after the war, and that the town would dry up.

Undaunted, Atkinson called on his Oklahoma City friend and fellow businessman, Sylvan Goldman, who owned a chain of supermarkets called *Humpty Dumpty*. He said Midwest City was here to stay, and Goldman agreed to establish a grocery in the Atkinson Plaza Shopping Center. Atkinson would build the store to Goldman's specifications, and Goldman would pay him one dollar for every person who came in. Goldman told Atkinson, "If you're so certain you'll have so many families [in this town], then you'll clean up." (26) The deal proved very profitable to both men, and Humpty Dumpty became the first supermarket in the shopping center, and soon anchored it.

Bill Atkinson was constantly considering and implementing win-win strategies for Midwest City and himself. He knew that whatever he could do to enhance the new community would also benefit himself. Yet his personality was such that he genuinely seemed to care about the people who were – and would be – inhabiting his town. One such review came from Pam Olson Boettcher, whose parents moved to the infant Midwest City in 1945.

Pam was born in the town and graduated from Midwest City High School in 1968, going on to the University of Oklahoma where she graduated, won a Miss Oklahoma title, and worked as a reporter and anchor for KWTV television in Oklahoma City before going to CNN where she covered the White House. Olson remembers Atkinson as a "kind, jovial, and upbeat person" who liked people and seemed very down to earth. (27)

Another native of Midwest City, Mary Clem Good Morris, remembers Atkinson being very friendly to children and teens in the city. "He was a good man. He paid us to watch for vandals in the area near his construction projects. I remember getting a check for $4 from him, and the lady at the bank said she had never seen a check *from* Mr. Atkinson!" (28) Morris, a 1964 Midwest City High School graduate, also recalled a time when Atkinson saw her brother and friends playing baseball in an empty field on the northeast side of Midwest City, and he stopped and asked them if they liked playing baseball. Sandee Springer, whose family moved to Midwest City in 1956, said she and her friends were playing and Atkinson also stopped and asked her brothers if they would like a baseball field built. He also invited all of them out to his pony farm to ride Shetlands on Sunday afternoons.

All these kids said they would love to have a baseball field and, before long, Atkinson had a construction crew turn an empty field on Midwest Boulevard into a baseball diamond. He did the same thing at another empty field on the northwest side. Both ball diamonds became used regularly by children and teens, which was a plus for them. But it was also a plus for Atkinson, because both ball fields abutted and enhanced his new Ridgecrest Heights subdivision, which was the third phase of Midwest City in the 1950s. Again, Atkinson's win-win strategy paid off.

Another Midwest Cityan, Kathy Jorgensen Stepenaskie, remembered how personally involved Atkinson was in the community and how kind he was to people. "Mr. Atkinson was my Sunday School teacher at Wickline Methodist Church," she said. "He had attended the inauguration of JFK and told us many stories of the events. My friend Linda and I attended his classes. If any of us attended thirteen classes, Mr. Atkinson promised us a lunch at the Uptown Cafeteria and a visit to his farm to ride ponies. This was in the early 1960s. What a treat for us! We had a ball!" (29)

As the city developed in its first decade, Atkinson never ceased to become personally involved in its growth and even funded programs that enhanced that growth and benefitted the residents. He donated the $250 prize money for various lawn and street beautification awards; each year he awarded the Outstanding Boy and Girl Awards to two Midwest City High School seniors; he welcomed town residents out to ride Shetland ponies on his estate, and he even donated some of those ponies for auctions that helped support charitable causes like the March of Dimes.

As Nancy Moeri Lee wrote in a graduate thesis at the University of Oklahoma, "As the city grew and town amenities became necessary, he helped finance community projects. He provided lumber for the new library and land for the country club. Of course, every addition to the town became an incentive for people to move there, and every new house meant a bonus to W.P. But no one could call him an absentee landlord." (30)

A School System Begins

As the city's housing and neighborhoods were taking shape, so was the city's school system. Again, the overall theme Atkinson envisioned called for a full-service community, and schools were a huge part of that theme. It cannot be overstated how important the youngest residents in Midwest City were to its future, and Atkinson knew that from the start. As homes were completed and families began moving into the new town in late 1942 and 1943, the only schools there were two rural, independent schools (Sooner Elementary and Soldier Creek) which only went through the 8th grade, and which were on the eastern and western edges of the original Midwest City limits. Midwest Air Depot, now Tinker Field, was a step ahead of Midwest City in its construction, and it offered its new post school and nursery facilities to non-military families for a time, as well.

To spearhead and develop the city's own school system, Atkinson tapped Oscar V. Rose, who had been hired by the Sooner School but who saw what was happening in Midwest City and told friends, "That's where the real school will be." So, he accepted Atkinson's invitation to start that school system. (31)The state approved Midwest City as its

Independent School District No. 52 in 1943, with full authority to tax for its revenue, and the new school board begin hiring faculty and staff. The state board of education accredited Midwest City High School, and it became the only high school accredited in Oklahoma *before* the first class ever began.

The original hutments that were the Midwest City School.
Artist David Fox, MCHS Class of 1959

When the hutment "kits" arrived, teachers, administrators, parents, and students alike all pitched in to put the plywood rooms together. Each one measured 16x16 feet, and they were all positioned in a square.

Amazingly, they were all finished in two weeks, in time to welcome the new town's school children in mid-September. Furniture was borrowed from Draughon's Business College in Oklahoma City, and the district's first school bus was borrowed from Bearden, Oklahoma, which was Rose's first school district. Altogether, the hutments housed 413 students that first year, grades K-12. (32)

Oklahoma winds being what they are, however, a few months later a strong wind struck the hutments and shifted the north and south sections to 45-degree angles. The decision was made to leave the structures that way, to build new foundations underneath them, and to run new gas lines to them.

The man chosen as principal of this Midwest City School, James E. Sutton, noted of the new layout, "Midwest City School was no longer a square; it was now a parallelogram." (33)

Permanent buildings would come soon for Midwest City schools, but classes were in session by 1943, and that was the important thing. Midwest City was just beginning, and it would triple in size in its first decade.

Looking back on what Atkinson developed, his daughter Eugenia Davis said, "the original square mile was arranged as a family-friendly community, complete with shopping centers, churches, parks, and schools. My dad wanted Midwest City to be a community where families could enjoy a good life, all the while supporting the ongoing work at the base." (34)

Although Atkinson was able to implement his vision of creating a complete town, his endeavor didn't come without personal cost. What had been a very close relationship with E.K. Gaylord in Oklahoma City turned into a blood feud when Gaylord learned it was Atkinson who had gobbled up all the land across from the Midwest Air Depot at a time when he and the Chamber of Commerce were trying to keep the depot location a secret. But most observers knew that, if Atkinson had not been the one to discern where it would be built, one or more of the other land developers who were feverishly searching for it might well have found it and bought the land themselves. Atkinson himself said later, "I cannot understand why others couldn't [find it]. It was very easy for anyone with any sense at all. Anyone could have figured it out." (35)

But anyone else didn't. Gaylord felt betrayed and worried Atkinson's actions might have cost the city the depot before it was even built. Apparently, he did not know or either overlooked the fact, that Atkinson had consulted with the War Department before he ever built his first house in the town, and that Washington had already green-lighted his planned community.

As for Atkinson's response to Gaylord's anger, Mikeman said, "Granddaddy always said, 'Gaylord gave me the roadmap when he published the site requirements for the depot land." And her own opinion of Gaylord? "I'll never say that Granddaddy meeting Gaylord was a bad thing. That's how Bill Atkinson's networking began in Oklahoma City." (36)

Nevertheless, the friendship between the two men was over and Gaylord would write devastating front-page editorials about Bill Atkinson in the years to come when the builder's career aspirations turned toward state politics, cutting short Atkinson's political future. In 1958, Atkinson ran for the Democratic nomination for governor of Oklahoma but lost to a young reform candidate named J. Howard Edmonson and his "prairie fire campaign." Edmondson went on to become a senator, and in 1962 Atkinson ran again for governor, won the Democratic nomination, but lost to Henry Bellmon, who would become the state's first Republican governor.

But Gaylord couldn't stop Atkinson from creating and building Midwest City, nor could he stop the city's growth which, by 1950, had topped 10,000 residents and would go on to top 60,000 in a few short decades..

All this history was unknown to me when my own family first became four of those early Midwest City residents, as Dad brought us to town in 1949 where he would become an advertising salesman for WKY-TV in Oklahoma City. From that point forward, the story of Midwest City became very personal to me.

3

New Kid in a New Town

One of the first classes of Jack & Jill Preschool Students in 1950. The Willis kids are circled (because that's what moms do).

Norman Warner Photography

My family's 1949 move to Oklahoma took us to this young town of Midwest City, lying only 15 minutes southeast of downtown OKC. By then, at least, the streets were all paved. Since the town did not exist before 1943, this 6-year-old place and I, age 3, would grow up together. In a way, the town was like my big brother, teaching me things about life. It was a new town with a new Air Force Base, and in the years to come I would see how important Tinker Field was to Midwest City and how it helped make the town so unique. But the town itself had its own can-do spirit and was probably as brash as any youngsters who felt they could and would conquer the world. My Oklahoma journey was just beginning, and the influence of this place would last an entire lifetime.

Today, I have a t-shirt that reads, *"Oklahoma: It's where my story begins."* The statement begs the question: Is that *all* this place did? Just serve as my starting gate? Or was its impact greater? I remember enough of my early years to know that Midwest City did help shape who I am today, as it did with so many of my friends. Understandably, those influences existed in greater or lesser degrees in all of us, but all of us were affected by the spirit and moods of Midwest City and Tinker in some way.

Of course, we all grow and change in different ways as we mature, regardless of early influences. But, as the writer Joshua Rothman asks in a 2022 article for the *New Yorker* Magazine, "Is the fix already in, or will our stories have surprising twists and turns?" He continues, "If we could see our childish selves more clearly, we might have a better sense of the course and the character of our lives. Are we the same people at four that we will be at twenty-four, forty-four, or seventy-four? Or will we change substantially through time?" (1)

Many of us do feel the intervening years have changed us dramatically, and that we bear only scant resemblance to who we were as young people. Rothman notes, that to those who feel this dichotomy, "the past seems like a foreign country, characterized by peculiar customs, values, and tastes ... But others have a strong sense of connection with their younger selves, and for them the past remains a home." (2) As I've thought about it, I fall into this latter category. There's a distinct thread that runs way back to my early years, although it has weaved and bobbed through several life-altering experiences along the way, snagging on several of them, losing its way on others, and nearly snapping on a few. Yet the thread is still intact to my present day.

The fact that I even think about it at all suggests my personal makeup is different from others like my older son, David, who is always looking forward, hardly ever in his rear-view mirror. He explains, "I don't look back, Dad. I don't see the point in it." But does not looking back mean the past hasn't affected who you are today? Or are you simply choosing not to see it? *Are you not noticing that you don't notice it?*

There are days when I feel like the poet William Wordsworth when he wrote, *The Rainbow*, an 1802 poem centering on this symbol of nature and of the poet's desire to stay close to his childlike self and keep it alive. It begins, "My heart leaps up when I behold a rainbow in the sky; So was it when my life began, so is it now that I am a man." (3)

Some 240 years later, in 1941, screenwriter Herman J. Mankiewicz resurrected that image, although using a simple snow sled to stand in for Wordsworth's rainbow. The result was the closing one-word line in the film uttered by the wealthy-yet-saddened Charles Foster Kane on his deathbed when he rasped the sled's name: *"Rosebud."* As Kane actor and director Orson Welles explains, Rosebud was "the representation of the simplicity, the comfort, and the lack of responsibility in his home, and also it stood for his mother's love, which Kane never lost." (4)

One Midwest City native, Barbara Manning Cox, told me a story in 2024 that depicts how a single element from the past can still represent something alluring. She said that, although she never worked at Tinker, she did go to school there in hutments the Air Force let Midwest City use while her school was being constructed. "Growing up, I lived on Turnbull, practically across the street from Tinker. My one memory is hearing the planes rev up. A tremendous roar heard for miles. I loved that sound as a child. It sounded all-consuming and *like there was an excited life happening out there somewhere.*"

An E-3 Sentry AWAC (airborne early warning control) aircraft
landing.
(U.S. Air Force Photo)

So it was to many of us, and so it was with me. My adopted
hometown and Tinker became much more than my starting gate. My
awareness of worldly adventures was, in part, driven by the sounds of
those jet engines powering planes coming from and going to all parts
of the globe.

*An E-3 Sentry AWAC (airborne early warning and control) plane is one of
the main aircraft serviced and maintained at Tinker Air Force Base. The disk
on top rotated to pick up blips from every direction.*

At first, I was oblivious to what this town was like, or that it even
hosted an Air Force base. But I did know there were a lot of airplanes overhead, and that they were taking off and landing just a few
blocks away. I remember feeling the same kind of sensation then that
I had when I sat and watched all the trains zoom past by back yard in
Columbus, taking travelers who knows where?

Now our home was right below the glide path that the jets and
bombers used every day and every night, to and from Tinker Field. I
came to feel the sound of airplanes was just another voice of nature,

as much as the birds and crickets in the back yard, and frogs in a nearby creek.

A small boy knows little about the new town his folks move him to, beyond what his house – and mostly his bedroom – look like, whether there's a backyard and maybe a swing set, and whether there are any other kids living next door. In my case, all these boxes were checked "yes," so I was happy when I saw our first place on Babb Drive. For one thing, it was not just one unit in a large apartment building like the one in Columbus. Yes, it was a duplex and not a single-family house, but that was okay with me, and I'm not even sure I knew the difference.

I had my own yard, and I was little enough to not mind sharing my bedroom with my older sister C.J. She and I got along better than most young brothers and sisters, and it would stay that way throughout our lives. Another plus was that our home and yard backed up to a city park, known as Lions Park, and that gave me even more room to romp and get dirty before suppertime. Soon the city would build a big public pool in that park, and that inspired my lifelong love of swimming.

One aspect of our Columbus experience that I missed, however, were the trains steaming past our apartment home. We had no nearby tracks in this new place, and I missed them. But the park was a pretty good substitute, and my sister C.J. and I made good use of it on sunny days. And, although I missed the chugging sounds of the trains, I came to feel the woosh and roar of the jets flying overhead was a pretty good trade-off as these sleek skyships approached the Tinker runways just a few hundred yards beyond our home. For a small kid, that was *definitely* not a bad trade.

I lost count of the times I would run out into my yard just to look up and read the numbers and insignia off some big bomber, transport, or jet fighter floating in on the glide path a couple hundred feet overhead. Sometimes the sound of the engines was deafening, and Mom often had to make sure none of the cups and saucers would get rattled and fall off the shelf in the kitchen.

We lived in this duplex for less than a year. During that time, my view of the larger town would grow, and my world would expand beyond our neighborhood.

I don't remember when I began hearing about the history of this "pop-up town" I had moved to, but I know it was something I learned over time. The lessons would come via what I witnessed and what I heard; from life experiences set in the context of the town and the era of the 1950s and 60s. Later in life, I would see that even though Midwest City was unique in some ways, it wasn't all that different from the American suburban culture that sprang up in the years immediately following World War II. That was especially true, I'm sure, for other towns that hosted military bases.

When the GIs returned from the war and reunions with sweethearts began producing what became the Baby Boomer Generation, housing was needed to accommodate the burgeoning growth of families. We boomers (in Oklahoma we were actually *Boomer* boomers) were born between 1946 and 1964, the years that birth trend lines were soaring in America. More babies entered the United States and Canada in 1946 than ever before in history.

Live births in the U.S. surged from 222,721 in January, to 339,499 in October. (5) World War II was over, and the long-delayed rush to start families began as American troops returned from the battlefields of Europe and the Pacific. The birth numbers totaled 3.4 million, which were a whopping 20 percent more than 1945 alone. Another 3.8 million babies came in 1947, and the trend continued until tapering off in 1964. Altogether by that year, there were more than 74 million baby boomers, comprising four out of every ten Americans. (6)

The young families of the late 1940s and 1950s preferred houses and yards instead of city apartments, so the suburban sprawl began. This produced entire towns in many cases, and in the Midwest and Southwest, a lot of these towns grew up out of farmland that once grew wheat and corn instead of families. Such was the case with Midwest City, but here the evolution from farm to town moved at warp speed. This was not a town that started with a gas station, general store, and a few houses. This town started with an *entire town* that would quickly spread over one square mile.

Two driving forces – World War II and the need to house workers at Tinker field – mandated that the air base and Midwest City be built as quickly as possible. By the time we arrived in 1949, there were already nearly 10,000 new residents here. Had we arrived just a decade earlier, we would have landed in the middle of the Dust Bowl desolation with a few dozen farmers struggling to provide for their families.

I remember enjoying the first year in that small duplex in 1949-50. I had plenty to eat, neighborhood kids to play with, parents who made me feel secure, and presents under the tree at Christmas. It was just my life, and I liked it. I suppose it's like that for most kids everywhere. Until someone told you you're middle-class or lower middle-class, you just never thought about it. Even if you did, it wouldn't have mattered.

It was a real-life version of the movie, *Pleasantville.* Dad would leave every morning for work in Oklahoma City, and Mom would see to it that my sister C.J. and I were kept busy during the day. Dad would come home at 6, dinner would be on the table, and afterwards we would listen to some comedy or drama on the radio. Television had made its entry, but it would be a couple years before our family could afford one, even though Dad worked at a new television station in Oklahoma City.

It's odd how memories work, but only a few things come to mind when I think of my family's first year on Babb Drive. The memories mostly involve the kindliness of other people in town. First, was having my tonsils removed by a very nice doctor at Mercy Hospital in Oklahoma City. Midwest City had no hospital, so Oklahoma City got the town's business. I had been having a sore throat for the past week or two and, in that day, this was usually a symptom that the tonsils had to go.

I think just about all my friends had gone through this procedure which, today, is widely seen as unnecessary. Anyway, it wasn't the little operation I remember, so much as the nurse coming in beforehand and pricking my finger to draw and test my blood. To me, that little prick has always hurt more than it should. More than that, however, I remember arriving back home and being presented a large ice cream cone by my parents as a reward for my heroism exhibited at the hospital. Or at least that's the reason they gave me!

Another memory that sticks is seeing several men in town who were missing one of their arms or legs. One of these was our laundry delivery man, who was always upbeat and flashed a genuine smile at me when Mom greeted him at the door. I still remember the image of him hooking the hangered dry cleaning over his left wooden arm while he reached into his pocket for change to give to mom after she paid him. I was probably at least 5 years old when I realized these men had lost their limbs fighting in the war. Even then I remember thinking how much they had sacrificed for the country. Later in my teen years, I would date a girl whose dad lost his leg in D-Day. I felt proud to be living next to a military base.

The third thing I remember about that year was our milkman. In those days, you could have cold bottles of milk delivered to your door, and most people did. The guy who serviced our route was Mr. McNulty, and he always had a smile on his face and a little mischief in mind when he took a moment to play with me on the front porch if I was home. He would reach over and do his little magic trick where he would reach down with his first two fingers, pinch my nose gently between them, and then quickly slide his thumb up between those finger as he stood up.

"Well how about that, Jimmy! Your nose wasn't attached to your face very well today! Here you go, I'll stick it back on."

And so he did, bending over once more to complete the trick.

In today's world, I'm afraid a neighbor witnessing that might misinterpret it as child molestation, call 911, and the poor milkman would be arrested before he made it to his truck on the curb.

Not unlike other towns and cities in America during and after the war, patriotism was an important part of life for Midwest City residents. It was made even more important because of the presence of military and absolute economic importance of being the host town of a huge military facility like Tinker. Air Force personnel and their families were part of the fabric of Midwest City, and you encountered them on the streets and in neighborhoods and stores every day of the week. I remember lots of parades in this Air Force town, lots of flags flew over front porch steps,

Tinker held an open house and big air show once each year, and the 4th of July was a bigger event than I'd ever seen before.

A relic of days gone by and the Oklahoma land run of 1889.

I was also introduced to another annual parade and festival – this one unique to the state of Oklahoma – called *89er Day*. Every April, cities and towns in Oklahoma pay homage to the Oklahoma Land Run, which was held on April 22, 1889.

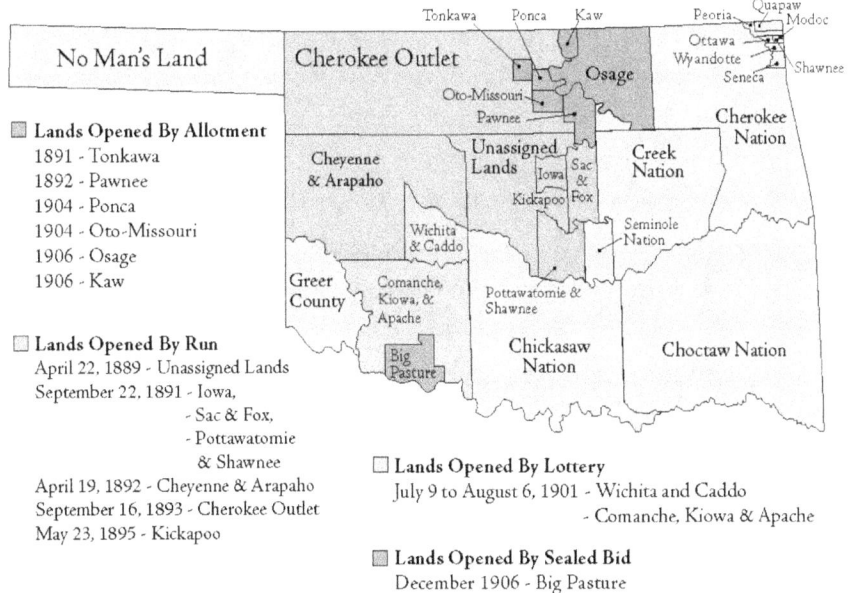

Oklahoma Land Openings

Oklahoma map showing the sections of the territory assigned to the tribes. The Unassigned Lands are in the center.
(Image by Branton Wiederholt/Sage Journals.)

It was the day that the government opened the "unassigned Lands," or 1.8 million acres in the center of Oklahoma that bordered reservations of the Chickasaw, Cheyenne, Arapaho, Shawnee, Sac & Fox, Iowa, Pawnee, and Potawatomi tribes.

Before Oklahoma became a state in 1907, it was known as Indian Territory where all these tribes lived. In fact, the name "Oklahoma" is the Choctaw word for "red people." As the westward movement gathered steam, this large chunk of central Oklahoma – which included Midwest City – was assigned to non-Indian settlement by 1889.

The Oklahoma Historical Society says this about the Land Run of 1889 that drew some 50,000 eager settlers to the starting points, stretching for many miles across the borders of the Unassigned Lands"Across America, prospective settlers began hitching their teams to wagons and loading aboard their families and scant worldly goods. Others saddled their fastest horses or caught trains for what they considered to be the most advantageous point of entry.

"The great dramatic moment came when, at the stroke of noon, starting signals were given at the many points of entry. In some instances, it was given by a blue-clad military officer firing his pistol or by his trumpeter, at times by a citizen firing his rifle in the air, or, as at Fort Reno, by the boom of a cannon. All produced the same results—a tumultuous avalanche of wagons and horsemen surging forward all in one breathtaking instant."

"Families that remained behind at the line cheered as a husband or father made his wild dash to choose his 160 acres. He would then determine its range and township from the surveyors' cornerstone markers and plant a stake bearing notice of his name and location. Some would immediately begin making token improvements such as digging a well or arranging logs for a potential home. Others would hurry to the land office to register their claim." (7)

If you've seen the 1992 Tom Cruise/Nicole Kidman movie, *Far and Away*, you get a pretty clear picture of what it was like to be a part of that land run of 1889. To say it was exciting is a gross understatement; to say it wasn't dangerous to be riding your horse at breakneck speed, surrounded by thousands of other stampeders, would be a lie.

The biggest and oldest of the 89er Day Festival is held in the town of Guthrie, 33 miles north of Oklahoma City. Guthrie was the original state capital of Oklahoma before some political scalawags devised a secret scheme to move it to Oklahoma City, making it one of several zany chapters to this state's colorful history. However, every April it seemed that every town and city in the state – including Midwest City – celebrated with an 89er Day Festival and Parade, as we all became 19th century cowboys and cowgirls again, eagerly awaiting our chance to claim our land.

This, then, was Oklahoma: my new state. It was a young, brash state and was only 42 years old when I arrived at age 3. Indeed, my Midwest City was much younger and – over my years there – seemed to exhibit the same brash pioneering spirit that Oklahoma itself did.

I turned 4 in my first few months in this new and curious and exciting place, as I began absorbing and internalizing elements of this new culture and its symbols of military aircraft, uniforms, rules and regulations. Within a year, when I would join the Cub Scouts, I think I felt I was in the very first stage of becoming a part of the Air Force and felt a kid's kinship to these warriors of the sky. For all my childhood and adult years, I would hold the military and its traditional values near and dear as I dreamed of becoming a hero protecting others and adhering to a strict code of honor.

These were not always conscious thoughts but, looking back, I can see their imprint was a part of my youth. As the teen years would ensue, I could see myself serving in the military, then becoming an FBI agent. I loved the idea of becoming a single-minded individual, maybe a low-key federal agent like Elliot Ness of TV's *The Untouchables* fame. I didn't begin having new and different visions of myself and a more diverse set of beliefs until I moved away from Midwest City and out into the larger world at age 22 and beyond.

I liked the world I was a kid in, and I felt very safe there. I liked Midwest City, even though we had yet to move into our permanent home there. That would come soon.

Jack and Jill Days

When you erect an airbase and a town to service it, the combination exemplifies the living, tangible truth of the classic line from the film, *Field of Dreams.*

"If you build it, they will come."

And come they did, starting in 1942, to work at The Midwest Air Depot – still under construction on the south side of 29th Street – and to consider buying brand new homes in the soon-to-be-chartered town of Midwest City, on the north side of 29th Street. Just eight years later, in 1950, the town was bursting at the seams with 10,166 residents. My family and I were four of them. By 1960, the town's population would more than triple, soaring to 36,058. Today it is around 58,000.

Military families were being transferred to Tinker and needed housing, schools, churches, parks retail, and family services. Additionally, thousands of construction workers and civil service employees were being added to the air depot payroll, and most of them chose to live in Midwest City. In the beginning, one school was built in town to handle all grades through high school, and that school was located on East Lockheed Drive, just six doors west of our home at 301 E. Lockheed. By 1949 when we arrived, other elementary schools were built, and the building was handling only junior and senior high students. Within a couple more years, Midwest City had built its stand-alone high school, north of 15th Street and between Lockheed Drive and Midwest Boulevard. Then the original school campus on Lockheed became Jarman Junior High School and then Middle School.

From its chartered beginning in 1943, Midwest City's population growth was staggering. In that first year, the town was home to 2,200 residents and those residents had a greater percentage of families than any other city in Oklahoma. (8) So, there was a special need not only for housing but for community activities like education and recreation. These early postwar years marked the start of the Baby Boom Generation as GIs and their wives got to know each other intimately after years of war separation. Babies were the natural result, and *by 1950 one-third of Midwest City's population was made up of kids under 10 years of age.* (9) Infants seemed to arrive as fast as oil gushed from the state's ubiquitous drilling fields.

A panel in the new Town Center Shopping Center remembers the earliest days of Midwest City.

(Photo by Jim Willis)

Since many of the families moving into Midwest City had infants and toddlers. Bill Atkinson, realized that he needed to build more than houses and a retail district to make good on the promise he had made to the War Department back in 1941-42 to create a full-service community for the people of Tinker Field. So, from the start, when he built the Midwest City School, on Lockheed Drive, he designated a portion of it to be used as a nursery. Many women in Midwest City worked at Tinker during the 1940s war years and needed someone to look out for their young children. Even after the war, some GIs were late in returning from the war theaters and their wives were still working, so the need for nurseries persisted. The Midwest City School nursery wound up accommodating 100 infants and toddlers. To help handle the overflow, some women in town opened up their own small nurseries and day care centers.

But there were no actual preschools that focused on early curriculum needs for children of ages 3-5, and that's where my mom, Hazel M. Willis, stepped in. Our family of four had only been in Midwest City for a few months when Mom recognized the need for a preschool to service the youngest children of the military and civilian families, so she planned one out, started it, and ran it for nearly a decade to 1958.

She chose the name Jack & Jill Preschool, partly because of the popular nursery rhyme of that title but also to make both boys and girls feel equally welcome. It became Midwest City's first curriculum-driven preschool. Here, young children could begin their educational journey into reading, writing, and arithmetic, while also learning about the fine arts in painting, music, and even the dramatic arts. And the truly amazing thing was it was located right in our own home.

This is how the *Encyclopedia of Oklahoma History and Culture* described the beginning of Jack & Jill: "The news coverage (of the new town) and the jobs being created at Tinker encouraged people to move to Midwest City for an opportunity to work and own a home. For example, Jim and Hazel Willis moved from Ohio with no guarantees and a lot of hope. In 1949 Hazel opened the Jack & Jill Preschool." (10)

These women were not alone. In her 1996 master's thesis on Midwest City, Susan Moeri Lee wrote, "As the city grew and established itself, its many active women deserve recognition for its cultural accomplishments. One of the early citizens, Mrs. Elsie Carlisle, taught speech and drama at the high school. She organized the first Study Group in the city, consisting of women who met together to better themselves spiritually, mentally, and morally ... Several female members worked alongside

Teacher Mom and one of her J&J students.

(founding School Superintendent) Oscar Rose fighting for federal funding and traveling to Washington, D.C. to lobby for school aid ... The League of Women Voters organized in 1948 and kept voters informed on the key election issues. The Business and professional Women's group helped begin a public library, and the town court used women as jurors for the first time in 1952." (11)

My family was able to move from our small duplex in town to what became our permanent home at 301 E. Lockheed Drive. It was only a 10-minute walk to the downtown Atkinson Plaza, and a 15-minute walk to my Westside Elementary School when I began first grade a year later.

Dad bought the home from his brother, Dr. L.L. Willis, the town's first dentist. It was a side-gabled brick, 3-bedroom home with one bath and comprised only about 900 square feet of space. Although small by today's standards, it

was actually one of the larger homes being built in the original mile, and our home was brick, whereas many of the others were clapboard siding.

All these homes were built for the young, working-class families who were just starting out in life after the war. Most of them were among the thousands of new civilian employees hired by Tinker. Few of them cost more than $3,500 brand new, and most were cheaper than that. Still, by 1940s standards, following the Dust Bowl and the second world war, many homebuyers needed the new, low-cost FHA interest-rate mortgages to buy them. Our home was the largest on our block of East Lockheed Drive, because my uncle had added another 300 square feet by building a large den across the back of the home before we bought it.

We would need it, because we quickly wound up sharing our home with some 40 kids a day, Monday through Friday, when

Mom became an entrepreneur and opened her Jack & Jill Preschool. Its campus was our den and our backyard.

Our home at 301 E. Lockheed. Jack & Jill Preschool was in the back den.
(Photo shot in 2024 by Jim Willis)

She went to work getting the word out, around town and at Tinker, about her new school. She would take telephone directories and start cold-calling families in town and at Tinker. She set up open houses so parents could come and see where their kids would be coming to school, and she hired two young women to help teach the kids. Together, the three of them welcomed two different groups of students each day, each coming for a half-day session, one in the morning and one in the afternoon. Each group would comprise 20 kids who would be learning their ABC's right there in our den. To this day, my sister C.J. and I still wonder how our family managed to pull this all off in such a small home, but we did. A bonus for us, however, was that mom had to have a large playground area built in our backyard for the students' recess periods. After hours, though, it belonged to C.J., and our beloved collie, *Laddie.*

Mom seemed to think of every-thing these young families might want in a preschool, and she sup-plied it for them. Three of these "value-added" services that I think most private preschools would be hard-pressed to provide even today were first, *pickup and delivery service* for the students, using our Ford "woody" station wagon; second, at least two *musical productions* each year in which the students were the performing stars, and third, full-blown *commencement exercises* at the end of each year.

Jack & Jill Preschool's Commencement was a big deal.

complete with caps, gowns, and the bestowing of student honors. The young graduates of Jack & Jill would not only receive their diplo-mas as they marched across the stage, but would be given a large pink or blue scrapbook containing much of the work they had done during their time at J&J. These became prized possessions for the students and their families, and many kept their scrapbooks in their homes until well into their adult years.

"I loved my Jack & Jill scrapbook," said Mary Clem Good Morris, who attended the school in 1951. "I kept it at my home for many years and only lost track of it a few years ago." (12)

In her tireless recruiting efforts, Mom did not overlook her own son, and I became a Jack & Jill student when I was 4. At age 6, C.J. was too old but frankly every member of our family felt we were part of this preschool in one way or another. After all, we were all under the same roof with it! In any event, Mom became my first classroom teacher in a long educational run that would wind up lasting 23 years for me, through an eventual Ph.D. Still, I often remember the book, *All I Need* to *Know, I Learned in Kindergarten.* In my case, all I needed to know, I learned in preschool.

Several kids who became my childhood friends through high school were classmates of mine at Jack & Jill, and I can still remember the 4-year-old faces of Marty Thompson, Steve Shriver, Mike Pickens, Marcus DeHart, Mary Clem Good, and others. In fact, Mary Clem, now a retired schoolteacher, told me recently about her first memory of Jack & Jill Preschool. One of those moments in time, she said, that she had no idea why she remembered it; she just did.

"I can remember sitting out in your backyard with you, Jim, while my mom talked with your mom about enrolling me in Jack & Jill," Mary Clem said. "Maybe the reason I remember it is that I realized I had red ants crawling up my legs! Midwest City did have so many red ants at the time. Anyway, I got enrolled and remember loving my time at Jack & Jill." (13)

Mike Pickens became a good friend for years until we each went our own way after high school. His dad, Cliff Pickens, was one of Midwest City's first mayors and – like the high-ranking Air Force officers whose kids went to Jack & Jill – helped to validate Mom's school as a solid educational foundation for Midwest City's youngest children.

"I think my best memory of childhood in Midwest City was Jack & Jill School," Mike once told me. "What Mrs. Willis was able to accomplish back in the early 50s was amazing. There were so many of us kids in that house!" (14)

Another Jack & Jill alum is Midwest City's Michael Hawk, who sent me a photo in 2023 of his framed, red and white J&J Preschool sweatshirt that he still displayed in his home. "My mom saved it for me, and many years later I had it framed," he recalled. "I was a student at Jack & Jill in 1952. My most memorable moment was hiding in the back of the school station wagon to skip school that day. Neither the driver nor my mom could find me, and it scared them senseless. I don't remember the final outcome, but obviously I was found!" (15) Hawk added that he also still has his Jack & Jill diploma, "signed by Mrs. W.J. Willis!"

One of the things I enjoyed doing a couple times each year was going with Mom up to Dowling's School Supply in Oklahoma City where she would buy a semester's worth of teaching materials, art, and music supplies for J&J. I could always count on her slipping in an extra set of crayons or watercolors, and maybe a coloring book or two, for me. Dowling's was a family-owned business and a real institution in Oklahoma that became part of the fabric of education in the city and state. It was founded and run by John Wesley Dowling, who came to Oklahoma in 1921 from Louisiana where he graduated from LSU. He owned and ran Dowling's for 65 years until his passing in 1987. It was the main go-to supply houses for educators and schools in and around Oklahoma City, including Midwest City.

The musical productions Jack & Jill staged each year, always during the Christmas season and in the spring would have impressed Gilbert and Sullivan, or even Flo Ziegfeld, producer of the famed Ziegfeld Follies, minus the scantily clad chorus line girls. Mom and her two assistants, Fairy Taylor and Betty Davis would compose the song-and-dance productions, then stage-manage, and direct them before packed auditoriums at either West Side. Soldier Creek, or Sooner Elementary Schools in Midwest City. Jack & Jill would rent the use of the auditoriums for the rehearsals and live shows, the kids would swing into the mood and ham it up, all to the delight of parents, families, and friends. Jack & Jill alum Mary Clem Good Morris recalled the role her own mother played in the stage shows.

"Mom loved to sew, and she made many of the costumes the kids wore in those productions," she said. "That was typical of how parents would get involved in Jack & Jill." (16)

Anne Patterson, who served Oklahoma City as a drama teacher for many years, said her first introduction to live musical comedy was as a student at Jack & Jill. "I still laugh when I remember all the fun we had performing some of those patriotic song-and-dance numbers at your mom's school," she said recently. "They were a tribute to the Air Force and the men and women of Tinker, and I still find myself humming *Off we go, into the wild blue yonder ... Nothing can stop the U.S. Air Force!*" (17)

Each student received their completed J&J
Scrapbook. Some still have them.

Jack & Jill preschool gave military and civilian families to mingle in Midwest City and pierce any walls that might normally exist between the two cultures in an Air Force or Army town.

The school had a successful run for its existence from 1949-1958. It could have run a lot longer except for two things. First, apparently not all our neighbors on Lockheed were excited about having 40 preschool kids a day converge in our home and back yard, because one of them asked the city clerk if our street was zoned for business.

Turned it, it was not, although the new zoning ordinance preventing businesses from operating out of homes didn't become law until after Jack & Jill had already been up and running for a couple years.

Mom could have fought and won, pressing an argument that her school should be safe under the grandfather clause of the ordinance. I think, however, Mom was feeling the stress of trying to juggle a business and raise a family at the same time, so she decided to go ahead and close the school. That was much to the dismay of young parents in Midwest City and at Tinker, many of whom urged her to fight the zoning complaint. But she didn't and decided instead to take some time off and be a full-time mom and – later – to take a civil service job at Tinker Field. For Dad, C.J., and me, it meant we had our house back for our own exclusive use. I remember that being a good feeling.

Mom's greatest legacy in Midwest City will always be Jack & Jill Preschool. She provided a structured curriculum for children ages 3-5 and, over the years of its operation, more than 500 children of Tinker and Midwest City families began their educational journeys on sound footing and had fun doing it. The legacy was long-lasting. In 2012, the founder of Jack & Jill passed away at age 103. At her funeral, several guests in their mid-60s came forward when it was over to tell C.J. and me they had begun their formal education as one of Mom's students at Jack & Jill. Some of them still had their pink or blue scrapbooks.

As J& J alum, Bob Ard confided in me in 2023, "When we began our nap time at Jack & Jill, your mother would play Braham's Lullaby, and I would start crying every time." (18)

Some Pioneering Leaders

One of the things I looked forward to doing in Midwest City was getting together with the family of my "Uncle Doc," more formally, Leroy L. Willis. I suppose my parents thought that was too much of a mouthful for a such a young boy, though, so he was always *Uncle Doc* to me. I never actually knew my uncle had a real first name until I saw it on the door of his dentist office in the downtown Atkinson Plaza Shopping Center of Midwest City.

He would later move his office to Air Depot Boulevard. Doc and my Aunt Margaret had three kids, Bill, Bob, and Sarah. Bill was three years older than me, Bob was two, and Sarah was two years younger. C.J. and I both enjoyed playing with them, and I came to perceive Bill and Bob as real-life versions of David and Ricky Nelson from the family sit-com of the early 1950s, *The Adventures of Ozzie and Harriet.* They were two down-to-earth popular guys. To me they were, in 1950s vernacular (and, come to think of it, today's too), *way cool.*

As for Doc, he was a jovial guy and actually looked a lot like my dad. He had a little more dash than Dad did, however, (sorry, Dad!) and cultivated something of a Clark Gable look and style. He was a good dentist and was a very outgoing guy around town, much more extroverted than Dad, and had pretty much been with the city from its beginning year in 1943.

Doc had been a Navy dentist and was actually on duty on the U.S.S. Whitney at Pearl Harbor when it was bombed on Dec. 7, 1941. He survived that attack, then spent two years on sea duty in the Pacific, was discharged and somehow crossed paths with Bill Atkinson and was recruited by Atkinson to set up shop in Midwest City as the city's first dentist. If you lived here in the 1940s through the 1960s, and you needed a dentist, you probably went to see my uncle. For a while, he was the only dentist in town. When he wasn't working, he was busy with leadership roles in the American Dental Association and serving as the founding president of the University of Nebraska Dental Alums.

Doc was very outgoing, loved people, and was the life of whatever party he hosted or attended. Many nights found my family over at Doc and Margaret's new home on Atkinson Drive enjoying their cookouts, trampoline, pool, and stories Doc would unreel. On some nights, Doc would grow less lucid as the evenings wore on and the liquid spirts flowed. He was still pleasant to be around; just feeling so good that his stories didn't always make much sense. However, he kept his party life separate from his work. He was a total professional as dentist, was admired for his skill, and I was a regular patient for years. I liked him and trusted him.

Doc and Aunt Margaret lived on the same street as several other prominent pioneers of Midwest City, and they were good friends with all of them. I came to know some, and they always seemed like nice folks to me. The group included H.B. Atkinson, a successful builder, state senator, and Bill Atkinson's younger brother; John Conrad, co-founder of the Conrad-Marr Drug Stores in town, and Dr. Meade Rutherford, one of Midwest City's first medical doctors. Two other friends were Marion C. Reed, longtime mayor of Midwest City, and Henry Croak, a pioneering banker in Midwest City whose American State Bank cum First National Bank funded many home and business mortgages for homebuyers in the young town.

Each of these men came to Midwest City with interesting backgrounds, and each of them helped the town grow from the ground up in their respective professions, as the following sample shows.

H.B. Atkinson had been making it on his own since he was 12 years old after he and his brother Bill had been assigned to others to raise after their mother died. H.B. succeeded in selling cars as a young man after moving to Louisiana from Texas, and he joined brother Bill in 1942 to help develop Midwest City. He wound up building 600 homes here, as well as the Lockheed Shopping Center, located at Lockheed Drive and 15th Street, and two other shopping centers later.

He also built the town's first auto garage, Midwest City Motors that later became H.B. Atkinson Chevrolet Co. It was sold to Paul Hudiburg who changed the name to Hudiburg Chevrolet Co. in 1957, which became the flagship auto dealership in town for many years. H.B. was also a passionate leader of various civic programs, was the charter president of the Lion's Club, sat on the administrative board for Wickline United Methodist Church, and served as State Senator of District 42, and later as wildlife Commissioner for District 5. (19)

Henry Croak, of whom my dad often spoke of fondly, spent 25 years in banking in Oklahoma City before buying the American State Bank in Midwest City in 1954. Eight years later, that bank became the First National Bank of Midwest City, and it became the leading bank in town for many years. It still exists as a $200 million institution, employing some 100 workers. Like both Atkinson brothers, Croak had a passionate involvement in many civic projects. He was influential in establishing the Midwest City Hospital, Rose State College, and the Midwest City Rotary Club. (20)

John Conrad and Ozzie Marr opened the first Midwest City drug store in 1943. In fact, the town's first shopping center, Atkinson Plaza, was anchored around it at Mid-America Boulevard near 29th Street. The store was initially a kind of general store for the town, selling dry goods, nylon stockings, and pharmaceuticals. Its most popular feature, however, was its soda fountain and lunch counter which was always busy around noontime. I can still remember the sublime taste of its vanilla ice cream sodas. It also had the first pay telephone in the area, and Conrad-Marr became a community hub for the city for five decades. (21) When Midwest City built its first 18-hole golf course, it was named the John Conrad Regional Golf Course.

Marion Reed became a notable and popular figure in the growth of Midwest City, having grown up on the family farm in Frederick, Oklahoma. Following service in World War II, he and his wife Gyneth moved to Midwest City in 1944, going to work first at Tinker and then setting up the first tax preparation practice, Reed's Tax Service, in the young town. Reed was one of the organizers of Midwest City government, served on the first city council and became the mayor a year later.

Altogether, he was elected mayor three times over the course of three decades, serving a total of 22 years in that office including all the years from 1962-1978. As mayor, he spearheaded the drive for funds for the development of Midwest City's first hospital, led in the creation of the first Midwest City Library and first swimming pools, as well as the new city hall complex on Reno Street. (22) His son Eddie followed him into the tax business and into the mayor's office, being elected in 1992.

Meade Rutherford was the town's early medical doctor who had the credentials to serve any city in the world, yet he and his wife chose to move to Midwest City in 1946. Born in Illinois in 1907, Rutherford received his Doctor of Medicine degree from the University of Oklahoma in 1932 and did post-graduate studies at the University of Chicago and University of Vienna, in Austria. He served in the Army Medical Corps in World War II, reached the rank of major and received numerous wartime citations. When he moved to Midwest City, he became the only physician in private practice, and he remained that for several years. (23) When Midwest City Regional Hospital opened, he served as its first chief of staff.

Apart from his medical service to the young city, Dr. Rutherford was an avid civic leader, was on the boards of Wickline United Methodist Church and the First National Bank of Midwest City. And, on the personal side, he was my own family's doctor during all my growing-up years wherein he made numerous house calls to homes all over town, including ours. As a small child, I still remember locking myself in the bathroom from him and his syringe, when he tried to give me a shot of penicillin, which seemed the cure for everything in the early 1950s. Unfortunately for me, Mom had the bathroom key.

The man often cited as being the "second father" of Midwest City was James "Jim" Mitchell Gregory, a man who was known for two separate and distinguished careers that intertwined with the young Tinker and Midwest City. Gregory spent 14 years in civil service, with the latter of those years spent at Tinker. Gregory's mother was born in what was then called Indian Territory, near the town of Wynnewood, and his father was a farmer in Indian Territory and built cotton gins.

The young Gregory graduated from Oklahoma Baptist University and then did graduate work at the American University in Washington, D.C. in business. A high school football injury kept him out of the Army in World War II, but he went to work as a civil service employee in Washington D.C. and was later transferred to Tinker. While there, he advanced quickly and, by the time he resigned in 1955, was one of the highest-ranking civilians working at Tinker. For his service, he was awarded the nation's highest honor for civil service as well as the two highest awards the Air Force gave for civil service employees. (24) In 1955, Gregory started a career in real estate management and became a key player in developing several residential subdivisions and shopping centers in both Midwest City and Oklahoma City. He served as the president of the Midwest City Chamber of Commerce and was chairman of the city's planning commission. The position allowed him to implement his vision for the growth of Midwest City, whose population increased dramatically during his tenure.

While Chapter 1 discussed the role that Lt. Col. William R. Turnbull played in the development of Tinker Field, he also should be discussed among the early leaders of Midwest City because of the immense importance that Tinker, and its growth was to the city itself. Turnbull is one of the Air Force leaders for whom a street in the Original Mile was named in appreciation for his tireless leadership.

He was the first base commander for the air depot in 1942, marking the establishment of Midwest Air Depot, before the name was changed to Tinker Field later in the year. In fact, Turnbull assumed leadership of the base six weeks after the bombing of Pearl Harbor and the entrance of America into the Second World War. He was tasked immediately with filling the massive hiring needs at Tinker, even as the first foundations were being laid for the first buildings at Tinker and the accompanying Douglas Aircraft Plant there.

When Turnbull left Tinker, in April 1943, the air base had grown to 22,000 military and civilian workers, and the Douglas plant was building C-47 cargo planes in what is now known as Building 3001. In honor of his service, Tinker's Gate 3, off Southeast 29th Street, was named for him. (25)

Turnbull was succeeded as base commander by Maj. Gen. Fred S. Borum, for whom yet another Midwest City street is named. Borum was the longest-serving Tinker base commander, leading the base from 1945 to 1954, and overseeing its postwar transition to its peacetime mission. During his tenure, Tinker prepared B-29 bombers, including the famed Enola Gay, for the 1946 Pacific atomic bomb tests, and received its first jet engine and became a P-80 fighter repair base. During Borum's years, the depot facility was renamed the Oklahoma City Air Materiel Area (OCAMA). (26)

Central to the growth of Midwest City were the early founders and developers of the Midwest City (later Mid-Del) School District. The two key names there are founding school superintendent Oscar V. Rose, and the man who succeeded him in that post, J.E. Sutton. Together, they built the Midwest City schools into a proud district whose graduates distinguished themselves and brought credit to the school system nationally.

The stories of these two men will be told in a later chapter, but it also important to remember the woman who worked for decades to help implement their educational vision. She is Shirley Shipley Nicholson, a 1953 graduate of Midwest City High School who spent 60 years as a key employee and volunteer worker for the school system. Nicholson was the professional right hand of both Rose and Sutton and, as class historian Barbara Winn Sessions noted, "[She was] an eyewitness to these leaders' accomplishments and a contributor to their success." (27).

After 40 years with the school district, Nicholson retired in 1995 from records management supervision for the district's attendance, personnel, and federal Impact Aid. She then turned her attention, as a volunteer, to founding the Midwest City High School Museum and managing it for nearly two decades. (10) She was honored by the 1964 Midwest City High School (MCHS) 50th reunion for her dedicated service to the high school and district at large.

Another key to the growth of Midwest City, and its popularity to surrounding communities, were its grocery stores which became large supermarkets. In fact, one of them would become the largest family-owned grocery stores chain in Oklahoma, and its founder was a man named Nicholas "Nick" Harroz, who came to Midwest City from Wichita Falls, Texas, in 1946 when its population totaled only 2,000 people. It is said that Nick Harroz got to know each one of them within a very short time. (28) Harroz' father had owned a small grocery store, and Nick worked in it for years with his five siblings, getting to know the business.

The family moved to Oklahoma City in the 1930s and, following the war in which he served as a Navy pilot, Nick moved to Midwest City and started his own grocery store, Nicks' Brett Drive Grocery, at the corner of Boeing Street and Brett Drive. Seven years later he moved to a larger location in town, and 11 years later moved north to Reno Street to an even larger building and changed the store's name to Crest Discount Foods. By this time, his store had gained a reputation as having a large inventory, sold at inexpensive prices. That had been the formula that his dad had taught him earlier in life: "Stack it high and sell it cheap!" (29)

The Reno store would grow to encompass more than 30,000 square feet, and Harroz also built a 20,000-square-foot warehouse nearby on North Air Depot. Over time, the increased traffic and sales necessitated another move for Crest Foods, to an even larger facility at 249 N. Douglas Blvd., where the store is located today. But Crest Foods, still under the Harroz family ownership, now has nine different store locations in Central Oklahoma. Most of the stores have grown to more than 100,000 square feet of space. Altogether, Crest Discount Foods employs some 2,100 Oklahomans, making it one of the largest non-governmental employers in the state. (30)

The man who took a key leadership role in organizing Midwest City's government was Royal A. Brust, who served as the first mayor of the new town from 1943-1945. Brust and his wife bought one of the first homes built by Bill Atkinson in the new development across from Tinker Field, where Brust went to work, serving there for 30 years as a contracting officer. Shortly after arriving in town, he quickly took a leadership role in the Original Mile development of Midwest City, helping organize the town's original government and helping establish its needed services that included the fire department, parks department, and sanitation services.

I knew his son, Ken, in high school (he was two years ahead of me) and spoke with him about his dad in researching this book. "My parents bought the first house in Midwest City, and my brother was a year old. Dad was a purchasing agent at the air depot. He started working at Tinker as soon as they opened it and he commuted from Oklahoma City until there was a house that he could buy. We were three blocks from the main gate. It was on the corner of Curtis and Turnbull ... He (dad) did everything to get the city going. He volunteered with the fire department, and he went to Ohio and brought the first garbage truck back." (31)

Royal Brust was a founding member of the city's first volunteer fire department and, when the city fire department was created, continued to serve as a volunteer fireman for 35 years. He and his wife were longtime members of the first church built in Midwest City, Wickline United Methodist, he was active as a Boy Scout leader and received scouting's highest honor for adult leadership. He was a life member of the Lions Club and served as president of the Midwest City chapter. (32)

The Skytrain theater was the weekend magnet for Midwest City.

One family name that deserves attention as Midwest City pioneers is the name Barton. It is also a name that many residents of that city never knew, even though they were entertained regularly by what the Bartons built: the town's first indoor movie theater – and only one for many years: the *Skytrain*. As noted earlier, this popular hangout was named for the famed C-47 Skytrain transport planes that Douglas Aircraft workers built across the street at Tinker Field, and it was one of several businesses in town with name tie-ins to aviation.

Dollye and R. Lewis Barton began their movie theater business in Stroud, Oklahoma, in the 1920s. Dollye was known as a creative promoter for the films that her Rex and Cozy Theaters showed, going so far as to give away free tickets, dishes, clothing, food, and anything else that might bring patrons into her movie houses.

One particular promotion that topped them all, however, came when Barton advertised she would be giving away a baby in a drawing to be held in her theaters. "People couldn't wait to see that baby," her son Bob Barton recalled. "The theater was jammed, and there was a crowd outside. They mayor drew the winning ticket, and they brought in a baby ... pig." (33)

The Bartons came to Oklahoma City in 1942 and built the Redskin and Knob Hill theaters in the Capitol Hill section on the south side of Oklahoma City. Soon after, they established the Skytrain in Midwest City during the Second World War, although unlike other early pioneers in this chapter, they did not live in Midwest City themselves. But the 972-seat theater they built was the entertainment anchor for the young city, located in the downtown Atkinson Plaza along 29th Street. The place was packed on weekends and on several nights a week.

As a newcomer to Midwest City in 1949, I quickly discovered it, along with my neighborhood friends. It was only a five-minute walk from our homes on Lockheed Drive, and few Saturdays passed without us trekking to the Skytrain to buy our 10-cent tickets and be swept away by double features on the big screen. Everyone who grew up in Midwest City in the 1950s and 1960s has fond memories of the Skytrain Theater.

The Bartons' penchant for promotions continued to be put on display at this new theater although, unlike the baby pig in Stroud, this new gimmick was the film's producer's idea and not theirs. As one former projectionist at the Skytrain noted, "At the Skytrain, I suffered through 3-D and 'Tingler' engagements and had to help install the seat vibrators throughout the house." (34)

The Tingler was a 1959 horror movie, directed by William Castle and starring Vincent Price. The plot revolved around a scientific theory that many people have a parasite growing within them that he calls "the tingler." Dr. Warren Chapin (Price), who makes the discovery, concludes that prolonged fear can cause the creature to harm a person's spine and may even produce death *unless* that person can start screaming loudly. So, at various times throughout the film, selected seats in the theater would start "tingling" from a low-level electrical device attached to them, producing a cacophony of screams from audience members.

As one of the Skytrain's regular patrons, I still have a clear memory of going to see that film and feeling the tingler in my own seat. When you're only 13 years old, it's pretty effective, not to mention loads of fun. I've sometimes wondered, in today's world, a stunt like that could at least get the theater owners sued, if not arrested, for child endangerment. But this was a different era we grew up in.

These then were some of the early Midwest City pioneers who helped to implement founder Bill Atkinson's well-rounded town that would service all the needs of the workers at Tinker Field. The list is only a sample of the many others who made their own contributions.

4

❧

Growing Up in Tinkertown

Oklahoma winds make kite flying a spring treat.
Photo by Pixabay/Shlomaster

"No one is ever free from their social or physical environment. And whether or not we are always aware of it, a home is a home because it blurs the line between the self and the surroundings and challenges the line we try to draw between who we are and where we are."

Julie Beck, *The Atlantic* (1)

From the start, Midwest City was envisioned to be a city of and for children. Bill Atkinson knew that the families moving in would be mostly young ones, and he knew they wouldn't stay long unless their children were happy there. It was imperative that the totality of the city's vision be one that served the needs of children as well as their parents. But that didn't happen right away.

When the first families began moving into the new housing in the summer of 1942, there wasn't much there for kids other than a home itself. As historian Susan Moeri Lee noted, "The small, nondescript houses sat in a barren wheat field, looking very much like the house next door and down the street. There was a little shade when the sun was out and lots of mud when it rained ... The community had unpaved roads, small one-room schools, and no stores. Yet families kept moving in." (2)

Within another year or two, however, that landscape would grow and include most of what these new residents – and their children would need. By the time my family moved to Midwest City in 1949, just about all the amenities were in place, albeit not what they would be a decade later. It became our new hometown, its culture began rubbing off on me, and I didn't feel we lacked for much of anything. The city was young, we were young. We would grow together and leave our mark on each other.

One thing that keeps writers from crafting a book about their hometown experiences is the question of much they can actually *remember* from those young years. And then there are those things that you *do* remember, some of which were so foolishly dangerous that you wonder how you survived those times at all.

I've learned that at least four things help open more closed-door memories than I thought possible when I began this book: First, writing about one event often triggers a dormant memory about another. Second, going back to my adopted hometown and seeing where I grew up and the places that made up my world help tremendously. Third, talking with childhood friends, most of whom I have not seen since school days, brings other memories back to life. And fourth, remembering *feelings* instead of trying to remember *events,* often leads me to those incidents and/or people who inspired those emotions.

For example, take the last of these triggers. Can you remember when you first thought you fell in love and why? For me, I was 1 years old and in the 7th grade when I walked down to the Skytrain Theater one Saturday afternoon to see the 1961 Disney movie, *Parent Trap.* It was hard enough for me to keep my eyes off its 15-year-old unknown British starlet, Hayley Mills, but the fact there were *two* of her in the film made it doubly hard.

If you know the story, you know she played identical twins named Sharon McKendrick and Susan Evers. The sisters' parents were divorced, and the two teens devised a plan to reunite them. I must have used up two weeks' allowances going back to see the movie several times, each time falling deeper in love with that blonde, smiling Hayley Mills, with the cute, upturned nose.

The thing I *didn't* notice was that if Midwest City founder Bill Atkinson had not included a movie theater in his vision for the city's "Original Mile'" there would have been no Skytrain Theater. That movie house was a prime example of how entrepreneurs were thinking about servicing the entertainment needs of children and teens, as well as their parents.

Hayley Mills and Hayley Mills in "Parent
Trap."
(Used with permission)

The Skytrain opened its doors in November 1944 and was an instant hit with the kids. The theater was built for $95,000 and featured first-run films, a modern sound system, air conditioning, padded seats and paved parking. The Skytrain showed five different movies each week, and Saturday morning matinees were designed for young children. The theater provided seating arrangements suitable for civic functions and presentations as well, and the Skytrain was used for those in addition to their regular movie showings.

In 1949, the *Midwest City News Leader* noted, "When C.L. Sanders of the Juvenile Department [of the Midwest City Police] suggested the reorganization of the Junior Police, the Kiwanis Club held the kick-off program at the theater. Six hundred kids attended the special film, had soda and hot dogs, and signed up to be Junior Police." (3)

And if I had not lived there where the Skytrain was in walking distance from everyone's front door (only two blocks from mine), I might never have seen that film at all, or at least not until I was older. If so, Hayley Mills would probably *not* have been my original love and, somehow, that doesn't seem right.

A postscript is that many years later, around 2008, I was living in Southern California and realized I had yet to bump into any movie stars. Then one day I was standing in the checkout line at a Chico's store in Manhattan Beach when I turned and noticed the woman right behind me.

It was Hayley Mills. She smiled at me and, before I could engage my mental filters and say something like, "It's a nice day, isn't it?", I let fly with, *"You don't know this, but I fell in love with you when I was 15."* Her smile broadened and said how sweet I was to say that, and we went our separate ways out into the Southern California sunshine. But my warm feeling inside came from just finally meeting my first teenage crush.

This chapter features scenes depicting other ways in which the design and culture of Midwest City's Original Mile,and the vision behind it, affected me and my friends as young people growing up there. For example, in elementary school, there were two main choices in town. One was Eastside Elementary, and the other was Westside. The town had two other pre-existing elementaries, Sooner and Soldier Creek, but they were on the outer borders of the Original Mile and drew a lot of students from outlying neighborhoods and villages.

East Lockheed Drive was the dividing line for kids going to Eastside and Westside. I lived on the north side of Lockheed, and my best friend Marcus DeHart lived on the south side. He would trek off north a few blocks to his school and I would head west a few blocks to mine, sometimes lingering just a minute or two in front of cute little Connie Vessels house on the way. She was a sweet girl with a blonde pony tale, and she was hte first girl I ever remember really noticing.

Midwest City was named America's Model City in 1951.

I've often wondered if I had lived on his side and one to Eastside, whether I would have chosen writing as my career or *In 1951, the National Association of Home Builders named Midwest City America's Model City.* chosen another path. That question may sound like a non sequitur (how could a career choice depend on what side of the street you grew up on?), but here's why I ask it: Each day, Markey would walk east to school, while I walked west. It was only a four-block stroll to school,

It was there that I developed an intense interest in reading. I clearly remember reading most of Walter Farley's *Black Stallion* books (*The Black Stallion, The Black Stallion Returns, Son of the Black Stallion, the Island Stallion,* etc., etc.) and I also remember being enthralled by Jack London books, especially *The Call of the Wild* and *White Fang*. But I also loved reading biographies, especially of early Western figure like Wyatt Earp. Buffalo Bill Cody, and Wild Bill Hickock. And this was all while I was still in grade school.

It wasn't long before I tried my hand at writing my own stories, not surprisingly about dogs, horses, and wilderness adventures. While some of this growing passion for reading and writing was undoubtedly fueled by the fun way of learning my mom introduced in her Jack & Jill Preschool, and while some was inspired by my dad's creativity as a writer and sketch artist, the Midwest City Public Library had even more to do with it.

If I had needed to go out of my way to get to that library, however, I may or may not have troubled myself in doing it. After all, I did know that reading took some focused mental energy while playing sandlot baseball or catching crawdads at the creek did not. But it was just so darn easy and fun to stop at the library on my way home from school and, once my fuse for reading and learning had been lit, there was on snuffing it out. I've often thought that Mr. Atkinson and Seward Mott, the urban planner who put that library smack in the center of the original mile, might be surprised to learn of the cultural and career impact it had on young people like me and several of my friends.

Certainly, growing up in a town that hosted a large Air Force base just across the street like Tinker Field influenced our interests as children and teens. Even as young kids in the 50s we understood that America had just emerged from a world war less a decade of less ago, and that the might of the U.S. military was the major reason for that.

And here we were, surrounded by artifacts of the victors in the form of bombers and fighter planes that were still transitioning into the early years of jet power. You could see them as they took off and came in for landings, with pilots often using the city's red-and-white checkered water tower, hovering over my backyard, as a visual aid to guide them in.

And the sight of Air Force uniforms on officers and enlisted troops in restaurants, grocery stores, and drug stores were constant reminders of the military presence in, and importance to, Midwest City.

On several occasions I recall my family joining the crowd of civilians invited across 29th Street to the huge Douglas Plant to view some of the aircraft being built and maintained and to watch the air shows and flyovers by big bombers and even the elite Air Force Thunderbirds jets. Tinker Field was fond of putting its airplanes on display, even though the daily military operations were generally kept secret, and civilians needed Air Force approval to enter the base at all except on air show days.

We couldn't help but feel that, somehow, we who lived in Midwest City were a part of this overall Air Force mission, and we took a sense of pride in that. Some did more than that, becoming so inspired by the Air Force that they chose it for their career. One was Robert K. Junior. "I'd say being close to Tinker made the Air Force an easy choice for me after 9/11," he said. "I work for the Midwest City now. Always admired those that stuck around and gave back to the community." (4)

Others found their career inspiration in other aspects of Midwest City as they grew up. For example, interior designer Judy Mikeska remembered how the artistic sketches of dresses, made for the newspaper ads of Streets Department Store in Atkinson Plaza Shopping Center, inspired her to take up a career in design. (5)

As kids, Tinker fueled our interest in aviation and the construction and flight of aircraft. That interest translated into hobby projects which our neighborhood gangs took on. Of course, this kind of "gang" was not the troubled urban street gangs that our evolving culture came to experience. In a suburb like Midwest City (if there were that many like Midwest City), we had the natural bonds of young middle-and-lower-middle-class kids growing up on the same street, coupled with the added glue that came from the fact everyone in town was relatively new and most were young.

It wasn't until 1953, in fact, that there were any homes or apartments older than a decade, and many had been built more recently than that. So, there were no "established" families here, and each family had come from somewhere else to this new town starting in 1942.

In some ways, we were similar to the characters in the television series, *Lost*, who had all crashed and washed up on this shore. The difference, of course, is that our families' decisions to move here was intentional, and the place we moved to was an extremely well-designed community that serviced just about every need we had. In short, all of us kids were on a pretty level playing field – at least for a while – and there was a sense of overall equality in town. It's important to note, however, as a later chapter will discuss, that this was an equality that attached itself only to white families, although many residents had Native American tribal blood in them, too.

There were no African Americans in town until the mid-1960s. But, as kids, we were pretty oblivious to this, and all that mattered to us what that we – which include Markey, John, Clayton, Mike, Charles (aka Bruda), Kay, C.J., Terry, Tina, and me – all enjoyed hanging out together and finding ways to while away our free time.

The aviation projects were part of our history, and they came in different forms. The guys in our Lockheed gang all seemed to gravitate toward model airplanes, and eventually to the kinds with fuel-powered engines and propellers you had to hand-crank to start. The plane itself was tethered by about a 25-foot line that was attached to a handle that you held as you guided the plane around you in a 50-foot cicle.

The only part of the flying process that worried me a bit was that business of cranking up the propeller. The process was similar to what you've seen in old movies where the pilot turns on the engine's ignition and gives a thumbs-up from the cockpit to the ground crewman standing just in front of the plane's propeller blade. That signal meant it was time for the crewman to physically take hold of that blade and jerk it down toward the ground to start the blade spinning when its gears engaged with the engine. Of course, it was always a good day when that crewman was able to avoid being caught up in the spinning blade himself. However, since our neighborhood model planes were only a small fraction of the size of those real planes, we used only a finger or two to flip the blade until it engaged and stared spinning under engine power.

That said, there was still some danger present, that is if you cared about reaching adulthood with all ten fingers intact. As far as I can remember none of our gang lost any fingers in the process, although there were a few minor injuries. You could always tell the models' "pilots" by just looking for the bandaged fingers. It all seemed worth it, though, to be flying our own miniature versions of the Air Force jets and bombers that would often be taking off or landing just a couple hundred yards above our model planes' flight path.

The other aviation adventure for me was a two-parter, helped along by the Boy Scout troop we belonged to that met at the Wickline Methodist Church just around the block from our homes. The troop had built a drop-off hut for old magazines and newspapers, which the Scouts collected and sold to paper recyclers in Oklahoma City. It was a pretty good fund-raising venture for them and gave townspeople somewhere to dump the stacks of old publications sitting around their homes or garages.

One of the side-benefits of this hut was that a few of us kids would use this shed as a kind of makeshift clubhouse. We would go over there after dark with our flashlights, climb in through the swinging half-door, and sit on the piles of magazines reading ones that looked interesting. And the ones that interested us most were *Popular Science* and *Popular Mechanics* magazines. We poured through the magazines looking for plans to build model planes, cars, and boats.

One night, when we were about 13, Markey and I were in there reading when a car drove up and the driver got out to drop in a bunch of magazines. They landed right on top of us, in fact, since he didn't know we were there. Anyway, one of those was a *Popular Science* magazine which had detailed plans on how to build a helicopter. Not a *model* one but a real, one-person flying machine that could be built – so the article purported – with scrap materials and a washing machine motor. The one piece that wouldn't be scrap was the propeller. Now, for a lot of kids, that would be very hard to find. But it happened that Markey's stepdad worked on aircraft maintenance at Tinker, and he had told us one day about the stacks of discarded propellers lying around the Douglas Plant, since most planes had converted to jet engines.

Enter Part 2 of the project. Mark and I were convinced we could build this "whirlybird" and fly it. We scrounged around both our garages to see how much of the materials, or reasonable facsimiles, we could find and then started looking around town for more spare lumber. The Humpty Dumpty grocery store often threw away used, heavy wooden orange crates, so we picked up several of those to deconstruct to make part of the frame on the small craft, which was only about seven feet long.

Then, as luck would have it, Mrs. Swanson, a neighbor lady had her husband put their discarded washing machine out on their front lawn, ostensibly for anyone who wanted it. A sign had been attached, claiming it still worked fine. So, Mark and I took our *Radio Flyer* wagon over, loaded the machine aboard, and took it to his back yard where we were constructing our flying machine. Mark was a budding electrician who knew how to rig a car battery to the electric motor.

We tested it and, miraculously, it worked. We decided not to dwell on the question of how *long* it would keep running, though. Then we needed a kind of rudder, and we figured we could use a bed sheet tacked to a frame made from the orange crates. I raided Mom's laundry basket for a spare sheet. At least I thought it was a spare. She let me know later that it wasn't.

The mini-chopper was coming along fine when Mark's stepdad brought home the single-blade propeller from Tinker. It was a little nicked in places, but we thought it would work fine. We also scrounged around for a steel rod on which to mount the vertical prop, connected it via a used car fan belt to the flywheel on the washing machine motor, then stood back and assessed our invention.

We were about to draw straws to see which one of us would be the first test pilot of this craft, and I don't remember if we decided whether the winner or loser would be the pilot. It was a moot point anyway, because two things happened that doomed the flight of our *Phoenix*.

First was a little discussion we had about whether this thing could actually fly or not. We were both confident the propeller would hoist it off the ground and into the lower reaches of the atmosphere. But one thing we hadn't talked about was how to get it to *come back down* to earth and do it slowly enough so neither the craft nor the pilot would land with a splat. Maybe we would need another bed sheet as a parachute?

As we were working on that problem, Mrs. Swanson -- the lady who had put the washing machine out on her front lawn two days ago -- came visiting and told us she needed her machine back. It seems her new one wasn't to her liking, and she wanted to keep her old one, after all. It was sitting there in Mark's back yard, still intact but without the motor, which was now set to power our helicopter.

Our reasoning for what happened next is somewhat hazy now, but we agreed to put the washing machine back together and give it back to her. I remember Mark and I convincing each other it was the nice thing to do, but I've often suspected we gave the motor back because neither one of us wanted to actually risk our lives in this alleged flying machine.

In the end, this saga went down as one that fulfilled our dreams for a few days and kept us out of other kinds of trouble. I'm not sure that *flying* the machine was ever the real point of the exercise, anyway.

I hadn't thought about this experience for many years until one day as an adult journalist, I found myself on assignment in Berlin, Germany, and the Checkpoint Charlie Museum, located at the infamous border crossing between the old East and West Berlin.

On display in the museum were many of the ingenious (and risky) homemade devices that East Germans had built to get them over the Berlin Wall and into the freedom of West Berlin. There, hanging from the ceiling was a homemade flying machine, made to transport one person over the Wall. It had been a successful flight, and the pilot did find safety in the West.

I was happy to know that, but I was even more interested in the escape craft itself because it reminded me of the contraption that Markey and I had built in his backyard many years before. And it was then – probably for the first time ever – that I felt sorry that we never took it up on its maiden voyage.

Other young people around Midwest City linked aviation to their lives as well. One popular program for boys (and, after 1970, for girls, too) was the Explorer program, the senior arm of the Boy Scouts of America for ages 14-18. From its beginning in 1949, the Explorers focused on career programs, some of which tied into one of the military branches. You could become a *Sea Explorer* or an *Air Explorer*, for example. Scouting was a big youth activity in Midwest City, and the first

Scout troop and Explorer post were affiliated with the original church in town, Wickline United Methodist.

In Midwest City, the Air Explorers drew the attention of several teenage boys, and the association the city had with Tinker Air Force Base was the main reason. In this program, teens could learn at least the basics of aviation ground-principles and often have a chance to go up in small training planes with accredited pilots.

The other aviation avenue for older teens and young adults was the Tinker chapter of the Civil Air Patrol (CAP), which was created during the war years, and which helped served as the eyes and ears of a civilian early-warning system for possible enemy aircraft. Following the war, the patrol became tasked with supporting American towns and cities with emergency response and rescue systems, and helped promote the needs for air, space, and cyber power. Some of my CAP friends would go on to become Air Force pilots.

But the interests of us young Midwest City kids didn't always skew toward aviation. After all, this was Oklahoma in the 1950s, we were the first generation to grow up on television, and a staple of TV and movies in this decade was the *Western*. In fact, some of the most celebrated and iconic Western books and movies were being written and made then. Among them: *Shane, High Noon, 3:10 to Yuma, Gunfight at the OK Corral,* and the classic John Wayne/John Ford collaborations like *The Searchers, Fort Apache, and She Wore a Yellow Ribbon.* Most of these films have spent time on the American Film Institute's 100 best American films.

More importantly, for youngsters growing up in the 1950s, however, they formed our perception of the heroes we wanted to emulate. The fact we lived in a western state that had itself been officially Indian Territory just 50 years before, made our interest in cowboys and Indians even more passionate. Add television's first real decade to the mix, with its nightly Western programming, and we had a cowboy mania on our hands.

Few of us would want to miss an episode of *Gunsmoke,* or *Rawhide, Have Gun will Travel, Maverick, The Deputy, Cheyenne, Wagon Train, The Rifleman,* etc., etc. But if there was one TV western figure who stood larger than life for us in those years it was *Davy Crockett*. Although it was only a five-part Disneyland serial of one-hour weekly episodes in 1954-55, this iconic ABC series anchored early Sunday night programming for all of us kids. We all wanted to be Fess Parker (oops ... I mean Davy Crockett), many of us badgered our parents into buying a coonskin hat like his and a toy rifle like his "Old Betsy."

But all our westerns weren't being made in Hollywood. Some were being made just a few miles away, in Oklahoma City. This was the heyday of local TV stations' original programming, and a lot of afternoon and early-evening programming was produced by the local network television affiliates. Since television was so new, there were few syndicated programs or series for stations to buy, because the cupboard would be bare until enough of them got made later in the decade and into the 1960s. Until then, local stations had to make their own talk shows, cooking shows, public affairs programs, and afternoon kids shows. The latter was of special interest to the kids in and around Midwest City. As kids, we didn't consider ourselves urbanites yet, and our town was still surrounded by cropland.

So, when we weren't building model airplanes or larger ill-fated flying machines, we were shooting up the block with our cap pistols and rifles, claiming victories over all the bad guys in town and, at times, defending our orange crate-Alamos. In fact, by the mid-1950s, the state's interest in cowboys and horses would provide the marketing impetus for a new upscale real estate development as the city pushed north past the original mile. More about that in a later chapter.

By 1957, my friends and I all had television sets, and some of our afternoon outdoor activities moved indoors. It was the era that journalist and commentator Linda Ellerbee would write about later in her classic essay, When *Television Ate my Best Friend*. In that story, after a 6-year-old Linda mysteriously loses the outdoor companionship of her friend Lucy to this new thing called a TV, she laments to her mother that television must *eat* people. Her mother tells her not to worry, that television is only entertainment, and that she is getting one, too. Ellerbee writes, "Christmas arrived, and Santa Claus brought us a television.

'See?' my parents said. 'Television doesn't eat people.' Maybe not. But television changes people. It changed my family forever." (6)

Admittedly, the late 1950s was a watershed period when outdoor group activities turned more toward indoor activity, and that activity was watching TV, often alone although sometimes with your friends. Either way, we kids were all treated every afternoon to a local cowboy show for kids, produced in Oklahoma City at my dad's TV station, WKY, Channel 4. It was the *Foreman Scotty Show*, with a longer title of *Foreman Scotty and the Circle 4 Ranch* (just to give the station itself a daily plug). It was produced right in the studio and on its spacious back lot.

Every afternoon Foreman Scotty became embroiled in adventures, chasing the bad guys around makeshift sets that looked very real to youngsters who wanted them to be. In between the scripted adventures, Scotty would be back on the established set for the show, made to look like the inside of a barn, with 25 live, invited kids who were perched on benches or hay bales. On at least one occasion, I was one of those kids who sat in awe of my afternoon hero. The whole thing was a must-see for those of us in and around Midwest City and solidified our wish list for Christmas. We wanted anything from cap pistols and holsters, to cowboy hats or wooden horses that reminded us of Foreman Scotty and his Circle 4 Ranch.

Said one of our friends who looked back on the show years later, "If you grew up here and you're over 35, you know about Foreman Scotty. If you were a youngster than, you possibly were on the show." (7)

The show ran for 14 years, and Scotty was played by a Tulsa acting student and WKY announcer Steve Powell, who died in 1994. As Ann DeFrange would write about his passing, "With other live television pioneers, he created characters who live in the cultural literacy of Local viewers. He created the corral where guest sat for the show; Woody the wooden horse where little birthday celebrants got to sit in honor on the uncomfortable saddle instead of the uncomfortable benches; the "Magic Lasso," which appeared on the screen to select the lucky kid who won the Golden Horseshoe; and the secret Password, *Nicksobilly*." (8)

The 1950s was the golden age of locally and regionally produced afternoon kids shows, and WKY-TV (which went on the air in 1949 and hired my dad that same year) was a true pioneer of this genre. It was part of the Oklahoma Publishing Company, owned by its founder E.K. Gaylord. He started the state's main daily newspaper, *The Daily Oklahoman*, and I would later work for it as a journalist.

As a child on Lockheed Drive, I became something of a neighborhood celebrity because Dad worked at WKY, and he often would invite me and my sister C.J., along with a few of our friends, to come watch some of the live shows from the observation booth above the studio. One of our favorite shows was the Saturday Night Wrestling program, where they set up a ring right on the studio floor, surrounded by chairs for the live audience, and brought in professional wrestlers to grind it out.

Not to be forgotten in the kids programming at WKY, however, was the 1950s interest in outer space. So, along with Foreman Scotty, WKY tapped one of its rising celebrities, Danny Williams, to become the futuristic spaceman, Dan D. Dynamo, or just *3-D Danny*. The latter name was a stroke of marketing genius, tying in as well to audience interest in the gimmicky new 3-dimensional-view movie exhibition fad. So, every afternoon, 3-D Danny would be furiously turning knobs on a control panel in the "Space Science Center" and, along with his trusted robot Bazark, would try desperately to save the world from aliens. It even got to the point where 3-D Danny's futuristic world intersected with the western world of Foreman Scotty as some of the skits featured both heroes and Bazark masterfully chasing and subduing the bad guys around the Channel 4 backlot.

As popular as it became, however, television didn't occupy all the afternoon and weekend time for my friends and me. For one thing, we loved to build "boys-only" clubhouses, using the wooden orange crates thrown away behind the Humpty Dumpty Store and any other spare lumber our dads were foolish enough to be lying around. We also loved to bike around our neighborhood.

One of the things non-Okies don't understand, when they critique the state topography for being so flat, is that flat land makes for good bike riding. And the kids I grew up with on Lockheed Drive made good use of that flat terrain. It was that love of bike riding that made my friend Gary Wiedeman, who lived just around the corner, another local celebrity.

Reason was, his dad Vic owned the only bike store in town, and he sold the Cadillac of the bikes then: *Schwinn*. Gary was exactly 10 days younger than me, and we developed a good friendship growing up. He would later join the Marines and serve a tour of duty in Vietnam, but that was several years down the road on which we rode those bikes we had.

When I think of my first bicycle that my parents gave me at the age of 9, I think of two concepts: *freedom and balance*. Freedom because my bike automatically enlarged my world (albeit it still didn't run much past Midwest City's original mile), and balance because you can't ride one without learning how to stay vertical.

Although we kids in the 1950s did a lot more walking than kids do today, a bike meant we could get their faster and take a long, circuitous route home if we wanted to drive through that neighborhood where that little blonde-headed girl lived. On weekends, we fantasized that our bike could take us to the moon if we wanted.

In my memory, my bike was my first taste of freedom. It seemed that way for my friends in Midwest City, too.

My first bike was a sleek, red Schwinn from Vic Wiedeman's shop, over on 15th Street. I called it my Red Rocket, and we became indispensable. One of the first bike memories a lot of kids have is learning that art of balance, and I remember the moment when it finally clicked for me. It was Christmas Day and Dad was coaching me on how to keep my body from becoming one with the pavement. Of course, I only half-listened, eager to give it a try and, of course, I took a couple spills. But I found soon that if I just stopped *thinking* about how to balance and instead just do it, then it worked pretty well. I was riding up and down the driveway by Christmas night.

From that lesson, I learned that I can't just *think* things into happening. I must trust my body's ability to apply what I've learned from people like my dad. That's actually a very useful lesson, and I've applied it to many challenges from learning to play the piano and guitar, to swimming and SCUBA diving. Given a chance, our bodies can get along fine on nothing but an innate instinct for survival, and a lot of muscle memory.

Summers in Oklahoma brought some suffocating heat of 100+ degree days where even the warm evening breezes brought no relief. None of the homes in the original mile had anything like today's central air conditioning, although those families with a few extra dollars of disposable income could afford a window unit or two. It took a while for my family to get one, but we finally did.

Dad and I installed it in a northside living room window where it could blow straight down the hall to our three bedrooms. But before we had that bit of luxury, the four of us would take the mattresses off our beds on the especially steamy nights and haul them out to the living room where we lay them next to each other. Then we'd open the front and back doors that faced east and west and let the cooler late-night breeze flow over us. Then there were nights when we, and some of our neighborhood friends, would just take our bedrolls out back and sleep in the yard with the starry sky as our canopy.

As I think back on nights like that, I see them as an example of how we early-1950s pioneers created minimal luxuries to make life a bit easier in what was then basically still a prairie town.

Winters could bring equally extreme conditions on the frigid side with plenty of snow and ice on the sidewalks and driveways that had to be broken up with a pickaxe. We kids turned the ice into makeshift skating rinks and we turned the snow into sledding courses. Of course, the biggest single event of the snow season was Christmas, and most families in our neighborhood pulled out all stops to make it a great time for us kids.

The windows of all the stores downtown in Atkinson Plaza were decorated and lined with toys, beautiful clothes, and the latest appliances. Patrons would stand on the facing sidewalk and watch TV programs played on sets in the display windows of Firestone and OTASCO (Oklahoma Tire and Supply) stores, while outdoor speakers played well-known Christmas songs.

TG&Y in the Atkinson Shopping Plaza was a huge hit in town.

As kids, our two favorite stores were TG&Y and OTASCO, both of which were stocked to the ceilings with toys, crafts, bikes, dolls, and teddy bears. TG&Y was Midwest City's version of Woolworth's, minus the soda fountain. It's worth a short discussion because it was so important to us youngsters. It was a "five and dime" store where you could take your weekly allowance of 50 cents in, buy your model airplane and some candy, and come out with enough change to go see a movie across the street at the Skytrain. It was headquartered in Oklahoma City but grew to more than 900 stores in 29 southern states. (9)

The company was founded during the Oklahoma Dust Bowl days and was named for the last initials of its three founders: Rawdon E. Tomlinson, Enoch L. "Les" Gosselin, and Raymond A. Young. The three men each owned their own Oklahoma variety stores but, after meeting at a 1935 trade show, agreed to join to form one store chain.

Doing that increased their resources greatly, and that allowed them to buy inventory in bulk, directly from manufacturers instead of through wholesalers. The result was cheaper prices for the customer, and the company's slogan became, "Your best buy is at TG&Y." (10)

Both TG&Y and OTASCO published Christmas catalogues delivered to our mailboxes, so kids like C.J. and me could circle those things we most wanted for Christmas before handing them off to Mom and Dad. It was a special time and, in our home, it was made more so by the lengths our folks went to make it memorable for my sister and me.

Ours was a home that began preparing for Christmas a month in advance, with everything leading up to that magical night of Christmas Eve. I always felt C.J. and I had the best Christmas on our block. I was sure of it when my best friend Mark was so envious that he asked my parents if they could adopt him. That was something I never shared with *his* mom.

It wasn't that my folks were rich; far from it. But our home was full of love, and our folks always found ways to provide a Christmas morning full of parents. In those days, my dad's bank, The First National of Midwest City, let customers set up special Christmas savings accounts, and I think my folks started making deposits the week after Christmas for next year's holiday.

I was probably the last kid on the block to doubt the existence of Santa Claus, and I have my folks to thank for that. Mom had me writing letters to Santa until I was 12, although I'm sure the last year or two I did that, it was more to please her and Dad than out of a belief for the Big Guy. For whatever reason, it always paid off on Christmas morning, and who was I to question a good system?

One Christmas Eve will always stand out in memory, as my dad nearby broke both legs in a valiant attempt to undergird my belief that Santa Claus was still in business. I was about 8 or 9 and Mom was having a particularly hard time getting me to go to bed. Knowing I believed Santa wouldn't come to a home where children were still awake, she knew she had the upper hand. She played it by having Dad drape himself in two long belts of attached bells and sent him outside into the snow to run around the house jangling them frantically, hoping none of the cops in the police station around the corner saw him doing it.

As quickly as I heard those bells, I remember lurching into my bed, followed closely by my sister in hers. Santa was not going to pass us by on this night!

I can't really say I remember hearing what happened next or whether I remember it from one of the many times Mom told the story over the ensuing years. Either way, it turns out that my dad's circular course around the house was interrupted suddenly on his third or fourth lap by our three large metal trash cans, hidden from view by a snow drift.

Or could it be that his accident was aided by too much Christmas cheer that he had to imbibe to overcome his better judgement in pulling this stunt in the first place? Either way, Dad collided with the cans at full speed on his way past the back door, catapulting him, the three 50-gallon steel cans, the trash, and the bells into the snowy night.

I was not a witness to this, because I had fallen asleep after Santa's first lap. But I do know my dad and I know that, in times of tumult, his words always sprang forth first from his deep, colorful pit of exasperation rather than from his library of measured reason. I am sure that when Mom rushed out to help him out of the garbage that night, she encountered what could only be described as trash talk coming from Dad. To approximate how much, try squaring the number of expletives uttered by Ralphie's *Christmas Story* dad in the cellar when the coal furnace erupted into a pillar of black smoke that came billowing up through the kitchen grate.

Alternatively, perhaps I did witness the great trash can collision after all and have just chosen to bury it in my subconsciousness. I never enjoyed getting in the way of Dad's angry outburst, short-lived though they were. I prefer to think, however, that it was a testament to Mom and Dad's parenting that – on this night of nights before Christmas – they shielded C.J. and me from this bad Santa hiccup and produced yet another magical Christmas morning.

Even though Dad seemed hobbled that morning by a mysterious limp while walking around the tree, passing out presents.

My father helped teach me about overcoming obstacles and about helping those in need in my growing up years in Midwest City. I never remember thinking we were similar in nature, but over the years I've realized that we were. He and I did several similarities, starting with our names. We were both born William James Willis, he the junior and me the third. We both served with the Navy, and both of our stints were cut short for medical reasons. Dad and I both had careers in the *communication* business.

Ironically, both of us have reputations for speaking softly or not speaking all that much. Over the years, Dad's *actions* came to speak more loudly to me than his words, and I suppose my two sons would say the same thing about me. Therein lies another similarity.

In several ways, Dad taught me that actions do speak louder than words. He was a kind man who sacrificed for our family, and he also had this habit of being kind to strangers whose paths he crossed in their moments of stress.

Over the years, one moment in particular has stood out in my memory, and I recounted it when I spoke at his funeral in 2006. It referenced a hot summer day in Oklahoma when Dad had taken Mom, C.J., and me to the town's Dairy Queen over on Air Depot, the street forming the eastern boundary of Midwest City's original mile. It was on the far southeastern corner of the playground of Westside Elementary where I went to school. Outings like this didn't come every day for our family because this was a time in our family when money was tight.

Anyway, we had all placed our DQ orders and were enjoying our cones and milkshakes at a picnic table as Dad waited to pay the cashier. On his way walking back to us, a little boy who had just bought his own double-dip cone, tripped. Both he and his cone hit the hot pavement at the same time, the ice cream starting to melt into the asphalt instantly. The boy began to cry over his lost treat. Dad saw and heard the whole thing, and went over to help the child up. Then he took the boy back to the DQ window and placed another order.

"One double-dip cone, please," he told the attendant. He laid down the last of his change, got the cone and handed it to the boy who was drying his tears by now. The boy's expression turned to a broad, check-to-cheek grin as he started licking his new cone. Dad just came over to our table, sat down, and ate his own melting treat in silence. I don't know that I was ever more impressed with my father than on that day.

I've shared that story several times with friends, and I was pleased to see that my DQ memories were also shared by many other people in town. Some happened at the second ice-cream drive-in in Midwest City which became as popular as the Dairy Queen. It was called Hilltop Dairyland, located north on Reno between Air Depot and Sooner Road.

The Hilltop Dairyland on Reno near Air Depot Boulevard.

"This is a true Hilltop story, 1970," Jay Gamble said in a 2023 Facebook post on the Midwest City High School Memories site. "My mother reminisced with me one day. She and I remembered our Country Estates Elementary baseball outings to Hilltop Dairyland. I got a large Coke for hitting a homerun. A fellow player named Roger Furlong began crying because he got a small drink. We were in t-ball.

My mom and I gave him my large drink voluntarily and exchanged his for mine. I was raised by good people, full of mistakes. I am, too. I'm grateful for them and grateful for Hilltop Dairyland."

As for my home, I remember it as being a safe and secure place. Most of my spare time and hobbies were focused there. Dad got me interested in photography in my early teens, and I set up a darkroom in the garage and spent many happy hours there. My sister C.J. and I got along very well and, since she was two years older and was so popular at school, she became something of a role model for me. Older kids would sometimes identify me as, *"Oh, he's C.J.'s little brother."*

I liked my home life so much that, when I started dating, I would bring my date over to the house to watch TV. I came to feel sympathy for those friends and classmates of mine whose family lives seemed out of kilter and hence places of tension.

My family took all our meals together, Mom always found time to cook us good meals, and on Friday nights, when Dad got paid, he would take us downtown to the only restaurant Midwest City had at the time. It was called Nick's, named for its owner Nick Panos, and it evoked what I felt was an elegant feeling of dining. Our favorite meal? A chicken-fried steak with mashed potatoes and vegetables, all for 90 cents. Another 20 cents got you pie and ice cream. Later, when the Uptown Cafeteria opened up on the north side of the Original Mile, we would troop over there and often run into my aunt, uncle, and cousins Bob, Bill, and Sarah.

Saturday mornings were equally fun as C.J. and I would spend most of the morning watching cartoons and series targeted to young people. The schedule usually started with *Howdy Doody and Buffalo Bob Smith*, and continued with *Fury, My Friend Flicka, Rin Tin Tin,* and *Sky King*. Sometimes my friend Mark and a couple others from our neighborhood gang would come over and we'd all watch together.

When Mom decided to close down her Jack & Jill Preschool, I was about 13. For two years she put her focus on making sure C.J. and I were happy and meaningfully occupied, probably spoiling us in the process but that was fine with me.

Many years ago, I heard a pastor preach a sermon on the theme, "Isn't it about time we realized that the best gift we can give is time?" When I heard it, I thought immediately of the time Mom devoted to my sister and me as youngsters.

Tinker Air Force Base wound up intersecting our lives directly when Mom decided to go back to work when I was in the 9th grade. It was 1960, Midwest City had grown to about 40,000 residents, and Tinker was the largest military aircraft maintenance facility in the country, with a huge payroll. A large percentage of Midwest Cityans worked there, so we all knew how important it was to our livelihood.

Mom had worked for the federal government years before in Washington D.C., but she still had to take -- and pass -- an exhaustive Civil Service Exam, for which she would need to study long and hard. This she did over a period of months. She even enlisted my help occasionally by popping questions at her from the study guide. As prepared as she was, she still failed the exam when she took it. But Mom was never one to be defeated so easily, so she went back to the books, studied a few more weeks, took it again, and passed it.

She went to work at Tinker shortly afterwards, accepting a position in the medical records division, which was located in the mammoth Douglas Building, known more commonly as Building 3001, and built to withstand a nuclear attack, or so the story goes. How appropriate for my determined mother, I remember thinking, because that's how *she* was built, too. This began Mom's second career and, before it ended some dozen years later, she had risen high in the ranks to a GS13, the civilian equivalent of a Lieutenant Colonel on the military side.

Unless our parents were employed at Tinker as military or civilian worker, most of us kids had only limited access to the base. So, the daily life of those at Tinker, including those living in the growing base residential areas, was largely cut off from us unless we were invited in. The main view most of us had of the base came during one of their open houses and accompanying air shows, which were generally scheduled once a year. When my mother began working there, however, I was allowed to drive in and see her for lunch or to take and pick her up from work if she needed me to do that.

For me, Tinker was the place where my lifelong interest in swimming began when an airman my folks knew, a lifeguard at Desert Oaks Country Club named Jim Miller, took C.J. and me over to the base pool for our first swimming and diving lessons. He was a good instructor and inspired me to become a lifeguard myself for several years. In fact, at least one summer between my sophomore and junior year at the nearby University of Oklahoma, I lifeguarded at Tinker myself at the NCO (non-commissioned officers) pool.

I could shop at the Base Exchange (BX) or attend the base movie theater since I had a Tinker employee I.D. I wound up spending a lot of time on base that summer, and my impression was it was very well groomed and seemed to run in an orderly fashion. In some ways, it was like driving around a large industrial district. From its opening in 1942, Tinker has grown to cover 9 square miles (almost a third the size of Midwest City today), is composed of 762 buildings under 15,200,000 square feet of roof. By far, the largest of those structures is the historic building 3001, headquartering the Oklahoma City Air Logistics Control unit, which covers 62 acres and stretches for seven-tenths of a mile. It is there that workers carry out a wide array of maintenance on airplanes and engines, along with all the administrative duties that accompany the mission. Some 9,400 of Tinker's 26,000 employees work in that building alone. (11)

Overall, the influence that Tinker cast on us Midwest City residents was not derived from the amount of time we spent on base, however. Most of us felt a little out of place there unless we worked there. It's similar to the feeling you might get visiting a college campus where you aren't a student or employee. Rather, the influence of Tinker was felt in ways that I've tried to describe anecdotally in this chapter as well as the very tangible economic impact the base had on all of us in town.

Over the years, both Tinker and Midwest City found they needed each other very much, and they worked hard to provide that help when it was needed as it would be in the years to come.

The Shetland ponies became a symbol of Midwest City.

The City of Ponies

All the features of this new Midwest City were designed to follow Atkinson's planned themes. In developing the roadways of the original mile, as noted earlier, most original streets were named alphabetically for military officers and aircraft companies. When Atkinson first expanded beyond his original mile north to add its second phase between 15th Street and Reno Avenue, he called the subdivision *Country Estates* and named the streets for trees and shrubs like Lilac and Mimosa. Upon purchasing one of these homes, the developer gave them a shrub or tree consistent with the name of their street.

When he finished that phase, he began work on his Phase 3, between Reno and Northeast 10th Street, which he called Ridgecrest Estates. This development differed from his previous ones in several ways, and it came to be the showplace of homes for Midwest City. Whereas the first phase consisted of small homes of 2 or 3 bedrooms and leaving a foundational footprint of only 800-900 square feet, Phase 2 homes were in the 1,100-1,300 square-foot range, while Ridgecrest homes were even larger and more expensive. Atkinson reasoned that Midwest City was growing quickly, and more professional people and senior Air Force officers were moving in.

The city lacked an upscale subdivision, and the developer knew it needed one for those new residents who could afford it, such as those officers and the growing number of lawyers and doctors who were moving in. The homes were all sprawling ranch style homes with square footage ranging from about 1,600 to more than 2,200 square feet, and they all had two-car garages as opposed to the one-car garages in the first two phases. They were also built on larger lots of a half-acre or more.

Matthew Pearce, historian with the Oklahoma Historical Society, said Ridgecrest and the city's Original Mile were parts of two different contexts. Whereas the original homes in the city were designed for families coming out of the dustbowl and into the war era who didn't have much money, Ridgecrest was designed for those who did. "Ridgecrest was designed to take advantage of the growing post-war affluence," Pearce said. "Even to draw some of those original working-class families who had moved into the Original Mile but who had improved their status in the middle class." (12)

But the most important difference, at least for the kids in the families, was that each of the first 100 buyers of homes sold on large-enough lots in Ridgecrest received a free *Shetland pony*, with its own little barn in the backyard. Additionally, Atkinson designated 10 acres of Ridgecrest to be used exclusively as a pony park, so kids could have an exclusive place to ride their Shetlands. This was yet another example of the developer's marketing talents, tying his homes into a nationwide "pony craze" that swept the nation in the mid-1950s.

As *Life* Magazine described it in 1956, "During the last five years the pony has galloped into a new place in the life of U.S. youngsters, who have rediscovered the old-fashioned fun of owning an animal big enough to ride and gentle enough to serve as a backyard pet.

Traditionally the luxury of the rich, the pony has now become a familiar plaything." (13)

Apparently the U.S. craze was ignited by the news coverage of England's Princess Caroline getting a new pony. Even the Montgomery Ward Shopping Catalogue was featuring ponies for sale by the mid-1950s, priced at $179.95 (the equivalent of $2,000 in 2024) for an untrained, purebred Shetland colt. Ponies in the U.S. are no more than 14.2 hands high (58 inches), with some small enough for toddlers and others large enough for teenagers.

To meet the new demand for ponies in America, the Shetlands were imported largely from Europe. The Shetland breed is often shorter than other ponies, measuring no taller than 42 inches. They originate from the Shetland Islands off the cost of northern Scotland and have been around for some 4,000 years. (14) Shetlands are known to be the hardiest of the ponies, able to withstand cold winters with their long coats, and that may be what fascinated Bill Atkinson about them so much. Oklahoma winters can be brutal at times.

As cute as the Shetland ponies were, they could also be spirited and mischievous with their riders. Joe Cole, one of the original residents of Midwest City who began working at Atkinson's Pony Farm when he was 12, found that out firsthand. "You know they're pretty stubborn," he said. "They bite and they kick."

The red barn of the Atkinson Pony Farm
(Photo by Jim Willis)

It was Cole's job to work with the ponies and tame them for children to ride. Atkinson hired local teens to serve as wranglers at the pony farm, and they would help the younger visitors get on their ponies and lead them around the track. When a family bought one of the eligible Ridgecrest homes, they could come over to barn and pick out the pony they wanted for their own. Sometimes, the pony turned out to be a bad fit, but Atkinson had already devised a solution for that. "Well, the family would try it out," Cole said. "If the pony wasn't right for them, there were a hundred other ponies here to choose from. I broke probably a hundred or more Shetlands to ride." (15)

On the second page of the *Life* photo essay is a picture of 7-year-old Mary Clem Good, of Midwest City, racing her Shetland named "Brownie" in her backyard, noting it was one of 30 (at the time) given away by Ridgecrest builder Bill Atkinson with the sale of $20,000-plus homes in the development.

"I loved Brownie," Mary said. "He was short and fat like me, and we would share a bottle of Coke and chocolate chip cookies. My friend

Linda, we could get on our ponies and be gone all day, as long as we would be home by dark. It was just an idyllic childhood." (16) Idyllic yes, but not without mischief.

The young rider recounted the time when she and Linda heard there was to be a new hospital built on the east side of Ridgecrest in a field they were using as a riding pasture. "We didn't want that hospital built on our riding pasture, so Linda and I would go over in the evenings and pull up the surveying stakes. We really thought we could stop the damned thing from being built. But then the school year started, and we weren't allowed out in the evenings on school nights, so they went ahead and built it anyway!" (17)

There were so many ponies in Ridgecrest that a pony club was formed (one of 40 nationwide affiliated with the U.S. Pony Club by 1956, according to *Life*). The Atkinsons hosted potluck suppers for members of the club at their pony farm on Friday nights. The club became such a fixture in the memory of the Ridgecrest kids that, as they grew to adults, they kept holding pony club reunions. Mary said she had just gone to one in the early 2000s, in fact.

It was there that she heard a man talking about the problems the hospital had getting off the ground. "This man said it had always been a question as to who tried to sabotage the hospital.," she said. "And it was never considered that it was two little girls!" (18) At that reunion, a photograph was displayed that showed the members as kids all sitting on a fence at the entrance to Ridgecrest, and they all decided to go back to that same fence and recreate that picture as adult pony club members.

*A statue of Bill Atkinson
and one of his famed
ponies.*

When Atkinson began his new housing development, word spread quickly around town about the pony giveaway over at Ridgecrest, and it wasn't long before there were plenty of homebuyers looking over there. And the fact that Ridgecrest was featured in *Life*, the leading national consumer magazine, only added to the popularity of the newest of the Midwest City subdivision. Home sales soared.

Atkinson didn't forget about the Ridgecrest families who *didn't* want a pony or, for other reasons couldn't have one. For their kids, and eventually for every kid in town who wanted to ride a pony, he built a large pony barn on his own estate that abutted Ridgecrest on the east side. He stocked that barn with more than 150 ponies, built a large riding arena on its east side, and invited any Midwest City family to come out and ride his Shetlands on Sunday afternoon.

There were many takers, and Atkinson offered the most unique and memorable fun activities for the children of Midwest City families.

Of course, while the kids were riding ponies, their parents had ample opportunity to talk with Mr. Atkinson or one of his associates about the homes in Ridgecrest, and there were more than a few appointments thus made for these families to tour available homes for sale.

My own parents made one of those appointments on a Sunday afternoon while my sister C.J. and I were riding Atkinson's Shetlands around the arena and having the time of our lives. It was 1955 when my sister and I were excited to hear that Dad made an appointment for us all to go and see one of the Ridgecrest homes, because we knew a pony would come with it.

When that day came, we were shown the home by Atkinson himself who seemed to have the tour all planned out. It was a beautiful, new ranch home, probably twice the size of our Lockheed Drive home, on a lot probably three times the size of ours. I thought it odd that Mr. Atkinson started the tour in the kitchen, but then I understood why. He wanted to show Mom all the newest conveniences of this home, one of which was something called a lazy Susan, or revolving corner cabinet. I don't think we had ever seen one before, and he seemed proud of it.

Then he suggested he take C.J. and me out in the backyard, where he had the pony saddled and tethered, awaiting to be ridden, while Mom and Dad looked through the rest of the house on their own. I still remember riding that gentle pony around that large yard, and thinking we *must* get this house! When the tour was over and our family got back into our car, I started working on Dad to get us that pony ... I mean *house*, of course. Mom was impressed by the kitchen, so it seemed to be going our way until Dad got home, sat down with his adding machine, and determined the $22,000 price was too much for us, given our home was only valued at half of that at best, with much lower monthly payments.

In conversations with other kids I knew, I discovered that many of them had gone through the same open house routine, starting with the kitchen and then the backyard pony ride. But, like my family, the price was out of reach for most of them, although some did take the leap and moved to Ridgecrest. One was Mary Clem Good who would be featured in that *Life* Magazine article, riding her "Brownie" a year later.

"One day my parents got a letter that said if you bought one of the first 100 houses in Ridgecrest, you got a pony," she said. "My dad was buying another Atkinson house in the Country Estates development, but it only had a one-car garage, and he wanted two. The Ridgecrest homes had two-car garages. When I heard they were giving away ponies in Ridgecrest, I pleaded with my dad to forget about the one he was buying and buy over there. So, he bought the Ridgecrest house instead. It was just across Reno on the corner of Mockingbird and Bella Vista. My dad had a pony when he was a kid, and I wanted one so badly, so Dad bought the home, and I got Brownie." (19)

Atkinson's granddaughter, Cindy Mikeman, explained the genesis of the pony idea this way: "Granddaddy always loved Shetland ponies and began buying several. He bought a Shetland stallion in 1949 and started expanding the herd. He started inviting kids out to ride Sunday afternoons from 2 to 5, and he and my grandmother would open their home to anyone who wanted to visit. My family had always envisioned Midwest City as a *family* town, and they wanted to offer those families some entertainment they could enjoy together." (20)

It all worked. By 1958, Midwest City parents would bring as many as 300 kids out to ride and tour the grounds every Sunday afternoon. (21) As one researcher noted, "The 167 ponies attracted families along with the farm's specially built club with game room and fireplace. He opened these facilities for any church or school event." (22) Mikeman reiterated that Atkinson liked things to match in theme. So, he painted his own pony barn red, filled it with red-colored animals like cows, chickens, horses, and turkeys, and invited families out to see it, too.

The Atkinson Estate was built on 160 acres on the north side of Midwest City at Midwest Boulevard and Northeast 10th Street. The original part of that home was called the "cabin," and Bill and Rubye Atkinson would invite officers and their families from Tinker out to enjoy the country life for a weekend day. The entire home still exists and is kept in pristine condition as the Atkinson Heritage Museum, owned and operated by Rose State College. Many community events and activities are held there.

The impact of the Shetland ponies went far beyond the boundaries of Ridgecrest Estates. The pony club created there drew in many kids and their club members proudly rode their mounts in various community parades that Midwest City staged.

As Susan Moeri Lee wrote, "The Shetland ponies became an appropriate image in the minds of Midwest City children. Whether owned, ridden, visited, or just admired along a parade route, the small horses symbolized Midwest City entertainment to most of its children." (23) And, since they were Bill Atkinson's idea and gift, each time someone saw a Shetland pony their thoughts often turned to the city's founder. Again and again, the win-win philosophy of Atkinson paid off in dividends for all sides. They not only became a symbol of Midwest City, but also of its founder.

Atkinson himself said with a smile, that the ponies were not only a hobby; they were also good business. "He soon realized that he needed some kind of representation so that people would remember his name," Lee wrote. "He chose a Shetland pony and bought a team of six. They pulled a coach, where Atkinson or some other personality sat. If he did not sit in the wagon, he would follow along

Bill Atkinson welcomes Pony Club royalty and their pony.
(Rose State College Foundation Photo)

behind in his car. It did not take many parades and ceremonies to make the ponies his trademark." (24)

Since Midwest City High School football was so popular on Friday nights, Atkinson would have some of the Shetlands taken to Rose Stadium where the cheerleaders would give the children rides as they led the small steeds around the track. Many would also advise the kids that staying active was a great way to stay out of trouble in life.

5

The Risks We Took

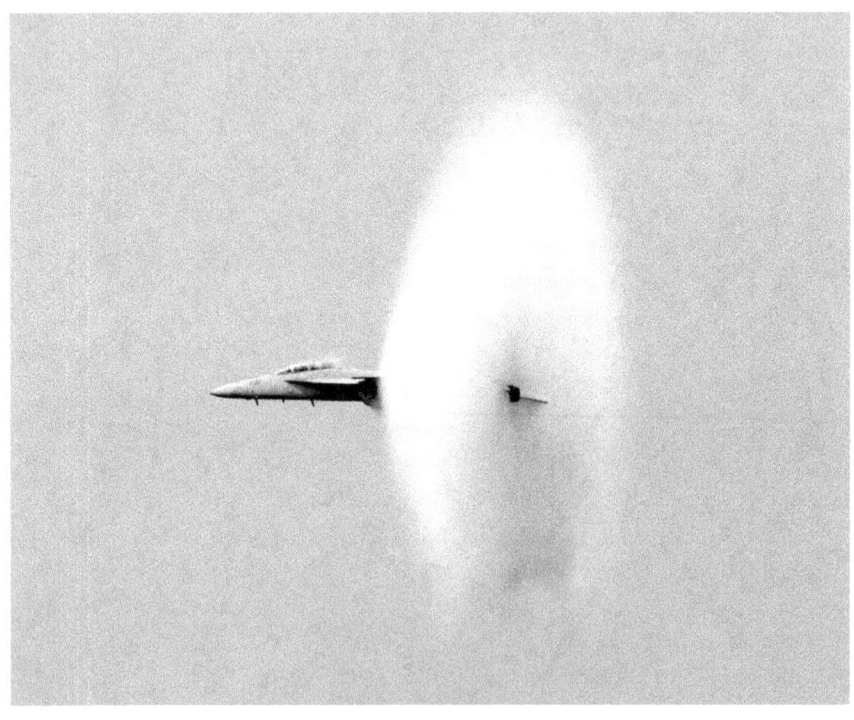

An Air Force jet breaks the sound barrier.
(Photo by Pixabay/No. 12012

The depth of Midwest Cityans' pride in – and reliance upon – Tinker Air Force Base was shown in several ways. First there was our willingness to live with the risks of airplane crashes in town, second, in withstanding daily sonic boom tests for months, and third, in realizing we lived within a mile (my own home was within three blocks) of this likely target for Soviet nuclear attack during the Cold War era of the 1950s and 1960s.

For some residents, there was also the fear that there could be Communist subversives operating at Tinker, stealing secrets and/or undermining the Air Force defense mission. Those who believed Sen. Joseph McCarthy's rants about "a Red under every bed," in the early 1950s were most vulnerable to these Communist fears, although others wondered about it, too.

Oh yes, and there were also the tornadoes, although the whole state of Oklahoma confronts those every spring and summer. We just seemed to get more than our share of warnings and, at least a few times, record-setting twisters.

This chapter looks at all these risks, in reverse order.

First, the fear of nukes and "Reds," as Communists were called disparagingly then. As a teenager, I felt I should attend weekly anti-Communist meetings for a while that were held each Tuesday night in a classroom at Midwest City High School. I wasn't even sure I knew what Communism was, but my church choir director, Dick Lykins, who also taught at the high school, was leading them and I thought he was a pretty smart guy. I was also influenced by a spirit of 1950s patriotism that came partly from my dad, partly from the presence of an Air Force base in town, and partly because of my own teenage fascination with the movies' depiction of the FBI, the popular weekly television series of *The Untouchables*, and my dream of becoming a special agent on a mission to save democracy.

Unfortunately, that was a dream that kept bumping into reality: at the time, the FBI required most of its special agents to have law degrees or accounting degrees, and I was struggling just to graduate from high school. College seemed like a bridge too far.

Nevertheless, I tried to do my part in protecting all of us from the encroaching evils of Eastern Europe, so the thought went. I went to the Tuesday night meetings. There, we were instructed on how to spot possible Communist infiltrators and what to do if we thought we found any. Problem is, spotting them was apparently not easy because we were also told they might look like anyone; even us. So, you had to look for "tells" like the following: Is someone making disparaging remarks about the way Democracy is working in America? Is someone arguing too much with elected officials at a city council or school board meeting or being too negative in their public comments? Is someone remaining too aloof at a public function and seen talking privately with a few selected individuals in a back corner of the room? Is someone making complains about Tinker or the officers or supervisors there? Is anyone refusing to exhibit their patriotism by not flying a flag at their home on Memorial Day or the Fourth of July? Are there any professors at your local college who are talking favorably about Communism or trying to show what the benefits of it can be?

If the answer to one or more of these questions is yes, you might want to think about informing authorities about them, or so the Tuesday night tips went.

One of several popular instructional film series of the early 1960s was produced by a private conservative organization called the National Education Program, located in Searcy, Arkansas, and associated with the faith-based Harding College there. None of us students knew this at the time, however, and we thought it must be a government-affiliated program or an offshoot of the National Education Association, which it wasn't.

Against an opening soundtrack blaring *The Battle Hymn of the Republic,* former FBI undercover agent Herbert A. Philbrick berated Communism and Socialism and gave tips on how loyal Americans could fight the threat in their own local communities. I remember this film from my sophomore year of high school, partly because Philbrick was a well-known name at the time due to a 1950s TV drama series on his anti-Communist adventures called, *I Led 3 Lives,* starring actor Richard Carlson as super-spy Philbrick.

In the third part of the school's propaganda series, called *What Can We Do About It?,* Philbrick instructs viewers to learn what

Communism and Socialism are, then spread the news of their threat via the civic, social, and church groups you belong to. He further advises against signing any petition or allowing your name to be used by any group or movement whose members have been listed as "suspicious" by the House Un-American Activities Committee (HUAC). (1)

That committee, created in 1938 to investigate alleged disloyalty and subversive activities in America, was formed by an investigative committee of the U.S. House of Representatives. It became a permanent committee in 1945 and was abolished in 1975. It was a highly controversial committee, whose actions were seen by many in America as a threat to individual freedoms and democracy itself. I came to agree with that, myself.

It was the most visible and feared element of the "Red Scare" era of the early 1950s, heavily promoted by Sen. McCarthy. During its many public hearings in Washington, the committee's collateral damage included destroying the careers – and sometimes lives – of many Americans who had only marginal association – if that -- with any suspected Communist groups and/or who refused to name the names of friends and even relatives whom the committee asked them about.

After attending some of these Tuesday night meetings at the high school, I lost interest in the group, mostly because I felt its pronouncements were too broad and even dangerous. If I were to look for all those "tells" among people I knew, I could interpret most of my friends as being Communists, which was insane. We were all upset about one thing or another, and we often disagreed about policies our government was enacting. Isn't that what being American is about?

In my later adult years, I realized that any good that came out of those anti-Communist meetings needed to be measured against the harm of turning Americans against each other by making us suspicious of anyone who disagreed strongly with us over a principle he or she thought was important.

It also belied the notion that all Americans view the country from the *same perspective*, and even then, I knew that wasn't the case, especially if you were not white. But since we lived in an all-white Midwest City, viewing the world from the viewpoint of an African American or Hispanic wasn't even in our frame of reference, except in the abstract.

If all this anti-Communism rhetoric focused on possible *future* takeovers by the Communists, the fear of what might happen *on any given day* in the form of a surprise, direct nuclear attack on Tinker took precedence for many in Midwest City.

We were not alone in that fear, because it was sweeping the country in the 1950s, partly because of rhetoric like *"We will bury you,"* coming from Russian Premier Nikita Khrushchev and transported into our living rooms nightly by the network newscasts. Khrushchev uttered the famous warning while addressing Western ambassadors at a reception at the Polish embassy in Moscow on November 18, 1956.

Khrushchev's personal interpreter, Viktor Sukhhodrev translated that phrase into English, and some latter-day translators say his translation was slightly inaccurate, although he was predicting the demise of the West. "We will bury you," became a rallying cry for anti-Communist sentiment in the West and especially the United States. It struck anger into the hearts of many Americans and raised the temperature of the Cold War to the point many were fearing that a nuclear attack could be imminent.

For those who – like us living near a major military installation – that concern ran even deeper. Six years later, on August 24, 1963, the Soviet premier said in a speech in Yugoslavia, "I once said, 'We will bury you,' and I got into trouble with it. Of course, we will not bury you with a shovel. Your own working class will bury you." (2) Some later authors suggested that a more accurate translation would have been, "We shall be present at your funeral." (3)

The result of this Cold War fear of nuclear attack (which, by the way, was also felt by Russians who viewed America as the threat) was an increased emphasis on civil defense in the United States. On January 12, 1951, President Harry Truman signed into effect the Federal Civil Defense Act of 1950 (Public Law 920) which had just been approved by Congress.

The president described it as follows: "[It] is designed to protect life and property in the United States in case of enemy assault. It affords the basic framework for preparations to minimize the effects of an attack on our civilian population, and to deal with the immediate effects of an attack on our civilian population, and to deal with the immediate emergency conditions which such an attack would create." (4)

The key benefits of this act were to award federal matching grants to the states for building air raid shelters and to order the federal government to procure and stockpile needed medical supplies and other survival materials, and to provide for suitable warning systems of pending attacks.

Five months before passage of the act, the government had developed a master plan for meeting attacks by an aggressor, following several years of studying that possibility. The plan was called "United States Civil Defense," and it served as the blueprint for American states and cities as they prepared to fully safeguard their populations possible.

As head of the new Federal Civil Defense Administration, the government named Millard F. Caldwell, a former governor of Florida. However, Truman noted in his announcement, "It is the expressed policy and intent of Congress, however, that the responsibility for civil defense should be vested primarily in the states and their political subdivisions. I, therefore, call upon all citizens to lend their support to civil defense in their own communities. Much has been done, but much remains to be done. It will require the best efforts of all of us to get ready, and to stay ready, to defend dour homes. No true American would want to give less than his best to that cause, and no one who knows the American people could ask for more." (5)

Of course, the matching grants meant that each state had to come up with its share of the money for the civil defense program designed by the Federal Civil Defense Administration, and Oklahoma's share was determined to be $804,000. A lot of money in 1951, and Oklahoma's Governor William H. Murray didn't want to raise taxes to pay for it. Nevertheless, that is what the administration's Millard Caldwell, asked the state to kick in for a two-year span of the program.

Oklahoma legislators balked at that amount, said it was too expensive for what the state needed, and counter-proposed a plan costing the state only $125,000. Caldwell, however, insisted the state stick close to the federal model civil defense bill. A week later, Oklahoma went forward with its modified plan nonetheless, and created the Oklahoma Civil Defense Agency, appropriating $125,000 for 1951, and an equal sum for 1952.

Under the plan, the statewide agency was established as well as county civil defense organizations. These would all be overseen by civil defense councils who were given emergency powers to invoke the plans in the event of imminent attack.

For Midwest City, it meant the creation of a civil defense program that drew on the support of many local volunteers. Having America's largest air depot right across 29th Street was both a great asset but also became a great concern for many residents here as the Cold War Era with Russia got underway just after World War II ended.

The worldwide Communism threat was now literally near our front porch. Local elected officials not only took the oath of office, but also signed an anti-Communist pledge to do their part in keeping us safe in Midwest City. As if that were really possible if the bomb was dropped here.

Tinker was a key target, because it played a vital role in national defense as it was tasked with producing and modifying both B-52 and B-47 bombers which were the planes that would go into action as retaliation for any nuclear attack by Russia. Both were designed to carry nuclear bombs.

Fallout shelters were being constructed in town, and civil defense classes were being held. The state began its CONELRAD (Control of Electromagnetic Radiation) radio warning system whereby certain stations continued in the case of nuclear attack on the 640 and 1240 AM radio frequencies, issuing instructions and keeping listeners informed about what to do. Midwest City constructed a Ground Observation Control (GOC) tower on the northwest corner of the high school campus, and the local chamber of commerce donating the construction materials to build the 28-foot structure.

As historian Susan Moeri Lee has noted, "Designed by concerned Midwest City citizens, it had a lobby and restroom on the ground floor, stairs to the second floor where an office space and glass enclosed observation looked over the countryside. Adult and teenage volunteers manned the tower." (6) Local volunteers were eager to serve in various functions including training their eyes on the overhead skies to spot any suspicious activity and/or threats. That's not easy in skies that are serving as regular flight paths for the military aircraft departing and landing at Tinker Air Force Base.

The state established more than 400 of these observation posts around Oklahoma, any of which could be staffed with volunteers with 15 minutes. Like other media around the state, the *Midwest City Leader* put out the call for these sky-watchers to maintain 24/7 monitoring of the heavens. (7)

But the civil defense initiative also meant organizing and implementing educational literature and seminars for local residents, offering tips on what to do in the case of an enemy attack which – in this era – probably meant a nuclear attack.

That instruction was also tailored to kids in Midwest City and across the nation. One of my earliest memories as a first grader at Westside Elementary School is of the emergency drills we did several times a year. There were three types of them.

The first was a fire drill, which all schools did – and still do everywhere. The second was the tornado drill, a staple for towns like ours located in "Tornado Alley." Just like tenpins would know a bowling ball is headed for them, so the residents of Oklahoma know that twisters would be coming in the spring and early summer. The hope is they will head back up into the clouds before they get to your street or, if need be, go down someone else's street.

The F-5 twister of May, 1995 was a killer.

Dodging tornadoes has always been a ritual of life here, and Oklahoma County has felt the brunt of 128 twisters from 1950 to 2022, 31 of which produced significant damage and deaths, according to the National Weather Service. (8) The number of tornado *warnings* heard over sirens in Midwest City has been many times that number. Warning sirens in spring are a frequent occurrence here.

The third, and most frightening, school drill was the *nuclear attack drill*. Of course, since kids were involved, it wasn't called that. Instead, it was called the *"Duck and Cover Game."* Our teachers showed us how to respond immediately to the warning signal coming over the school's intercom by crawling under our desks, bending over forward, and covering our heads with our arms and hands. The purpose was to avoid any injuries that might occur should America's enemy launch an attack on Tinker Air Force Base. The drill was sold to us as a way of being brave and patriotic by not letting the enemy harm us.

Of course, I don't remember of anything being said about the fact that Tinker was located just a block or two away from our school and that, if the blast were nuclear, we wouldn't have to worry about fallout from it, because we'd all be vaporized instantly. And I do understand why this was *not* said nor explained. The thinking was that it's better to give kids a shred of hope and a sense that they had some control over their safety by crawling under their desk or covering against a wall in the hallway, even if they were in the epicenter of a blast zone.

In any event, it was probably better to keep this low profile than be standing up during an attack, right?

Duck and Cover was not an original drill with our school or community. It was happening all over the United States in the 50s and 60s as the United States and the Russian-led Soviet Union rattled the sabers of nuclear war the loudest. "Duck and Cover" was the official preparedness measure designed to be a civil defense response in the event of a nuclear attack.

In the post-war years of the 1940s when Russia achieved nuclear capabilities, Americans began prepping for the possibility – some felt probability – of nuclear war. Constructing fallout shelters was a key response to the threat, but also were the air-raid drills like Duck and Cover practiced in schools and workplaces around America.

To make it a little easier for kids to deal with this attack threat, the Federal Civil Service Administration contracted with Archer Productions to make animated films in 1951 about a snappy-looking turtle named *Bert* who wore a bowtie and a chin-strapped helmet and walked on his hind legs with his shell on his back. Background vocalists provided a jaunty song about Bert that went like this:

> "*There was a turtle by the name of Bert and Bert the turtle was very alert;*
>
> *when danger threatened him, he never got hurt; he knew just what to do...*
>
> *He'd duck! And cover!*" (9)

In the 9-minute black and white cartoon, Bert would stop, drop, duck and cover into his shell whenever he sensed danger afoot. He told the students they needed to do the same thing and, after the film ended, the teacher would instruct them to duck and cover under their desks or, if outside, drop to a sidewalk next to a wall, just like Bert did in his shell.

Bert the Turtle showed school kids how to "duck and cover."
U.S. Government/Archer Productions

As more and more children were exposed to Bert's advice, the phrase "duck and cover" spread across the country as a kind of battle cry for American domestic preparedness against a foreign attack. If they weren't in a place where an alarm would sound, they should look for a "blinding flash of light," then duck and cover immediately. The Library of Congress designated the turtle film as "historically significant," and inducted it into the National Film Registry in 2004, saying it had been seen by millions of school-children in the 1950s. (10)

The film has been on YouTube for several years and has had well over 4 million views there on one channel (Nuclear Vault) alone. Viewed in today's context and culture, the film seems silly to some, but others remind us these were different times when the country was on edge because of Russia's nuclear capabilities, actions and rhetoric. The following YouTube comments on the film show these different reactions from residents: (11)

- "I love how the civil defense worker, completely unscathed, helps the little kid get on the bike and sends him on his way as if nothing happened."
- "It doesn't matter how old this is. It still manages to give me chills. I don't know why, but it must be because this was actually a serious issue back then and, even though it would have been minimal help in protecting you, it still gave you a sense of hope and protection. But there was still like a 90 percent possibility that you would die."
- "When I watched this film in grade school in the 50s, I believed I'd soon be dead; crispy-fried. I just watched it again here and laughed so hard I couldn't finish!"
- "While your chances of surviving a nuclear weapon are slim, duck and cover is still by far your best shot at survival. When [an attack] shows up unexpectedly, that is."
- "This actually made me really sad that people had to live in such fear."
- "I'm always gonna' carry a newspaper with me from now on, because [laying it over me] will help protect me from severe burns in the event of a nuclear blast. Thank you, Bert!"

- "Would love to see the version of this the USSR put out for their children."

Despite the naysayers, "the duck-and-cover campaign remained a standard response to potential nuclear attack, through the 1950s and into the 1960s," according to the Encyclopedia Britannica. "Eventually, it waned, however, partly because of thaws in U.S.-Soviet relations. Despite its eventual demise, the encyclopedia said the policy remains one of the most pervasive and successful homeland-security initiatives in U.S. history." (12)

One former Midwest Cityan, Jane Vickers Bogan, remembered that her father had served as the head of civil defense at the Oklahoma State Department of Education, and that she had fears of a nuclear attack as a child. "I once asked my dad what if a bomb hit Tinker," she recalled. "'Honey, we'd be a greasy spot,'" he said. (13) Now there's some honest parenting!

Schoolkids practice duck and cover in the hallway.

That grim assessment seemed backed up by formal data. The *Midwest City Leader* cited the results of a recent simulated an atomic bomb exploding at Tinker, which was the most sophisticated of several such experiments done around the country. The estimates were that, within 200 miles, some 35,000 people would die 50,000 would be injured, and 40 trained squads of first responders would be needed for search and rescue operations. (14) Midwest City, which had fewer than 20,000 residents at the time, would be hardest hit.

Such was the threat that Midwest City – and the entire Oklahoma City metro area -- lived with during the country's Cold War Era. Like the other challenges of having Tinker as a neighbor, however, the city survived and continued to strengthen its bond with Tinker in the ensuing decades.

More importantly, however, was the fact that we were all able to carry on with our normal lives and few were freaking out over all these worries. It was similar to our

situation in the current day when we live with the daily threat of mass shootings and terrorism, both foreign and domestic.

The difference is that, today, we are exposed to graphic visual presentations of these threats 24/7 thanks to television and social media. So they are probably on our minds more regularly than were the threats of nuclear strikes back in the 1950s and 1960s.

Fire in the Sky

"Jimmy, come out and see this!"

It was a sunny morning in my sophomore year of high school, 1962, when my mother called me out into the front yard. There was urgency in her voice, so I hurried out and saw her looking up to the northeastern sky, using her right hand to shield her gaze from the sun. "Jim, Look!" She shouted as she pointed to the near horizon.

At that second, I turned and saw an Air Force jet streaking low and toward us, not that far above the rooftops down our Lockheed Drive. The plane's canopy was gone. We stood transfixed for the few seconds it took for the plane to stream over our house, with its landing gear down. As it passed across Lockheed, its gear seemed to clip the top branches of our neighbor's tall elm tree down the street, and it streaked past the city water tower just to its right.

At that point, it was still a few hundred yards from the runway, but had to clear Atkinson Plaza Shopping Center and a busy 29th Street before it could catch the end of that runway. A couple blocks later, the plane dipped too low to see it, and we began hearing emergency sirens from the fire station around our corner and from Tinker Field. A news alert came over my transistor radio a few minutes later that the plane had, in fact, just made it to the apron of the runway and was down safely. We heard from neighbors that the pilot had ejected about three blocks north of us and landed on the roof of a home on Lockheed.

That was the only airplane going down that I witnessed personally growing up in Midwest City, although I had seen the aftermath of a fatal crash a year before in the Glenwood Subdivision, east of us by about a half-mile. Both events showed me clearly the dangers of building housing so close to active air base runways, and I counted my family as lucky for not having this jet land on us that day.

It is the kind of challenge that military bases and their adjoining towns and cities face across the United States: residential areas encroaching too close to the military action zones, such as the runways at Tinker, and the dangers they can pose. A 2002 federal government report describes that challenge this way:

"The U.S. Department of Defense (DOD) maintains over 10 million hectares of land to house and train troops, test weapons, and conduct readiness exercises ... Despite the economic and environmental contributions of military installations to their surrounding areas, areas of conflict sometimes arise between installations and local neighboring communities ... Military installations are increasingly being asked to alter activities within their boundaries to alleviate these conflicts ... These constraints have all resulted from local community conflict. The growing friction and restrictions to such operations and land use may put installations at risk for meeting mission requirements." (15)

In brief, this assessment done for the U.S. Army Corps of Engineers in 2002 lays out a key ongoing challenge in the relationship of all military bases with their host communities. It's not always easy for the military base to pursue its mission and keep residents feeling safe and happy at the same time. Air Force base operations can be very noisy, and some can pose danger of crashes to the adjoining communities. Such has been the case over the years with Tinker Air Force Base and Midwest City, Oklahoma.

Tinker is a very large aircraft maintenance facility, there are a lot of jets, bombers, tankers, and early warning aircraft flying in and out on an hourly basis, 24/7, they produce noise taking off and landing, and sometimes these planes develop catastrophic failures and fall from the sky. These latter incidents are rare, but real and tragic when they occur.

This is why the Air Force worries about residential encroachment
near runways..

When Tinker was just starting out in 1942 and Midwest City was, too, the aircraft were flying over mostly cropland that was spare in populations. But, within a couple years, there were some 1,500 new homes built in the town built just across Southeast 29th Street from the base; by 1950, Midwest City had a population of just over 10,000, along with schools, a shopping center, and several churches.

By 1960, that population had more than tripled and a city of 36,000 sprawled north across 29th Street from Tinker. Some neighborhoods had encroached very close to main Tinker runways, and many worried there was an accident waiting to happen. There would be more than one, but the biggest of them threatened the future of Tinker's ability to carry out its mission and Midwest City's ability to keep all its residents safe and still allow them to thrive economically.

In a conversation late in 2023, retired Air Force Gen. Roger A. Brady, himself a former Midwest Cityan, told me, "Local communities take 'ownership' of a base and have a significant impact on the vibrancy and actual longevity of the base. It is really a symbiotic relationship that may sometimes go unnoticed or be taken for granted. Things like noise and allowing development to encroach on a base can lead to a 'divorce,'" and failure on the part of either the military or the community to think strategically can lead to outcomes that neither want."

In the 2002 Army Corps of Engineers report, some 99 military installations in eight states were deemed to be at risk because of residential encroachment, with 13 of those labeled "high-risk." (16) Happily, for Tinker and Midwest City, the air base did not appear on that risk list.

Such has not always been the case, however. In preceding years, fatal air disasters have occurred; the damage has been done. Afterwards, there were hard questions about the continued viability of Tinker's mission and to the economic health of Midwest City. But these were those moments when civilians and military worked together to reduce futures risk levels and keep Tinker on mission.

The first of those air crashes came within the first three years of operation for Tinker in 1945. It happened on April 30, while school was in session, shortly after the permanent Midwest City School building (which later became Jarman Junior High and Jarman Middle School) was constructed. Tragedy struck when a Lockheed Lodestar transport plane crashed just north of the school building on Lockheed Drive, on what is now its athletic field. The plane had just taken off three minutes earlier from Tinker at 10:23 a.m. It was carrying 14 passengers and crew.

The plane developed engine trouble, and the pilot had to tilt the plane's wing to miss hitting the smokestack atop the school complex but crashed just yards away from it and burst into flames, narrowly missing the packed school itself. Four Tinker employees on the plane died, and 10 were injured. (17) Seeing the crash unfold, several students and teachers rushed from their classrooms to help. Principal J.E. Sutton would later note with pride, "Many were saved by the efforts of our students and teachers who, in the face of danger, dragged several from the burning plane." (18)

Donna Elledge, an early resident of Midwest City, remembered that crash and said, "I was in Mrs. Sutton's second grade class [at Midwest City School] when the plane crashed where Rose Field is today. "It had rained the night before, so we went for a walk at recess instead of playing on the field [where the plane crashed]. God's intervention for us." (19)

When you live in an Air Force town, you get used to the sights and sounds of low-flying aircraft overhead on a regular basis. It didn't take long for all of us in Midwest City to feel that the roar and swoosh of jet aircraft engines were just part of the background noise of the city. The sonic booms, which would come in the early 1960s, were harder to ignore because you felt a physical jolt from some of them. But it was all part of trying to be a good neighbor to an important government facility in our midst which our city depended upon in many ways. In fact, when I think of the hundreds of regular missions flown out of Tinker in a given week or month, I count it as amazing there weren't more accidents over our heavily populated town than there were.

Most of us felt very safe, trusted the pilots at Tinker, and the city continued to grow and prosper. Always, we knew, the major reason for both was this huge Air Force base across 29th Street.

Nevertheless, there was one subdivision that paid a heavy price with two fatal crashes and one near miss, all of which came in the 1960s. When it was all over, the incidents put a spotlight on the advantages and disadvantages of building a town next to a military base, the dangers that can arise, and the extraordinary lengths a town will go to let that base complete its intended missions. This subdivision was called Glenwood, named for its developers Glen Breeding and N.D. Wood. It sprawled over 283 acres, included 836 houses, and one large elementary school.

Glenwood was built as the decade of the 1950s began, and it abutted the easternmost boundaries of Midwest City. It was located between 15th and 29th Streets on the north and south sides, and between Midwest Boulevard and Douglas Boulevard on the west and east. When its first homes were built, Glenwood was not inside the city limits, although Midwest City annexed it in the fall of 1952. But the location would prove dangerous for residents there, as future events would show.

As The Oklahoman noted in a 2017 retrospective by Richard Mize, "Times changed along with developments in military aircraft and weapons systems, and the place became dangerous, situated as it was almost abutting the base, directly under the northern approach to Tinker's main runway ... Glenwood faced the potential risk – tragically realized –of deadly accidents from the air traffic just overhead. The property and people living in the area themselves were a danger to the future of the base, which the U.S. Air Force was threatening to close." (20)

The planes coming in for landing were so close to the ground, that one of my childhood friends remembers seeing pilots smile and wave at them, and recalled how she and her best friends would try to hit an occasional plane with water balloons from their backyard.

Then one day, on a Friday afternoon August 26, 1961, all of us school kids in Midwest City were readying for the last weekend of summer. But that would be the day the future of the Glenwood Subdivision began to change for the worse. I was heading into my sophomore year at Midwest City High School and was outdoors shooting pictures with my new 35mm Minolta camera Dad had bought me. Photography had been my hobby for about three years, and I'd taken pictures of just about everything in Midwest City during that time.

Meanwhile, over at Tinker, one 27-year-old Air Force officer named

Lt. W.H. Barbour, was going to work, taxiing his F-100 Super Sabre fighter jet, fully tanked up with 1,800 gallons of fuel, out onto the main runway. He was taking the jet home to Myrtle Beach Air Force Base in South Carolina, where he was stationed with the 354th Tactical Fighter Wing. He no doubt considered this just another routine run after getting his plane serviced at Tinker. But the young pilot had just taken off when his F-100 lost its directional control, and Barbour had to eject at only 800 feet when his plane failed to respond to his attempt to turn it back to the base.

It was later determined there was a fire in the fuselage and, as the jet crossed north over 29th Street above Glenwood homes, it went down immediately, crashing into a home at 325 Ferguson Drive. Two little sisters, Tibbie Lynn Tuttle, 2, and Judith, 4, were in the home when the jet hit and exploded. Tibbie was killed in the blast, and Judith died the next day. Seven homes on Ferguson Drive were in the path of the resulting fire and were destroyed, as several residents were injured and rushed to the hospital when first-responders could get through the flames and smoke to rescue them. As for the plane's pilot, his parachute landed him safely, two blocks away. (21)

"If I could have stayed aloft one more second, the plane would have missed hitting the houses," Barbour told reporters later. "In 20 more seconds, it would have made the runway." (22)

The Oklahoman wrote about the proximity of homes to the runway saying, "A spokesman for the Air Force noted that while Tinker was one of the least congested Air Force bases, officials were growing uneasy with residential areas directly in any bases' flight paths." (23)

Glenwood was the subdivision he was describing, and I witnessed the destruction that can happen from that encroachment myself the next day when I rode my bike over to the neighborhood with my camera and shot several photos of burnt homes and aftermath of the F-100 crash in this crowded neighborhood. None of us knew at the time that this would *not* be the last such tragedy there. But before the second one would occur in Glenwood seven years later, two Air Force pilots would lose their lives less than a mile away in a wooded Midwest City field in 1962.

That incident involved a Martin B-57 E Canberra bomber on a routine training flight from Edwards Air Force Base, in California. The pilot was Maj. Thomas J. Deegan, a 37-year-old father of eight, and his crew member was A-1 Bobbie L. Rolland, 25, also married and father of two. A Tinker spokesman said the plane left Tinker at 10:28 a.m. after refueling, enroute to Willow Grove Naval Air Station, in Delaware. Seconds later, Maj. Deegan radioed the Tinker control tower that the engines were failing. Two minutes later, the light bomber crashed into a timbered field at the intersection of North Douglas and Reno Avenue on the northeast side of Midwest City.

The field was surrounded by a heavily populated residential area, school, and a shopping center, and the doomed two-man crew was credited with heroic action as Deegan guided the twin-engine plane past the houses and into an empty 500-yard field between two homes. The bomber was loaded with fuel and would have done serious damage, probably involving civilian casualties, had he not guided it over and be-tween those two homes. Wreckage was strewn over the entire field, but no homes were damaged and no one in the housing area was hurt. (24)

There were more tragic air accidents yet to come for Midwest City. Six years later, on Wednesday, December 18, 1968, I was a senior at the University of Oklahoma when I heard the news that Glenwood had once again been the site of a jet mishap, although this one wound up thankfully as a near-miss. Just after noon that day, a crippled F-4C Phantom jet fighter needed to make an emergency landing at Tinker as it flew from Bermuda to Ogden Air Force Base in Utah. At the controls were Air Force Capt. Alex W. Sapyia, 34, and his navigator Maj. Thomas R. Adams. The pilot managed to guide the plane onto the runway before discovering his plane had no steering. He immediately took off again, but he was unaware that the jet had snagged 300 feet of steel cable and parts of a runway barrier system Tinker used for emergency landings.

As the F-4C ascended, this trailing debris snapped electrical power lines, poles, and treetops across some 10 blocks of the Glenwood addition. Despite this, the pilot was able to bank the jet and returned it to Tinker for a second runway landing. This one was successful, and no one was injured in the mishap. Nevertheless, neighborhood residents were horrified, and the memories of the 1961 disaster came flooding back. (25)

Then, ten months later, on October 7, 1969, a TF-100 Super Sabre training jet developed equipment trouble on a routine flight from McConnell Air Force Base in Wichita, Kansas. The crew consisted of the instructor pilot, Capt. James L. Kirkhuff, from the 184th Tactical Fighter Squadron, and the co-pilot, Lt. James R. Nelms, of the Kansas Air National Guard. They were attempting to make an emergency landing at Tinker. Once again, the glidepath brought him over Glenwood and, once again, a jet crashed into the eastside neighborhood.

Kirkhuff managed to eject and was found dazed but walking a block and a half away. Nelms was killed in the crash, and that crash occurred only five blocks from Glenwood Elementary School. It was 2:15 p.m., and the school was in session. But three homes were destroyed, and others were damaged. (26) At least one unconfirmed report said co-pilot Nelms saw the Glenwood School just before he was supposed to eject.

He turned the jet slightly southeast to miss the school, which it did. Even though it only took a couple seconds to do that, it was too late for him to eject, and he rode the plane down to his death.

One witness, Bonnie Hill, wrote, "I was 8 years old, out riding my bike when I saw a person bailing from a plane. I lived on Shortway Drive, one street from Ferguson on the other side of the railroad tracks. I then saw and heard the explosion and saw red flames and huge cloud of black smoke from the crash. I rode over on my bike to see what happened. It was the most horrific image of my childhood, seeing the burning homes. I'll never forget the thick smoke and ashes everywhere." (27)

The question of pilots ejecting before their planes crash into heavily populated areas was one discussed by Midwest City residents who

wondered what the Air Force directs pilots to do in these dire circumstances. In 2023, a veteran Air Force senior command pilot told me the
following about this:

"As to policies regarding bailing out over inhabited areas, there is a
lot of judgment and not a lot of firm guidance. Airbases who support
aircraft with ejection seats usually have what they call a 'controlled bail-
out area.' We always had one at the training bases when I was a pilot
training instructor. It was an area close to the base where you would
go to eject if you could control the aircraft to get to it, or if you were
under control but ejection seemed inevitable.

'For example, if you could get a main and nose gear down, but one
main was still stuck 'up,' you would not be able to land safely and were
probably facing an inevitable ejection. The 'ethic,' though I never saw it
as a directive, was that you would try to maneuver your aircraft away
from inhabited areas, but I don't remember it ever being suggested you
should 'ride it in' or put yourself at risk to avoid casualties on the
ground. However, I remember several cases where accident investiga-
tors suspected the pilot had done just that. Those are obviously difficult
decisions, and there is often little or no time to contemplate it." (28)

In sum, within a period of seven years, the Glenwood neighborhood
alone had experienced two jet crashes, one near-miss, three resulting
fatalities, and several other injuries. Tension had been building not only
in the neighborhood from worried residents who feared more crashes.
Several homeowners tried to move, but found difficulty selling their
homes, even below market value. Others did sell and did move out. But
tension was also rising in the ranks of Tinker and Air Force leadership
who knew the town's residential encroachment near the main runway
was creating danger for residents and threatening the Air Force mission
at Tinker.

The problem was huge for both the city and the base. Leaders in
Midwest City knew of other bases that had to either downsize or close
because of threatening residential encroachment. But the Glenwood
subdivision encompassed 836 homes and as many families living in
them. It also encompassed the school servicing the area's children. It

would be a huge displacement and cost a lot of money, yet in 1971 the Midwest City Council felt it had no choice. It proposed an urban renewal authority be recreated to relocate the Glenwood residents, buy the whole 283-acre subdivision, and raze the homes and school.

The price tag to the city would be $2.8 million, funded by bonds that would need voter approval. In the hearings on the bond issue, some Midwest City residents wondered why Glenwood was ever allowed to be built so close to the base in the first place, two decades before. But was not in the Midwest City limits at the time, so the city had no say in it. Others said there was no way of predicting the advances in technology and weapons systems that would create a future danger after the neighborhood was established. Even the Veterans Administration had insured many of the mortgages on the homes when they were bought.

Both the Air Force as well as former Oklahoma Governor, Henry Bellmon, supported the razing of Glenwood. In fact, the Air Force said it *must* be cleared. The area's congressman, Tom Steed agreed. "The next five years," he said, "would bring a life-or-death struggle for the survival of military bases like Tinker. There could be no stronger insurance for Tinker than the resolution of the Glenwood problem." (29)

The Glenwood proposal was the most important of six bond issues that confronted Midwest City voters on December 28. None of them passed, and only one of 20 voting precincts (the one housing Glenwood) voted for purchasing and razing the Glenwood neighborhood. So now the problem remained unsolved, and attention turned to voters in Oklahoma County, which includes Midwest City.

Glenwood's future became not only a city issue but a county-wide issue because of the huge economic impact Tinker had on central Oklahoma residents. There were upwards to 26,000 jobs on the line and an annual payroll of $300 million, and many of those employees lived outside of Midwest City; some commuted for many miles to and from Tinker and lived in Oklahoma City, Del City, Moore, and other area towns. If Midwest City wouldn't pass the bond issue, then maybe the county would.

It took some time for that to happen, and the Mid-Del School Board did what it could in agreeing to close Glenwood Elementary School if arrangements could be made to relocate the area's homeowners. The Oklahoma County Commissioners responded by calling a county-wide bond election in May 1973, asking voters to approve a $10.8 million bond issue that would fund the purchase of Glenwood and the removal of the homes that would be sold at auction

Leaders from all levels of Oklahoma government supported the bond issue, and the rallying cry of *"Save Tinker Now!"* began appearing in advertising. May 8 was proclaimed as "Save Tinker Day," by those supporting the bonds approval. The state's most influential newspaper, *The Daily Oklahoman*, carried a front-page editorial urging passage of the issue under the headline, "Save $300,000,000 Today." It was an obvious reference to Tinker's annual payroll.

The bond issue was approved overwhelmingly by nearly 9 out of 10 county voters. Oklahoma County purchased the first Glenwood home two months later, paying the owners $14,000. The entire neighborhood of 836 homes took five years to be cleared, with the last homes auctioned in January 1978. Four years later, the county leased the property to Tinker for $1 per year, for 50 years. It still stands vacant and fenced by Tinker, which uses it for some training purposes.

While the air accidents in Glenwood were the most impactful for Midwest City and Tinker, both because of the lives lost and the eventual clearing-out of an entire subdivision, they were not the last crashes to occur. *The Oklahoman*, in a 2017 retrospective by Graham Lee Brewer, described two other fatal air crashes to occur in the 1970s and 1980s.

The first came in May 1974 when a Northrop T-38 Talon, on a training mission with a crew of two, was approaching the base to land when the plane lost power, according to Brewer and cited Tinker historical documents. "Witnesses also said the plane's engine backfired just before impact, indicating a possible engine failure. The pilots were able to

The Glenwood subdivision is shown in the bottom half of this photo, after it was cleared of all its 836 homes and the elementary school was closed in the 1970s. The upper portion of the photo shows the runway system at Tinker. Southeast 29th street runs between them and was the only buffer separating them. Glenwood's razing and the relocation of all those residents were the price Midwest City and Oklahoma County paid to keep residents safe from more air accidents and to keep Tinker on mission so it wouldn't have to relocate.

regain control enough to avoid an apartment complex, however they crashed into a home on Del Casa Circle before they could eject. Both pilots were killed." (30)

The $35,000 home belonging to Paul Shofner and his wife Lisa, was not occupied but was destroyed in the crash. According to witnesses, the plane clipped some trees before careening off the pavement of the cul-de-sac and shoving a car in the Shofner's driveway through the home.

The second crash happened in 1985 when an air support aircraft, just repaired at Tinker, took off on a test flight, according to Tinker acting commander Lt. Gen. Richard Burpee. "The engine caught fire about six miles north of the base, and the pilot weas trying to find his way back to the base for an emergency landing, Burpee said. The plane was not going to make it back, and the pilot found an open field in which to land. The pilot ejected just before the plane skipped off the ground, plowed through an oak tree, and crashed into the only home in the immediate area, killing an elderly attorney and his sister." (31)

These and the previous crashes caused the Association of Central Oklahoma Governments (ACOG) and the United States Department of Defense to hold joint meetings and study better practices of development land around Tinker. Burpee noted, "Planes are a lot safter today than they were 20, 30 years ago, but every once in a while ... You just never know. The most critical time of flight is the takeoff and the landing." (32)

According to *The Oklahoman*, Tinker created several large acreages in the immediate area as "accident potential zones," which were to be left clear of development to avoid more such crashes. The former Glenwood subdivision, razed by 1978, was one of those cleared zones.

As late as 2008, the commission that did the land-use study was still recommending keeping those zones clear of development and encroachment that "negatively affects readiness and is often gradual, going unnoticed, until its impact cumulatively erode the military's ability to complete the mission of training and deploying combat-ready troops and equipment." According to Brewer, "The study found previous guidelines for development were being exceeded and warned against future construction in those areas." (33)

These were some of the most significant of the accidents occurring over Midwest City by planes either taking off or landing at Tinker, and they were painful chapters in the history for both the city and the air base. But today both Tinker and Midwest City continue to function side by side across 29th Street. And now they have the benefit of several decades' experience in how to work together to be good neighbors and keep residents feeling safe and glad that the base still thrives.

As one veteran Midwest City resident, who grew up in the ill-fated Glenwood subdivision, everyone who bought homes there understood what could happen if a plane crashed there. "As my dad used to say, 'we all knew the risk.' He said, 'the noise from landing and departing aircraft was the sound of freedom!'" (34)

Sonic Booms and Broken Stuff

Compared to the tragedies of occasional jet crashes in Midwest City, the noise and jolts felt from advanced jets breaking the sound barrier over your home would be inconsequential. Or so many of us thought in Midwest City, especially if these booms were somehow helping Tinker Air Force Base complete part of its mission. Even though it was more a case of helping the then-Federal Aviation Agency (FAA) complete theirs. Either way they were Air Force jets, and that was good enough for us. After all, keeping Tinker in business was good business for all of us in its host city.

It's just that, for a period of months in 1963, there were *a lot* of these jarring booms. They came eight times a day for six months, and they affected all of us to one degree or another. Those of us who lived through them still talk about those booms and, if we think about it hard enough, we can still hear and feel them. So, it's worth taking a chapter to remember them and to explain why they occurred and with what results.

The Bell X-1 was first to break the sound barrier, in 1947.

What is a sonic boom? When an airplane streaks through the air, it creates a series of pressure waves, both in front of the plane as well as behind it. It can be likened to the waves created both by the bow and the stern of a ship as it moves through water. Pressure waves travel at the speed of sound which, in the air, is around 750 mph. As the airplane moves faster, these pressure waves are forced together (compressed), simply because they cannot get out of each other's way fast enough.

Eventually, they merge into a

single shock wave, which is a critical speed known as Mach 1, and is approximately 741 mph at sea level and 68 degrees Fahrenheit. When the aircraft hits Mach 1, it produces a "boom" because of the sudden change in air pressure. In actuality, you hear two booms: one when the initial pressure-rises reach a ground observer, and a second when the pressure returns to normal. (35)

These booms can cause some ground-level damage such as shattered glass and broken stuff when dishes, pictures, and other family heirlooms break, falling off shelves. Buildings in good condition should suffer no structural damage, although that depends on several factors such as the size and intensity of the air-pressure change, the size and shape of the aircraft itself that produces the boom, and the distance that aircraft is from ground level. The threat of *ground motion* itself resulting from sonic booms is seen as rare and has been measured as well below structural damage thresholds accepted by the U.S. Bureau of Mines and other agencies. (36) In other words, the danger of *earthquakes* being caused by sonic booms is very rare and would need extreme fluctuations in air pressure as well as unstable ground layers.

For a period of 178 days, starting on February 3, 1964, the FAA supervised sonic boom tests over the metro Oklahoma City area and particularly Midwest City. The aircraft used were Air Force supersonic jets, most of which were housed at Tinker, right across 29th Street from our town. The purpose of the test was to gauge the effects of sonic booms over an extended period of time. More specifically, the results were meant to provide quantifiable data about the impact of transcontinental supersonic transport (SST) aircraft on a city, to measure the effects of these sonic booms on the structures and public opinion, so standards might be developed for boom prediction and insurance data. The experiment was known *Operation Bongo* and was to consist of 1,253 sonic booms generated by aircraft flying through the sound barrier.

It had been less than a year since President John F. Kennedy, whose November 1963 death was fresh in America's mind, had challenged Americans to not only put a man on the moon, but also to welcome supersonic air passenger travel as a means of dramatically cutting international flight times.

The Greater Oklahoma City Chamber of Commerce hosted a celebratory dinner when Oklahoma City was selected as the test site. City leaders saw in this experiment the chance to become a national SST aviation hub, having already landed Tinker Air Force Base and the FAA's training, logistics, and research center at Will Rogers World Airport (then Will Rogers Field) in Oklahoma City. The Chamber had been told in 1961 by New York engineer Glen Williamson that this metro area could become one of a dozen U.S. transportation centers or hubs with the advent of 2,000-mph commercial aircraft in the 1970s. (37)

However, in a move that would portend future trouble, the Chamber apparently did *not* secure agreement to the tests from the Oklahoma City Council, nor from the citizens of metro Oklahoma City, either. The move angered some of the council members, with Ward 1 Councilman William Kessler saying, "The people's basic human rights are being ignored and violated. We're being used as human guinea pigs." (38)

Nevertheless, the council put off asking for the FAA to suspend the tests until near the end of the scheduled testing period five months later. The Chamber agreed to the sonic boom experiment to see how metro-area residents would react to the repeated booms, and the FAA set up monitoring stations to measure the impact at several homes and at the First National Bank skyscraper in downtown Oklahoma City. (39)

Here is how a retrospective story in *The Oklahoman* described the extensive promotion campaign to metro residents for the then-upcoming sonic boom tests, and the immediate public reactions:

"In the weeks leading up to the testing, the FAA and Greater Oklahoma City Chamber engaged in a public relations campaign to educate and prepare residents. Several hundred residents attended a demonstration of supersonic T-38 Talon trainers and were told the city was on the threshold of a new era in aviation. By the time the city council met to ask that the testing be stopped, residents were reporting damage to their homes and an unhappy co-existence

with supersonic travel. The packed city hall chamber, however, was dominated with proponents of the testing who far outnumbered critics." (40)

I was finishing the last semester of my senior year at Midwest City High School when these tests were conducted. The FAA had determined our town, along with much of Oklahoma City, would likely be more tolerant of the effects of these tests because we lived daily in an environment where high-speed aircraft were flying overhead all the time. Also, we were economic benefactors of Tinker. We also hosted the FAA's important Mike Monroney Aeronautical Center, located nearby at Will Rogers World Airport on the south side of Oklahoma City.

We were all alerted about the tests, although many paid scant attentions because we were so used to noise caused by the Tinker jets. Why would these new tests be any different? Those who did try to ignore them were the ones who wished they had listened more carefully and heeded the suggestions that they take down the family China from the shelves during the designated testing times that were posted publicly. The tests began on schedule on February 3, and there were eight booms scheduled each day. They started at 7 a.m. and ended in the afternoon hours. Aircraft used in the tests consisted of F-104 fighter jets and B-58 bombers, occasionally joined by F-101 and F-106 fighters.

I remember the first couple weeks of testing were somewhat unnerving because wherever you were in Midwest City – as well as much of Oklahoma City itself – you heard and felt the sudden jolts of the booms as the sound barrier was broken time after time overhead. My mother had decided to pack up the family valuables for the entire period of the testing, rather than take stuff down and put it back up eight times a day. Such was the case in many homes on our block. We also noticed, over time, more cracked windows, as well as some hairline crack lines appearing in our ceilings and walls. The eight booms a day could be harsh, but we were told the peak air pressures were below the levels needed to break glass, although that would be disputed many times. After a few weeks, many doubted it was true.

These suspicions seemed validated when a front-page story in *The Daily Oklahoman* reported later that the director general of the

Aeronautical Research Institute of Sweden said 5-pound [per square foot] sonic booms had been measured in Oklahoma City during the six-month test program. A spokesman for the FAA countered, however, that the highest boom measured was 3.79 pounds, although there were several of the booms over the 3-pound level. However, the maximum level for booms that the FAA had set for the entire test period was only 2 pounds. (41) And the Air Force fact sheet on sonic booms states, "Typically, community exposure to sonic booms is below two pounds per square foot." (42) Still, most of us seemed to take the tests in stride. We were used to jet noises and we knew the specific time that the boom tests were coming. Eventually, we just tried to forget them, yet were still caught by surprise at times.

If the tests didn't rise to the level of serious aggravation for many, it did for others.

"Within the first week of the FAA's flyovers, which produced eight sonic booms every day, 655 complaints were registered," wrote *Slate* Magazine in 2014. "John Lear, the science editor of the defunct *Saturday Review*, wrote that the FAA's spokesman sympathized with the townspeople. "Nervous people might have to rely on tranquilizers," the spokesman told reporters." (43) It was reported that, during the first 14 weeks of the sonic booms, 147 windows in the two tallest downtown Oklahoma City buildings (the First National Bank and Liberty National Bank) were broken. Those and other damage reports from around the city caused organized civic groups to rise up in protest of the tests. Some of the complaints stretched the imagination more than others, including the following chronicled by *Slate*.

"There were strange and menacing forces at work in Oklahoma City during 1964. 'An Oklahoma City woman says her furniture is shrinking,' reported the *Washington Post*. 'A man is worried that fish may take to deeper than usual water this spring and affect his favorite sport' ... One woman demanded that the FAA stop dropping atomic bombs. Others called in furiously, the *Washington Post* reported, to complain about 'broken chinaware, fallen mirrors and events—by their own timing— [that] occurred long after the booms had ceased for the day. A resident claimed the booms ruined television reception. Another claimed the booms improved it. Both were wrong." (44)

Oklahoma City politicians pushed back against the protests, however, pleading for residents and groups to show their support for the program to state legislators. Nevertheless, a lawsuit seeking an injunction against the sonic boom tests was filed in federal district court in Oklahoma City. But Judge Stephen Chandler eventually denied the injunction, saying the plaintiffs could not establish that they incurred any mental or physical harm and ruling that the tests were serving an important national need.

By this time, the FAA's spokesman Gordon Bain had weighed in and said his agency was actively monitoring public opinion as well as any damage to structures in the metro Oklahoma City area. "I can say, in general, that there was a broad range of reaction to the booms in Oklahoma City, from indifference to extreme annoyance," he said. Seeming to dismiss most of the damage complaints the FAA received, Bain added, "One of the most important factors ... is fear on the part of an individual that sonic booms will damage his property. In the great majority of cases of damage claims, however, there does not appear to be a reasonable engineering basis for attributing the alleged damage to sonic booms." (45)

But the court of negative public opinion took its toll on the testing as these news stories continued, and the federal government found itself taking a lot of heat. The federal Bureau of Budget criticized the FAA, saying it had designed the experiment poorly, and citizen complaints continued to pour into the office of U.S. Sen. Mike Monroney. By July, the *Washington Post* reported on the tension at the local and state levels of government in Oklahoma, and Oklahoma City council members were starting to support the citizen complaints by putting pressure on Washington to do something.

Something *was* done finally, although by that time only a few days of the scheduled tests remained. The Oklahoma City Council was poised to meet Tuesday night, July 28, and formally call for an end to the sonic boom tests immediately. But the FAA beat the council to the punch by announcing the day before, on July 27, that it would end the testing for good by Friday, July 31, at 1:20 p.m.

That was only two days shy of the originally scheduled termination date. An FAA spokesman said its decision was made independently of the city council's pending vote. *The Daily Oklahoman* wrote that Gordon Bain "praised the people and leaders of the Oklahoma City area for their 'major part' in the SST development program ... Bain had suggested an immediate halt of the booms last Friday, before he left Oklahoma City following a court hearing on the testing." (46) This was the hearing in which Judge Chandler ruled against ordering an *immediate* cessation of the program. Even though the testing program ended 48 hours earlier than planned, all the originally scheduled sonic booms were completed by the July 31 termination date.

Formally, the FAA praised the people of metro Oklahoma City for their contribution to what it felt was a successful six-month experiment. "The sonic boom presents the most imposing challenge to the design and operation of the SST plane," Bain said. "And the people of Oklahoma City have helped explore this challenge and have, in effect, played a major part in the nation's SST development program." (47)

Nevertheless, the kind of opposition that was heard from disgruntled Oklahoma City-area residents had grown into a larger chorus of objections to supersonic passenger flight. Environmentalists were especially concerned about how the earth's ozone layer might be depleted because of high-altitude SST flights. One way to diminish some of the ground effects of sonic booms was to fly the supersonic planes higher than regular passenger jets, creating more distance between the originating booms and the cities below. The Oklahoma City tests were often cited by groups opposing SST flights, because they produced 9,594 complaints of damage to buildings, 4,629 formal damage claims, and 229 claims for a total of $12,845.32, which were mostly for broken glass and cracked plaster. (48)

There were also complaints from professionals, such as surgeons, who do delicate work, as well as from hearing specialists who said sonic booms could damage people's hearing. Then there were those people with nervous pathologies who didn't react well to sonic booms.

All of this, plus the needed redesign of SST aircraft to help minimize noise (which made the planes heavier and limited their range) made it too costly for the Boeing 2707 SST Project to continue, and eventually the government stepped away from the idea of supersonic air travel on civilian passenger jets. What had been the hope of designing a large aircraft with seating for 250-350 passengers and cruise speeds of approximately Mach 3, came to a halt, and the Oklahoma City tests and the public reactions to them were major parts of the reason. More than $1 billion had been spent on the project's development. (49)

Interestingly, results of a public opinion poll done at the University of Chicago showed in 1965 showed that 73 percent of Oklahoma City respondents said they could live indefinitely with eight sonic booms per day. Twenty-five percent said they couldn't, and 3 percent of the Oklahoma City/Midwest City population issued complaints and/or sued. But that 3 percent represented about 15,000 residents. (50) And from this 3 percent came thousands of claims for real damages, such as broken windows and cracked walls. With the tests now over, all these complainants could do was wait for the FAA to respond to their claims. And for most of them, the responses were "no."

As former Saturday Review science editor John Lear wrote in 1964, "Even if it were assumed that all the claims were valid – that the seeing eye dog of a sightless vendor at the capitol was too frightened to perform its customary guiding function, that human victims of heart disease and muscular spasm were detrimentally stimulated, that older people had suffered falls and other accidents, that a schoolroom ceiling lamp had dropped and knocked a boy out of class for an hour ... that flocks of chickens had been crazed into erratic flight with considerable loss of egg yield and some loss of life – Judge Stephen Chandler of the U.S. District Court said the only redress was to wait for processing of damage claims, only 132 of which have been paid to date; a total reimbursement of $7,239 compared to a single claim of $15,000 by a chicken grower." (51)

Although the FAA rejected 94 percent of all the claims it received, that action alone cause the level of anger to rise after the tests were over. By 1965,

Sen. Monroney had received hundreds of letters from constituents complaining about the FAA's seemingly cavalier manner of dismissing claims. The senator, who had once been a champion of the SST program, pulled his support from it altogether. (52)

The end came to the government's support of developing supersonic air travel in March 1971 when Congress shut down funding for the Boeing 2720 SST program. Longtime Oklahoma Congressman Tom Steed called the action, "the biggest mistake since I've been in Congress." (53)

A personal postscript to the question of damages related to the sonic boom tests is this: Four months after the booms had ended, I was a freshman at the University of Oklahoma in nearby Norman. One day in early December I received a call from my dad in Midwest City telling me that the ceiling in my bedroom had just collapsed. Everything that had been above it in the attic, was now piled on my floor. He said it was the accumulated effect of 1,253 sonic booms over our home.

And he said he remembered every one of them.

Sixty years later, in January 2024, NASA and Lockheed Martin's Skunk Works unveiled to the public their latest aircraft designed to reach speeds of Mach 1.4 (925 mph) while cruising at 55,000 feet yet producing ground noise no louder than a car door closing. According to a company press release, the X-59 is a

The X-59, a joint project of NASA and Lockheed Martin Skunk Works.
NASA/Lockheed Martin Skunk Works

"significant milestone in a project to create an ultra-quiet supersonic passenger jet" that it calls the QueSST. "We're thrilled to take on this challenge, alongside NASA, whose quiet supersonic technology mission will have lasting, transformational impacts for people around the world," said John Clark, vice president and general manager, Lockheed Martin Skunk Works. The new sonic boom tests were scheduled to start soon.

6

Just Look at our Names

The entrance to Midwest City High School

*H*ow closely were Tinker and Midwest City aligned? Just look at the fighting spirit names we gave our schools. While other schools were naming their teams for some fierce wildlife like Tigers, Wildcats, and Bearcats, we teens of Tinkertown were proud of our Jarman Junior High *Rockets*, Monroney *Thunderbirds*, and – most of all – our Midwest City High School *Bombers*. In the early 1962, when Carl Albert, a second high school was added on the east side of town, they became the *Titans*, as in (what else?) the Air Force's Titan Missiles. Just across the town's western line (but in the same Mid-Del School District) there were the Del City *Eagles*.

The names still surprise some around the Oklahoma City metro area, among them a friend and former managing editor of *The Oklahoman*, Joe Hight. "I have always chuckled about that name, the *Bombers*, he said in a 2023 conversation. "I have never heard of any school sports team named the Bombers!" (Well, okay, the New York Yankees are *informally* known as the Bronx Bombers, but they're no school team.)

If these schools' nicknames were connected to the Air Force, the two junior highs were named for state politicians: Congressman John Jarman, who served for 26 years, U.S. Senator Mike Monroney, who served for 18 years. Later, the second high school was named for Congressman Carl Albert, former speaker of the House of Representatives who served in the House of Representatives for 30 years. Additionally, two of the elementary schools were named for Congressman Tom Steed, who also served for 30 years., and U.S. Senator Robert S. Kerr, who served 14 years in the senate after four years as Oklahoma governor.

The interesting thing about these men is that, in the current red state of Oklahoma, four of them were Democrats. Only Jarman was a Republican. The connections illustrated the high regard Midwest Cityans held for their national elected leaders and authority figures in general.

As Oklahoma City newswoman Pam Olson Boettcher pointed out, "We had great political leaders in Tom Steed, Mike Monroney, Carl Albert, and John Jarman. The city was more liberal then than it is now. These men helped Midwest City get federal funding, especially for schools. The education was great, and there was money there from the federal government." (1)

That federal money has always been an important piece of the funding for Midwest City schools, and it comes from the Federal Impact Aid program whereby cities and school districts that are heavily impacted economically by the presence of a federal facility (and all its employees and families).

The idea is that if the federal government is responsible for putting my students in the classrooms, then it should help subsidize the cost of educating those students. For example, in 1943-44 when the very first operational year for the first Midwest City School, the federal aid amounted to $192,406, which was a big sum in that day and which the new school district needed to get rolling with its original 104 students.

Oscar V. Rose

Just seven years later when that one school had grown to several around town, the

federal aid totaled $2,304,344 for the 1950-51 school year for a district that had ballooned to more than 2,500 students. (2) This is operational and capital money over and above what the district collected from local taxes and bond issues, and it made a huge difference in the quality of education offered by Midwest City (and later Del City) schools.

Securing that funding in the first place and maintaining it has always been a key job of the school superintendent. The Midwest City (now Mid-Del) School District had an excellent founding superintendent in Oscar V. Rose, followed by his successor, J.E. Sutton.

Rose was a former high school dropout who enlisted for service in the Army during World War I. Following the war, he returned to school, eventually graduated and went on to receive undergraduate and graduate degrees at Oklahoma State and Oklahoma University, and became a teacher in Quesada, Oklahoma. He once quipped, "I was a teacher, coach, principal, superintendent and even swept the floors and built fires in the heating stoves." (3) Rose came to the rural Sooner School, at 15th Street and Sooner Road, in 1943 as superintendent of that independent district, adjacent to the newly chartered Midwest City in 1943.

At the time, the small school housed first through eighth grades. Rose's wife, Virginia. was named Sooner Elementary School's first principal and continued in that post until her retirement, whereupon the school's name was changed to Sooner-Rose in her honor.

Oscar Rose quickly realized, however, that the area's main school district would be built in this town of Midwest City just under construction. Like many early professionals, he was encouraged by Bill Atkinson to start Midwest City's educational system, and that's just what he did. The area's first three-member school board elected him school superintendent of the fledgling Midwest City public school system and, as writer Hugh Cosby noted, "inherited two typically country school buildings (Sooner on the west and Soldier Creek on the east) on the outskirts of town, five teachers and 125 students." (4)

One of the true early pioneering students in Midwest City was Clo Ann Davis, whose home was on Le Jean Drive, on the far east side of the new Midwest City. In fact, Davis was a student at the original Sooner School in 1940, two years before Atkinson founded Midwest City. As noted earlier, Sooner was a country schoolhouse on the far northeast side of what was to soon become the Original Mile. At this point, though, it was just a rural school serving students of farmers in an area of wheat fields.

"I started first grade there, so I remember a lot of happenings!" she said. Her timing put her there when Oscar Rose was hired, just before taking over as founding superintendent of Midwest City schools.

The Sooner School would become part of that new school district in 1943. Davis recalled that it was her dad, "Shorty" Kane, who drove the first school bus for Sooner School. "As I recall," she said, "the school term was to begin, and the bus hadn't arrived yet. My dad had a black van, and he carried the kids from the area south of 29th Street and Sunnylane. We piled into that van and away we went to Sooner School."

Davis also remembers the extreme weather on the central Oklahoma prairie. "One time when we got to school, the pump was broken on the well and my brother Tom, always handy to fix things, soon had it operating. He was the hero of the day. Altogether, I've seen Midwest City, Del City, and Tinker Field rise right from the ground up! We traded dusty roads for nice streets, and we are grateful." (5)

Rose's first challenge as superintendent was raising funding for the new district, and he started by seeking and obtaining support from the 1941 Defense Public Works Law, or the Lanham Act as it was called. That act provided grants for water, sewer, housing, childcare, and schools in communities affected by the growth of the war industry. It was that initial federal funding that purchased the "hutment" buildings where the district started in 1943 on the site of what would be the first high school and, later, Jarman Junior High and Jarman Middle School. This Midwest City School opened in the hutments in 1943 and moved into the newly constructed permanent building in 1944. (6) The school served K-12 grades plus a childcare center.

Oklahoma Congressman Tom Steed was a driving force behind developing this federal impact aid legislation, and he was influenced by a good friend who happened to be Oscar V. Rose. The aid program benefitted schools nationally, and Steed would later say of that bill, "That was the most important piece of legislation I ever introduced in Congress."

As local historian Barbara Winn Sessions wrote, "Federal grants continued until after World War II, and this K-12 school would grow and divide to comprise the district of elementary, junior high, and high schools of Midwest City and Del City ... By the time the Lanham Act expired in 1950, the federal government employed 70 percent of the workers in the school district." (7)

It should be noted that, following the war, Tinker had begun its own on-base school called the Post School, that ran from 1948-1953, and that this school took some of the impact off Midwest City schools. (8) Additionally, Midwest City had its own private Catholic school, St. Philip Neri, named for the Italian priest who was known in the 16th Century as the "Second Apostle of Rome" after Saint Peter. The school, located at 1107 Felix Place, was completed in 1954 and began offering classes through the 8th grade to some 223 students. Seventy percent of the student body is Catholic, while 30 percent is non-Catholic, according to the school's 2024 web site. Two members of my own "neighborhood gang" on East Lockheed Drive, were Catholics attending St. Philip Neri. They were Kay and Mike Donohue, and they lived right across the street from me on East Lockheed Drive. We all remained friends into adulthood.

With the wartime Lanham Act gone, Rose realized his school district would need more funding than it could get from local taxes and bonds. After all, the huge chunk of real estate taken up by Tinker Air Force Base was federal property and, therefore, non-taxable. But the Midwest City school system was not alone in this quandary, as some 600 of America's 80,000 school districts faced the same problem. They serviced children of federal workers whose place of business provided no tax revenue for the schools. (9)

Sessions writes, 'Working with Oklahoma's powerful Congressional delegation, he was able to gain passage of bills known as "Impact Aid." Aid went for school construction and for maintenance and operations. The bills were approved, and Midwest City recognized their Washington delegates by naming five elementary and junior high schools after them in the 1950s, as noted earlier.

In assessing the relationship between Midwest City, its schools, and Tinker, historian Susan Moeri Lee has written, "Midwest City and Tinker always tried to work hand in hand to develop plans beneficial to both parties. From the beginning, the base needed the city and the city existed only because of the base. Built as a cooperative venture, Midwest City provided a place for the military and government employees of tinker to live, buy merchandise and send their children to school.

A dilemma began when the community could not supply federal families a satisfactory education because of the government facility ... Encouraged by the Lanham Act funding during the war, Oscar Rose knew that government money offered the only answer to communities within federal impacted areas. He became the savior of not only Midwest City education, but other schools throughout the country." (10)

Here's how Impact Aid worked, according to Dr. Vernon McAllister, a former longtime assistant school superintendent: *"A" aid* is based on the number of children whose parents are in military service and live on a military base, while *"B" aid* is based on the number of children of military parents who reside off-base and the children of civilian parents employed by the federal government at military or other federal installations.

The "A" aid compensates the district for both commercial and residential ad valorem taxes lost, while the "B" compensates only for the equivalent commercial ad valorem taxes lost. "The Impact Aid laws, adopted in 1950, were set to expire four years later, but Rose worked relentlessly to make sure they continued each year after that," wrote Sessions. (11)

By 1960, Rose's hard work had paid off not only for Midwest City schools, but for 4,000 other districts who received funding from the Impact Aid Act. (12) When Oscar Rose died in 1969, Speaker of the House Carl Albert proclaimed of him, "No single person has done as much to make the case for children living in federally impacted areas as Oscar Rose." (13)

Rose would leave a living legacy behind to continue his contribution to the Mid-Del School District. That legacy is his and Virginia's grandson, Morri Rose. When Morri lost his dad at age 11 while living in Okemah, Oklahoma, he and his mother went to live with his grandparents in Midwest City. His mother would later teach at Monroney Junior High School for 12 years, and one of her students was Morri himself. Much of what he has learned about education and about handling students came from his grandparents and mother.

"Granddad loved the school kids, and he treated them with respect," Morri said. "He and my grandma were country people, and very innovative in their teaching methods. Granddad was very much against food being wasted in the cafeteria, so he developed an incentive system called the *"Clean Plate Buttons."* If students would clean their plates during the week, they would earn these buttons and were allowed to go to the snack bar for free and to a free movie on Friday afternoons."

Morri Rose would graduate from MCHS in 1970 and then went on to Oklahoma City University where he graduated and returned to teach for three decades in the Mid-Del School District, also serving as principal at Pleasant Hill, Cleveland Bailey, and Soldier Creek elementary schools on the city's far north side, and as vice-principal for Del City High School. Wanting to return to the classroom as a teacher, he assigned the last 12 years of his career at MCHS to teach government and history.

The right-hand man for Rose was James "Jay" Edgar Sutton Jr., a young Oklahoma educator from Boynton who Rose tapped to help him organize Midwest City's first high school. For the school system to become a state-certified independent school district, it had to have a high school. So, Rose and Sutton set about forming one and, by June 1943, that school was accredited by the state board of education. Now that Midwest City had an independent school district, it had the power of taxation for school revenue. The thing about this new high school is that it was the first one – and only one since -- accredited by the State Department of Education as Midwest City Independent School District 52 *before a single class was ever held.*

JAMES E. SUTTON JR.

The challenging story of the school district's first year in 1943, made harder by the fact there were no school classrooms yet built, is told in an earlier chapter. Then there was the polio outbreak in Midwest City that year which delayed the start of classes in the fall of 1943, which did however give enough time to import temporary hutment structures from a company in Dallas. Teachers, parents, and students volunteered to put them together in time to start the school year just a couple weeks late. The first school year began on

September 20, 1943, with 413 students and 17 teachers. The enrollment would increase to more than 1,000 by the end of that year.

Despite the hardships, the first school year was completed successfully, and the high school graduated its first class on June 2, 1944. The first one receiving his diploma was Van Buren Appelman, Jr. That class numbered 14 graduates, but there would be thousands more to come in the decades ahead.

Just two years later, after the permanent school building was constructed, tragedy struck when an airplane crashed just north of the school building on what is now is the athletic field. That story is told in Chapter 13. The pilot of the plane tilted his wing to miss the smokestack on the school building, but crashed just yards away from it, narrowly missing the school building itself. Several Tinker employees on the plane died but, as Sutton would later note with pride," Many were saved by the efforts of students who, in the face of danger, dragged several from the burning plane." (15)

Rose and Sutton continued to build the Midwest City school system and, by the end of the 1950s, the federal impact funding was accounting for 24 percent of the district's annual revenue. (16) Along the way, a new stand-alone campus was built for Midwest City High School, just north of 15th Street, and that is still the school's campus, although the original building has been greatly enlarged and modernized. By the late 1940s and early 1950s, more and more school buildings were added. The original Midwest City Public School became Jarman Junior High and then Jarman Middle School, while a second junior high (Monroney) was built when the city expanded north to Reno Avenue.

While Midwest City was growing, an adjacent city to its west on S.E. 29th Street was being formed, largely in the image of Midwest City. It was called Del City, and its founder was a developer named George Epperley, who became that town's Bill Atkinson.

In 1946, Epperley bought the original 160 acres that became Del City, at the intersection of S.E. 29th and Sunnylane Road. In many ways, the original plan of Del City was nearly identical to Midwest City. The main entrance to the town was on 29th Street, anchored by a semicircular shopping center like Midwest City's Atkinson Plaza Shopping Center. You continued north on Epperley Drive and encountered the same kind of city hall plaza that Midwest had, with residential streets fanning off that circle. Del City was incorporated in 1948, three years after Midwest City received its charter.

The borderline between Del City and Midwest City was Sooner Road, which ran north and south from 29th Street. Del City had no schools at first, so students had to be transported east to Midwest City's first schools (three elementaries, a junior high and high school). In 1949, Del City Elementary School was built and, two years later, the city built Del City Junior High, which transitioned into Del City High School, a building that looked identical to Midwest City High School. Before long, the Del City schools were annexed into the Midwest City Independent School District, along with several outlying rural schools. The district then became the Mid-Del Independent School District, and it encompassed 55 square miles. (17)

Overseeing all of this growth were Rose and Sutton, along with members of the Mid-Del School Board. Looking back on it all in 1982, Sutton said he was proud of what had been accomplished and the spirit and values with which it was done.

"In all these years of growth, there has developed a spirit of real caring.," he said. "[This is] a school that cares for its students, employees, and its patrons. A great character has been passed down to all of us. I think of the cold, the crowding, and the mud... I think now of the togetherness, I appreciate the teachers who

The first MCHS graudating class, 1944

taught for the joys of teaching, and I think of the students who shared with ius and gave their best. Many of them are illustrious alumni ... Selflessness was our aim; selfishness was a forbidden word. It took grit, termination, and sacrifice for this dream to come true." (18)

Sutton retired in 1982, after serving 39 years with Midwest City schools, 35 of them in administration, including 19 years as the founding principal of Midwest City High School and later as school superintendent. He took leadership roles in many educational groups and projects statewide, and he helped organize the Oklahoma Association of Schools for Impacted Services (OASIS) and served as its president until his retirement. And, like many of Midwest City's early leaders, he was a deacon in his church, which was the First Baptist Church of Midwest City. In 1992, he was inducted into the new Midwest City High School Wall of Fame. Seven years later, he was inducted into the Oklahoma Educators Hall of Fame. He died in 2001 at age 84.

With the passings of Oscar Rose and J.E. Sutton, the torch of school leadership was passed to the next generation of superintendents and principals who would take the Mid-Del School District into the 21st Century. They would be building a modern school district on the solid foundation that Rose and Sutton had left for them.

7

Ups and Downs of School

Youth is the time for dreaming.
Image via Pixabay

All this was the institutional history of Midwest City schools, and it was a story that few of us students knew, mostly because we didn't ask.

Yet it was extremely vital to the quality of our education and what came after that in our careers. In years to come, we would look back on those early years in Midwest City and see ourselves as modern-day pioneers who tried to do our part in making people proud of the town, while minimizing the mischief that can give a town a bad name. Often, we succeeded; sometimes we failed. But hey, we were kids, right?

Several years later, when the hit television series *Happy Days* premiered, we realized we had already created our real-life version of it at Midwest City High School.

What follows are some of the human anecdotes that came from MCHSH graduates of the 1960s, many of whom started in elementary school in the early 1950s as I did. These were my classmates, and I knew most of them pretty well. I know the nuances of my own story best, so this is where parts of my own memoir will re-enter the narrative.

Some readers may wonder why my focus doesn't include Del City schools and Carl Albert schools, since they are now a part of the Mid-Del District. When I began school, however, Del City was not in our district and Carl Albert had not even been built. So, I write about the realities I experienced, along with my Midwest City friends. I didn't attend these other schools, so anecdotes about life there must be left for another storyteller's book. There are as many stories waiting to be written about life at those two schools as my own.

My educational journey after Jack & Jill Preschool started in the first grade at Westside Elementary School in 1951. By then, the Original Mile was an active and fairly settled place. I was fortunate in having both my elementary school and Jarman Junior High School so close by. Westside was a four-block walk, while Jarman was only six front doors away on my own East Lockheed Drive. So, I walked to the first nine years of school without breaking a sweat or freezing my feet off.

I know this runs counter to the traditional septuagenarian tale of walking three miles over treacherous terrain in a howling blizzard, but it was what it was. Then, by the time high school years arrived, my older sister C.J. was already there as a junior, so I would ride to school and home with her until I was old enough to drive myself. All told, I never had to ride a school bus during my entire K-12 school experience.

I used a lot of that walking time to do what sometimes I think I'm best at: imagining and dreaming. Since our Midwest City world was a safe one, we never worried about encountering serious trouble on those walks, and few of us ever did. I also got to know where the cute little grade schoolgirls lived and sometimes would alter my route to walk by their houses, stopping momentarily to ostensibly tie my shoe that was already laced up, hoping they might be out in their yards and maybe we could walk to school together. If I was ever lucky enough to have that happen, I don't remember it.

The library stoked a lot of my dreams.
Photo via Pixabay.

Surprisingly, one of the key benefits of my walks to Westside was stopping at the public library on the way home. It was right on my route, so why not? It was in that library, two blocks away from Tinker Air Force Base, where my imagination and dreaming would take serious flight. I developed a lifelong love of reading, which led to my passionate career as a writer.

I remember loving my time at Westside, where I attended grades 1 though 6. In fact, those were probably my best years academically until I began graduate school many years later. I think it was my curiosity about life and the world; everything was so new to me when I was between the ages of 6 and 12, and I wanted to learn as much as I could. I felt more comfortable in my own skin than I did during my junior high and high school years, because being popular in elementary school wasn't such the big deal as it would become later. The quest for popularity is a tough fight for most kids; at least it was for me.

Two highlights of my Westside Warriors experience were playing football and becoming captain of the school's Junior Police. I also remember a system the school had worked out in the 5th and 6th grade years where students could do individual reading exercises and proceed at their own pace. I enjoyed the challenge of trying to finish my work and pass the different levels faster than my classmates. It was a good motivator for learning, and I felt it was innovative even though I was only 11 or 12 at the time. Even at that age I remember thinking that this was an innovative learning method that the school was using, and I liked learning that way.

The dream of football. With or without a face mask.
Photo by W.J. Willis Jr.

In football I was a lineman (most of us played on both offense and defense then), and I remember my helmet always seemed to be a bit too large for my head. I have memories of getting up off the field after a tackle and looking out through the helmet ear hole. But the main thing I recall is that I was the very first guy on the team to wear a helmet that had a face guard attached to it. The early 50s were the transition years from maskless helmets. I had seen some pro players wearing the face bars, though, so I talked my dad into buying one for me. It took a couple weeks for the local sporting goods stores to order and receive it, but it arrived and my dad drilled holes in my helmet and screwed it on for me. I can still remember the envious look on the faces of the other players, and I probably was the only guy on the team that year that wound up without any chipped or missing teeth.

The other memory I have of our school football games was getting up off the field after a block or tackle and picking "goat heads" out of my skin. These are the hard, multi-pronged stickers (some looked more like the head of a longhorn steer) produced by weeds in the plains states like Oklahoma. All of us who played football got used to them, but they sure did bite.

The dream of enforcing the law.

As for the Junior Police gig, we young law enforcers, sponsored by the Kiwanis Clubs of the Oklahoma City metro area, who were used as the school's crossing guards to separate passing cars from school kids. We also helped with traffic control at some school events. Our badges were made of hard, gleaming metal, and it was not hard to fantasize you a position of authority.

I don't remember how I was chosen as *captain* of the force, but I was, and I got to wear a badge and different color chest sash that said so. It seemed to catch the eye of a few cute girls in the 6th grade, so it was worth the added responsibility I shouldered which, I must say, wasn't much.

In Junior High and High School, the things we focused on then are the same things school kids still do, minus the cell phones and social media of course. But we did great without that technology and spent our time trying to do what it took to get through another year of schoolwork. Of course, we loved the extracurricular activities at school – which, in Oklahoma, often revolved around football – and lusting for our free time on weekends, Christmas break, and summers.

We had deep respect for the "smart kids" in class. For many, however, being popular was more important. For others, finding satisfaction in doing our own thing away from school activities and the chase for popularity. I pretty much fell into this latter category, probably because of how comfortable I felt at home and on my block with the neighborhood kids, but also because I had my hobbies of writing, photography, and the guitar which were more individual pastimes than group-oriented ones.

In truth, I went through a period during my Jarman Junior High years, when I just felt out of place in school, and I discovered later several of my friends felt the same way during those awkward years. I didn't understand that feeling, since I had enjoyed elementary school so much.

Many years later, though, I read an article from the publication, *Raising Teens Today*, letting me know I wasn't alone in my awkwardness. In that piece, Katy M. Clark wrote, "Middle School [which was junior high in my day] is so darn awkward. It's filled with greasy hair, smelly armpits, pimples, acne, and swinging hormones that are hard as heck to keep up with. It's when our kids leave their old young selves behind and learn who this new kid is inside of them. It's when they finally realize the opposite sex isn't quite so bad and they suddenly have the urge to talk to them but they're clueless and utterly clumsy about how to go about it." (1)

That pretty much summed it up for me, although I could have tossed a couple more causes into the mix. Nevertheless, we kid/teens did learn some useful lessons from those years as Clark continued, "The good news is, middle school, however embarrassing and awkward as it may be, is teaching our kids that they're not alone. Everyone is going through the same, crazy, unrelenting stage, fumbling their way through it. And, even though they may feel alone at times, all they have to do is look around and they're reminded ... hey, I'm not the only one going through this."

I guess I didn't take the time to look around, because at the time, I sure felt like I was the lone apple in a basket of oranges. And that made me do a few stupid things, the zaniest one was the following that had my folks scratching their heads for years. I've always considered myself a relatively intelligent guy, a bit of a loner, and an imagineer, prone to daydreams and impulses. At age 12, I took that profile into Jarman's 7th grade in 1958. Two years later, those emotional impulses threatened to wreck my education and my future.

It was a sunny October morning in 1960 as I walked into the principal's office at Jarman Junior High. I was 14 and just starting my 9th grade year, but I was on a mission of personal liberation to rid myself of school. The plot involved presenting a typewritten note, carrying Mom's alleged signature, to Principal Ray Polk's office staff and announcing that my family had just bought a home in Florida. We would be moving immediately, so please give Jimmy Willis his school records so he can transfer to a new school home down there. Simple enough, right? The problem is the note contained two screaming lies, and that's why my hand

Jarman: the vexing years.

delivering it resembled Tom Hanks' shaky hand in the war film, *Saving Private Ryan*.

For one thing, the signature was not Mom's. I had forged it. And for another, we were not moving to Florida or anywhere else, for that matter. I was simply checking out of school, period. Even then, I thought it a drastic idea but the worst that could happen, I reasoned (and that verb is a serious stretch) is that the principal would see straight through my ruse and, in a fit of anger, toss me out of school.

However, since parting company with Jarman was my goal, anyway, would that be so bad? I not only thought it could happen; I was pretty sure it *would*, and I knew the school office would be filled with a lot of loud voices, full of invective, all aimed at me. I mean, c'mon, the office was staffed by adults, yes?

As a wise newspaper editor would counsel me as a young journalist years later, "Son, never assume anything." Years before he uttered it, he was right in this case, and I chalk it up to either an Oscar-worthy performance on my part, or a busy day in the school office that distracted the secretaries, or both. In any case, I did an inner jaw-drop when I realized my plan was actually *working*. The secretary bought my whole scam, hook, line, and winker. She simply smiled, said the school would miss me, and wished me sunny days in Florida. Then she handed over all my school records and warned me to watch out for the swamps and alligators.

That proved to be prescient advice, as events would soon prove.

"Free at last!" I remember feeling as I stuffed my school records into my backpack and biked to the neighborhood Conrad Marr Drug Store to have a celebratory ice cream soda. Of course, I had no plan on how to hide any of this from Mom and Dad that evening, nor did I know what to do with myself the next day, or for the rest of my life for that matter. In short, although the word "clueless" would take years to work its way into the American vernacular, it defined me completely in October 1960.

This event was the culmination of nearly three years of feeling just plain weird in school. In 6th grade, I'd been a class stud; by the 7th, I was lost. Even my dad was unsure of how to read me, and his loving nature just got it flat wrong one day in March 1959, when I turned 13 at Jarman. It was the worst day of my life that year in school, and it involved a rabbit whose name was Crusader. Since Dad worked at WKY-TV in Oklahoma City, he knew the local celebrities, including Tom Paxton who changed it slightly to *"Tom the Paxton"* in hosting an afternoon animated cartoon segment of the *Foreman Scotty Show*.

The most popular cartoon character was Crusader Rabbit who each day voiced birthday greetings to special kids whose birthday was on that day. I should have read the tea leaves when Dad mentioned to me the night of the 18th that I should tune in to *Crusader Rabbit* tomorrow afternoon. I did just that, just in time to hear this crazy rabbit wish "little Jimmy Willis" a happy birthday! Did it matter this was my 13th birthday and that I was trying hard not to present myself as a kid to my classmates anymore? Did it matter that when I got to school the next morning, the whole classroom erupted in laughter aimed at me?

"Hey Little Jimmy! Did you bring your friend Crusader Rabbit with you?"

That day continued to live as my own personal day of infamy for years, and junior high just seemed to go sideways from there. When Mom returned to work, as so many other moms in town were doing at Tinker Field, I was left on my own in the mornings to navigate my day; make choices on what to do with it, starting with the question of whether to even go to school or not. Dad and Mom left for work just after breakfast, C.J. went off to high school, and I was still in my bedroom putting on my socks. I'd look at my collie Laddie, he'd look at me, and I'd think about the awkwardness facing me up the street at Jarman.

I began skipping school and, by the time I reached my 9th grade year, I had started putting my creative writing talent and typing skills to a different use: typing notes to the school principal to excuse me from school because of illness, then forging Mom's name to the notes. There were only a few of these, but they were the first times I put my writing skills out for public view. I suppose it was an inauspicious start to my career as a journalist and author, albeit better than taking up a career as a felony forger.

In any case, on those home-alone days ditching school, I was ensconced in my personal, creative world of words. I would spend the day reading the *Hardy Boys* book series, and I'd write short stories and crafted other kinds of fiction, usually involving a rugged loner of a man and his dog in the wilderness. I would break that up with watching some game shows on TV, having lunch, and playing with Laddie. I knew the family wouldn't start coming home until late afternoon, and I made sure I had a cover story for how my day "at school" went.

There were a couple snags, however. One was my dad, who would pop home unexpectedly for lunch. A couple times it happened so fast that I had to make a dash for my closet where I sat in the dark with a flashlight reading a book until he left.

A few times Dad stayed home a couple hours past lunch, and I wondered if he was doing the same thing I was: ditching work. One problem on those days was Laddie. I couldn't take him into the closet with me because he would bark when Dad came into the house and, even if he didn't, Dad would wonder where he was and start an in-house search. So, I'd leave Laddie out in my bedroom, but he would lie just outside my closet door and occasionally scratch at it and whine, wanting in.

Those days were touch and go.

Even so, there came a time in my 9th grade year when I decided to make this home-alone thing permanent, because home was much more peaceful and secure than school. I knew I was stretching my luck with those letters I was writing, so I resolved to write one *final* note checking myself out of Jarman Junior High for good. That brought me to this October morning in Principal Polk's office.

After making my great escape from Jarman, the first few days of my new-found freedom worked pretty well. But I noticed boredom setting in toward the end of the week, and I missed having some classmates to talk with. So, I thought, am I really meant to be a recluse and living a lie to my parents? I decided the next week to write yet one more note to Principal Polk. Possibly recalling the school secretary's warning about Florida swamps, I crafted this one:

"Dear Mr. Polk, this is Hazel M. Willis, the mother of Jimmy Willis who was recently checked out of Jarman because were moving to Florida. This is to inform you that things have changed because we discovered the house we bought there is built upon a swamp, and it is sinking. So, we aren't leaving Midwest City after all, and we need to enroll Jimmy again in Jarman. Please reinstate him. Thank you. Yours truly, Hazel M. Willis."

I have no memory of the day I delivered that particular note to the principal's office, and that's probably due to PTSD. Apparently, sometime during the two-week period between my check-out and check-in notes, the distracting office pace had slowed down to the point where the staff saw what I was up to. It was then I heard the loud invectives I'd expected when I gave them the checkout note.

The roof was finally caving in on Jimmy Willis, just as the roof to my bedroom gave way years later after accumulated stress from the Air Force sonic boom tests flown over Midwest City. What ensued in the principal's office were calls to Mom and Dad, followed by a meeting of the minds that night at home, followed by a regular schedule of visits for me and the school counselor. Everyone was straining to solve the math puzzle of what kind of brain this Willis kid had. The 2+2 was coming up to 3, and that's pretty much how I felt about myself, as well.

Still, they persisted, and they wound up being very supportive and kind in attempting to replace my missing cranial link. For her part, my mother's loving words were, "There is nothing you can do, Jimmy, that will separate you from my love for you." To this day, those words still mean the world to me and have motivated me to try and be a better man.

In the end, the grownups' plan proved more effective than mine did and -- thanks to the unmerited grace of Mom, Dad, the school counselor, Principal Polk, and an understanding algebra teacher -- I graduated from Jarman and moved on to high school where life improved greatly. The awkward years faded into the shadows, and the kid who hated school, but loved reading and writing, wound up loving learning and eventually received a Ph.D. in Journalism from the University of Missouri. I look back on my life now and wonder how my life would have worked out if the support group of family, school teachers, counselors, and principals had not been there for this young teenager who was on the brink of taking his life in a much-less fulfilling direction. If I had, maybe I would have gotten back on track; maybe not. I'm glad I didn't have to find out.

There is no doubt this was a key turning point in my life, and the fact that I wound up going in the right direction is credited to the caring of people in the Midwest City School District, like Principal Polk, his counseling staff, and most of the teachers who taught us. I've always remembered that math teacher, in particular, who worked with me after my "Florida" escapade that could have wrecked my school career.

His name was Jessel V. Williams, and he was the kind of teacher I tried to be years later

Jessel V. Williams
U.S. Air Force photo

when I, myself, became a teacher. Mr. Williams (notice how we refer to our past teachers as *Mr., Mrs., or Miss, even when we're adults?*)

took extra time with me and other troubled students to help us understand Algebra and pass his class. My grade point average was minimal in my 9th grade year, and Algebra was my worst grade. I needed to pass it, though, to graduate on to high school.

Mr. Williams had a plan for his students to let them keep taking tests (with different math equations each time) until we passed them. I know not every student took advantage of that but, given the mess I'd almost made of my young life that October, I knew a good thing when I saw it. It took me two or three times on some of his tests to pass them, but I did and actually came to understand math. When the term was over, I not only passed Algebra but received an *A* in it.

Many years later, I realized I couldn't remember Mr. Williams' name, and that vexed me because he had been so important to my future. Former classmates helped me remember and, in 2023, I checked to see if my algebra teacher might still be living. Sadly, I found his obituary instead. He had lived a full life, died at age 96, in 2020. In reading about that life, though, I was amazed at the things I didn't know about Mr. Williams. Kids often think their teachers have no life outside the school. Somehow, they're just teachers and are totally defined by that role. Rarely is that the case, and it certainly wasn't with Mr. Williams.

It turned out that Jessel Williams was also an *Air Force pilot*, who reached the rank of Lieutenant Colonel, and who spent a lot of his Air Force Reserve career training other officers to fly. He was still doing that concurrently with his Jarman job. While he was teaching me math and helping me climb out of a hole I'd dug for myself, he was also teaching Air Force officers to become jet pilots.

My 9th grade year in 1961 was his last year of teaching, as he moved on to become a supervisor with the Federal Aviation Administration. As I discovered that, I hoped it wasn't his bonehead students like me that made him move on to a career change. Knowing something about him as a caring and patient man, however, I rejected that thought and realized he was built for complex kids like me. Clearly, he inspired his own daughter Debbie, who would become superintendent of Moore, Oklahoma public schools.

In researching this book and talking with other former classmates, I kept hearing that same theme repeatedly of teachers, principals, and counselors who cared enough to have high academic standards but who also knew each of us was working out way through some kind of growing-up issues. As if they weren't already overworked enough, they often went the extra mile to help us when we asked for it or, as in my case, when we didn't but it was obvious we needed it.

One story came from MCHS grad Rusty Weller in a post on the Midwest City High School Memories Facebook page in 2023. In it, he discussed the role an English teacher played in his ability to overcome challenges.

"The possibility of one day being a sportswriter or photographer or newspaper editor, etc., never entered my mind until I actually was one of those," Weller said. "With bad eyesight and seated alphabetically far from the teacher, I was a horrible student. I would have ridden the short bus to special classes had they existed. I literally was written off by everyone until the ACT test by junior year at Midwest City High when I shockingly scored in the 98th percentile or higher in all subjects. A teacher actually slammed the results on my desk, gave me a long stink eye and hissed, 'Slacker!' But those scores must have elevated me to the Honors English homeroom with the great, "Momma" Van Dusen who instilled grammar and righted my course during my senior year in 1964.

Perhaps impressed by those scores, my junior English teacher, Mrs. Barber, planted a valuable seed by writing in my annual that she expected to see my byline in the *Daily Oklahoman* one day – a wild prediction that unbelievably came true and was the reason I signed up for OU's Journalism 101, which surprisingly made me a staff writer on the student paper the very first day of class. Looking back, MCHS served me well."

It's good to know I'm not the only teen who faced varsity blues. And I'm sure my mom and dad not the only parents who would write to the faculty of their kids' schools and offer up heartfelt gratitude for helping Jim or Rusty or whoever make it to graduation. I was going through an old scrapbook recently and here is an excerpt of the letter my folks wrote to the principal, counselors and faculty at Jarman:

"This is a difficult letter to write because no matter how few nor how many well-chosen words are written, it will still not convey the extent of our feelings of appreciation.

"Jimmy has had his problems during his school years, but through the personal interest, guidance, and cooperation of the counselors and faculty – both with the children and their parents – these problems were solved and proved to be both beneficial and enlightening experiences for all concerned.

"This spring, or son Jimmy will graduate from Midwest City High School. If it were possible to pin medals on teachers for 'outstanding performance over and beyond the call of duty,' you would all be medaled this spring."

... Eternally grateful, Hazel and W.J. Willis Jr.

I don't believe I ever knew Mom and Dad wrote that until I saw it in scrapbook this week.

We were all given a great opportunity to experience a wonderful school spirit at Midwest City High School (MCHS), starting with the opening days called *"Howdy Week."* The school had a large, enclosed patio (a gift from the class of 1960), and the first week there was time set aside for students to congregate there during school hours and get to know each other. Every senior was wearing a name tag that read, "Hello," while Juniors wore tags that said, *"Hi,"* and we sophomores had name tags that said, "Howdy!" The different iterations of the same greeting were meant to indicate (somewhat tongue-in-cheek) our different levels of sophistication.

It's been six decades from my MCHS years, yet I still remember Howdy Week with a smile. For us sophomores, we were finally starting to feel more like real teenagers with a grasp on reality than we ever had before. After all, our role models in town all those years had been high school students, whom we considered very mature. So here we were at MCHS. We were now Bombers, and it felt pretty good. An added bonding influence was that many of our parents worked at the same place: Tinker Field, either as military or civilian employees. And, finally, we all shared the same experience of growing up in a town that was now less than 20 years old itself in our sophomore year of 1961. It was a young town, we were young high schoolers, and we were ready to rock and roll.

A few memories stand out above the rest for me at MCHS, and Howdy Week was one. I remember how sophisticated I thought I was when I got to switch from a Howdy name tag to a Hello tag as my senior year began. But it was in high school that my dating life began as my focus turned too much to girls starting in my sophomore year. I went through the same angst other guys did until, at some point, I got the hang of conversing sanely to females.

The fact I was a lifeguard every summer automatically earned me more attention from girls than I probably would have otherwise received, and I was grateful for that. The first pool I worked – and continued to work through high school summers – was a would-be country club called Desert Oaks, on the eastern edge of Midwest City off Reno Boulevard. It was not a country club in the traditional sense, mostly because what was planned to be its golf course never went beyond being a cattle pasture.

But it was in the country, and it did have a nice supper club, and a large patio veranda that overlooked is swimming pool nestled among the surrounding forest of blackjack oak trees. Membership was required for swimming there, and families would bring their picnic baskets and quilts and sit among the shade trees around the pool. It was a pleasant summer gig, that also produced more than a few dates for me.

The owners and managers of Desert Oaks were Bill and Minnie Sheppard. They were extremely nice people and fine hosts for those dining there at night. There was a shuffleboard and pool room across the back, and my dad and I enjoyed playing both. Upstairs was rumored to be a gambling room or two which was, so the story goes, a big draw for men.

Whether true or not, it added a touch of mystery to the place. I remember the first time I saw the old movie Casablanca on TV, the character of Rick reminded me of the suave and well-dressed Bill Sheppard and that *Rick's Cafe* had the same feel as the Desert Oaks Club where members dined on tables covered with linen tablecloth and fine silver.

Bingo games with cash prizes were held at Desert Oaks on Sunday afternoons, and they were very popular and well-attended. Mom would play several times, and I went with her occasionally and enjoyed the afternoon. But I do remember one summer afternoon when I was lifeguarding the pool, and my friend Kay Donohue was working the concession stand. She sent me a hand signal to come up to the front, which is where police cars came cruising into the parking lot on Bingo afternoon, and officers went inside to talk with the owners.

It provided for an exciting afternoon, and I think Desert Oaks benefitted from some of the stories of the exciting nightlife that went on there, especially on weekends. The Sheppards offered the supper club to civic groups in Midwest City looking for dinner and meeting venues, and Bill was well-connected to some top Oklahoma politicians and was even a national convention delegate himself. Mostly, though, I just remember Bill and Minnie as being nice people to work for who treated people fairly and made them feel at home.

I played football in my sophomore year, but opted instead to focus on swimming, which had been a big part of my life for several years. I worked my way through all the Red Cross aquatic levels of advanced swimming and lifesaving certifications. I joined the school's swimming team and did well in the distance races. I also taught swimming to young children in Midwest City, and I still remember how cold the pool water was in those early-morning swimming lessons.

In my earlier years, I had a mentor in an airman from Tinker, Jim Miller, who was himself a lifeguard and who taught me and my sister to swim at the Tinker pool. In the ensuing years, I worked alongside other airmen who spent their spare time lifeguarding at Desert Oaks. My mom always said I seemed to spend as much time swimming *under-water* as on top, so I guess I took that to heart and became certified as a SCUBA diver in my senior year of high school. My love of the water then led me to join the Naval ROTC program as a student at the University of Oklahoma.

Much of time during the high school years was spent on dating and sweating over whether girls would actually want to go out with me. The idea of calling up a girl and asking her for even a Coke date evoked a nervousness that I had to work to overcome.

I had to plan out what I would say long before I made the call and wondered if I could keep the conversation going much past hello. To assist me in that effort, I wrote notes to myself about topics we would talk about and even pop in a joke or two I thought would be funny. Girls liked guys who made them laugh, no? But when the phone calls began, they usually went off-script immediately because I forgot the girl might have her own things she wanted to say! So, I improvised as I went along and, usually, it worked out and I got the date.

I made friends with a guy in my junior year speech class named Randy Staley. He was a fun guy and we hit it off almost immediately. We decided to double date one weekend, something I'd never done before. As the evening ended, I was in the front seat with my date, and Randy was in the back with his. Suddenly, I heard this strange sound coming from back there. It was a kind of muffled speech pattern, accompanied with a metallic clink. When my date and I turned toward the back seat, we realized Randy must have planted a passionate kiss on his girl because his front teeth got tangled up in her braces, and he couldn't disengage.

So, my date and I got out and went back to help pull the two of them apart. That is an experience I've never forgotten.

Randy is one of the many friends whom I haven't seen since high school, but he went on and became a successful actor in Hollywood after graduating as a drama major at OU. His professional name is James Staley (he went by his middle name in school), and I read he retired recently after 30 years in movies and television.

Most of his 74 roles were supporting characters, but some of those were very memorable. If you've seen the Chevy Chase film, *Vacation*, he plays the Arizona hotel clerk whose frustrated, dry humor works perfectly in denying Chase's credit card when it's time to pay for the room. He also appeared in films such as *Firefox*, with Clint Eastwood; *Sweet Dreams*, with Jessica Lange and Ed Harris, and *Pacific Heights*, with Michael Keaton and Melanie Griffith.

Randy – or rather James – was inducted into the Midwest City Wall of Fame in 1993. I recently discovered we missed seeing each other there by six years, because my own induction didn't come until 1999.

The story of that strange night will come later.

8

Moving Toward Maturity

The MCHS Wall of Fame honors those graduates who have been recognized for their achievements in life.

Photo by Jim Willis

In 1963, I remember two tragedies which deeply saddened me and my classmates and introduced us to the realities of life beyond our high school bubble. One occurred in March, and the other occurred the following November. The latter, of course, was the assassination of President John F. Kennedy on November 22. Life turned to slow motion on that day for all of us at MCHS. The announcement of his shooting came over the intercom, and we all gathered around classroom television sets to watch live updates from Dallas and to hear CBS' dean of news anchors, Walter Cronkite, tell us the president died in surgery at Parkland Hospital. I had never heard silence in the halls of that high school like I did that day, with the only sound coming from the noises that accompany disbelief and grieving.

Classmate Mary Kay Clemons Havens said of that day:

"I was in English class, just after lunch on Friday, November 22, 1963. The teacher was attempting to bring order to the class when the intercom came on unexpectedly. A lot of static was on the announcement and the rowdy boys in class made the message even harder to hear.

Then we heard: President Kennedy ... shot ... Dallas. A pall came over the room as we listened. We thought surely a president could not be killed in the United States in 1963. That was something that happened only in far off, uncivilized countries. Soon after, school was dismissed and I don't remember how I got home I do remember walking in the door and seeing my dad in tears, staring at the television.

We were all in disbelief. We had been to Dallas, and even in Parkland Hospital. We had gone to downtown Oklahoma City to see Kennedy in a campaign parade. My family had been Democrats forever, and still blamed Herbert Hoover for the Dust Bowl and the depression.

President Kennedy was young, enthusiastic, handsome, had a beautiful family. Surely, no one would have wanted to kill him. We prayed he would not die. We were glued to the television for two days, trying to process this terrible event and wondering what was happening to our country and our freedom." (1)

I've often wondered, in this age of social media where few people seem to get their news and information from the same source, if there would be such a unified reaction of grieving were a current-day president to be assassinated. The television era before the cable-splintered audience, and then the further splintering that came from social media, was one where three television networks delivered essentially the same fact-anchored stories, with little or no opinion or commentary added.

And the one dominant news anchor, often voted as "America's Most Trusted Man," was CBS anchor Walter Cronkite. As some called him, "Uncle Walter." Here is how a special edition of *TV Guide* Magazine described America's reaction after Cronkite broke the news on mid-day television:

"At that moment, there began something that could only happen in the age of TV. As a nation we were able to live out our grief in concert and at the same time begin the arduous business of picking up the pieces. Moreover, we were able to prepare ourselves for the new order to things. At the end of the four days [of official mourning] we were to know the new President intimately, who he as, where he came from and, most important of all, how he behaved in a time of extreme stress.

As Cronkite was later to comment: 'We saw before our very eyes a smooth transition of government. No confusion. Only a man in command moving ahead to the problems at hand. And [ABC newsman Ron] Cochran was to add: 'Television had actually become the window of the world so many had hoped it might be one day.'" (2) But again, Television at that time consisted of only three national networks, and all TV-viewing America got their same information from them.

The other sad moment that stands out was more personal for me, and it came on March 9, 1963, when I read in the afternoon *Oklahoma City Times* that my friend from Westside Elementary, Ben Braswell, had died violently that morning in a head-on automobile crash in dense fog east of Midwest City. Ben was born on March 23, 1946 (only four days after me) and was on the threshold of his 17th birthday when he became Oklahoma's 122nd traffic fatality that year. It shook me to the core. As I look back on it, that was a classic example of how young people expect their lives and the lives of their friends will somehow go on forever. Then a classmate dies, and your disbelief and sadness spiral into a surreal series of days.

I remember standing near Ben's grave at the funeral on a day when the winds really did come "sweeping down the plains," as our beloved state song says. I was feeling very sad and very confused. I was in shock and already missed Ben. It was the first time I remember thinking seriously about the thing we call *time*, how it related to Ben – and me – and I had no answers. Ben had been so young, so full of life, and so much fun to be around. My friend whom I played football with over at Westside, was always looking ahead. And then, in one foggy and decisive moment on the road, he wasn't. And that perplexed me.

As the preacher was delivering the sermon (to Oklahoma pastors, funerals are always a good time to deliver one) I was thinking instead, "What should I make of Ben's death? Does time just really stop, or is our definition of time just really wrong? The stock answers (i.e. "God needed him there more than we needed him here") may have worked for a while, but not for long. I guess because Ben was my friend, and I didn't have a chance to say goodbye, I couldn't let his passing go with such a quick fix. So, I tried in vain to solve the puzzle. Absent an answer, I finally let it go. Or maybe I didn't since I'm still writing about it today.

But when you are 16, your day-to-day reality of school, friends, sports, and dating all manage to shove those weightier questions of harsh reality to the back corners of your mind. The immediate questions become: can I convince that cute girl in my homeroom if she will go out with me Saturday night, and who's our team playing this week?

One of the reasons Midwest City was a great place to attend high school was that it fielded outstanding athletic teams. Especially noteworthy was the black and gold Bomber football team that won state championships in 1960, 1985, 1988, 1994, and 1995. In Oklahoma, football comes next to God, country, and family in priority, sometimes jockeying for higher position in that list.

Friday night action at Rose Field
Photo by Bomber Beam

It seemed every year the MCHS Bombers managed to post winning records over the toughest competition Oklahoma had to offer. In my sophomore year of 1965, the Bombers won their Mid-State Conference Championship, playing in the big-league class of Oklahoma high school football teams. These were the halcyon days for the football team, and their success was largely due to their long-time coach, Jim Darnell.

Darnell had grown up in Chickasha, Oklahoma, and had been a standout athlete there in football, basketball, and track. Graduating in 1947 he attended college at Cameron College and graduated from Central State College (now the University of Central Oklahoma). He received his master's degree in secondary administration from OU, began his teaching and coaching career at Altus High School and came to Midwest City in 1953 as assistant football coach.

Two years later he was head coach and began compiling his record of 186 wins, against 50 losses and 10 ties. His teams won nine conference championships, a state championship in 1960, and three runner-up finishes in 1967, 1969, and 1971. He never had a losing season at MCHS, was named Coach of the Year in Oklahoma in 1970 and was inducted into the Oklahoma Coaches Association Hall of Fame in 1978.

Midwest City High School named him to its Wall of Fame in 1995. He was described by his players as well organized and disciplined in his coaching, and most said they have remained loyal to him and are grateful for the life lessons he taught them. In 2001, the Midwest City football stadium was named Jim Darnell Stadium at Rose Field. Coach Darnell passed away in 2007.

At our neighboring Mid-Del School District high school, Del City, those Eagles later pulled off a state championship in football in 1976. At the time, the teams from Enid, Northwest Classen, Putnam City, and Lawton provided some of the main rivalries. After the games, we would drive up to Oklahoma City to General Jack's or Sussy's pizzerias to relive the excitement of the game in conversation with friends.

Also noteworthy was the MCHS men's basketball team, coached by John Pratt, that played Oklahoma City Northwest Classen in the state championship in my senior year of 1964 and lost by a narrow margin of 47-41. In the later years of 1998, 2000, 2001, and 2007, however, the Bombers won those state championships and also the 2024 state championship. The girls team won in 1992, 2010, and 2016.

An interesting thing about high school basketball in Oklahoma high schools: there never has been a shot clock used in games. That has produced some bizarre games, and one came during my senior year, albeit at another school in another district. On January 24, 1964, Sumner High School beat Coyle High School by the unheard-of score of 2-0. One basket in the third quarter accounted for all the scoring as both teams slowed the game down, holding the ball and stalling for long periods on court, and intentionally shooting only occasionally. Fans on both sides were upset about the boring pace of the game. Even today, only eleven states mandate the use of shot clocks in their prep school basketball games.

On the baseball side, the Bomber team picked up a state title in 1988 and has sent several players into the pros over its years of existence.

The sport of wrestling has always been big in Oklahoma high schools, as well as at the University of Oklahoma and Oklahoma State University. Midwest City wrestlers won state titles a whopping 16 times between the years of 1971 and 2008. And, not to be forgotten, were men's and women's track teams that have combined for eight state titles.

Former student athlete John Carpenter, posting on the Friends of Midwest City Facebook Page, Jan. 14, 2024, remembered his Midwest City coaches – and one in particular –with fondness for his kindness and helping him to grow. That man was Ed Jacobsen, a former state high school wrestling champion from Oklahoma City who founded the high school wrestling team in 1954 and coached it until 1964, serving also as a math teacher at MCHS. He then refereed various athletic games and was inducted into the Oklahoma Coaches Hall of Fame in 1984. He died in 1995.

"I was playing 8th grade football at Monroney Junior High in Midwest City back in 1967. I wasn't very good; I was third string center and nose guard," Carpenter said. "As dire as that sounds, things could have been worse; we had four full teams back then. Most games, we would have to be ahead for me to see any playing time, so during a lot of the games I would be standing on the sidelines just watching the action. One of our last games that year was in late October, and I remember a cold front had blown in and we were all standing on the sideline just freezing to death. Besides wanting to be able to play in the game, I also knew it would be a lot warmer running up and down the field than standing on the sideline in a short sleeve football jersey.

"Our team finally had a big lead. The game was out of reach, so with about a minute to go, our coach, Al Bagley, yelled for the 3rd team defense to get on the field. I ran out full of energy, but almost as soon as the ball was snapped the opposing team quarterback tripped and went down and the whistle blew to end the play. It had happened so fast that I didn't have time to make a tackle or even make contact with anyone. So, perhaps out of frustration, I found a smaller kid standing nearby from the opposing team and banged him on the helmet a few times with my elbows.

"Suddenly, there was a referee standing next to me yelling, 'Boy, what are you doing?' I recognized the referee as Mr. (Ed) Jacobsen, who ran the bowling alley at the high school and had refereed some of our prior games. I could tell by the look on his face that he was not happy with me, and I thought maybe he would throw a flag or maybe even kick me out of the game! That concerned me because I had never known anyone who had been kicked out of a game before. I worried needlessly though as before he could admonish me further, the whistle blew ending the game. Mr. Jacobsen immediately forgot about me and yelled, 'Game over!' I quickly got lost in the crowd of our celebrating football team and felt better knowing my helmet provided some anonymity.

"That good feeling didn't last long as I realized I had a big No. 75 on both sides of my football jersey. It took a few days before I understood that Mr. Jacobsen must have had more things on his mind than worrying about hunting down an 8th grade football player who had committed unsportsmanlike conduct on the last play of the game.

"My junior year (1970-71) at Midwest City High School, I was in Mr. Jacobsen's high school math class. Math was my weakest subject. That is, until I took his class. It was fourth hour, right before lunch. Mr. Jacobsen would give us an assignment and then take orders for 'Round Charlie's.' A Round Charlie was a type of cinnamon roll with a big dab of some sort of chocolate sauce on top that he sold at the bowling alley. I believe they were a quarter apiece.

"He would leave the room and go across the street to the bowling alley to get the Round Charlie's and bring them back to us. When he returned, he would dispense the sweet rolls and then go back to his desk. The deal he made with us was that we could leave early as soon as we got our work assignment done and he checked it. If you missed anything on the assignment, you had to stay until the end of class when we went over any missed items. I found that math wasn't as hard as I had convinced myself and with the reward of getting out early, I could figure out most of the problems if I applied myself.

"Another break in my favor occurred early on in wrestling season that year. Mr. Jacobsen would drop by our practices occasionally and one day he spotted me in the crowd of wrestlers and walked over and said, 'I didn't know you were a wrestler!' I am not sure I ever benefited from this revelation, but it did seem my status in his high school math class was elevated ever so slightly and he always remembered my name.

"In January 1972, I was wrestling at the Geary Tournament. My first match was at 168 pounds against Danny Addington, a wrestler from Del City High School, our archrival school. As I walked out on the mat, I looked over and the referee was Ed Jacobsen. Danny beat me 13-8. The next year Danny and I were teammates at Oscar Rose Junior College where our coach was the legendary Virgil Milliron. Danny, who became a wrestling coach at Del Crest Junior High in Del City, and I live a few miles from each other and are good friends all these years later. I always figured Danny and I would always remember the match, but that it had been forgotten by most people who were at Geary that day.

"However, one day in September 1976, I was walking across the campus at Oklahoma State University where I was taking my last semester of classes. This young student stopped me and asked me if I had wrestled at Midwest City and had wrestled Danny Addington at the Geary Tournament. I looked at the kid and realized it was then freshman and future NCAA Champion Leroy Smith who had asked me the question. I had never met him before that day and was somewhat taken aback that he had remembered our match!

"As for Mr. Jacobsen, I would run into him a few times over the ensuing years. Turned out that, like my dad, he had gone to Capitol Hill High School. My dad had been an All-State football player there and they had been a few years apart in age but had known each other for a long time. Mr. Jacobsen and I would discuss many subjects, but I never reminded him of the 8th grade football game and the identity of the kid wearing No. 75!"

A major event that happened during my high school years was the 1962 addition of a *second* high school in Midwest City: Carl Albert High School, whose building would also house Carl Albert Junior High. In the Mid-Del School District, it would join MCHS and Del City High Schools. It was in my 1961 sophomore year at MCHS when we heard about it, and it was important to us for a number of reasons. First, some of our classmates who lived on the far east side of town would be going there, and we were worried about losing contact with our friends. Second, we were told that the Carl Albert school building, would not be completed until 1963.

That meant that, at least for the first semester of our junior year at MCHS, Carl Albert students would share classroom space in our own high school. We would be two different high schools on the same campus, at the same time. I remember also that any MCHS student who wanted to transfer voluntarily to Carl Albert could pursue that, and some of us considered it. I was glad I decided to stay put, although the idea of starting in a new school building with new athletic teams and probably less competition to start for those teams, was intriguing.

By 1960, population growth on Midwest City's east side had necessitated that a second junior high and high school be built there, so the Carl Albert School was sited on South Post Road, just north of 29th Street, and a mile east of Douglas Boulevard. Construction began in 1961 and it was completed in January 1963, when the school opened for business. Over the years, Carl Albert High School grew quickly in size and today competes on the same athletic level as Midwest City High. In fact, by 2023, it had captured an amazing 17 state titles in football, several more than MCHS. The annual game between the two schools has become a key rivalry game in town every year.

Alas, for the Bombers, more gridiron glory has gone to Carl Albert and Del City in recent years and the two teams squared off in the 2023 state football championship with the Carl Albert Titans winning.

Midwest City High School put a lot of effort to developing its fine arts and performing arts departments, as well as its vocational programs like shop and auto mechanics. But those two original programs have expanded geometrically as other programs have been added over the years. Midwest City has since developed an entire adjunct campus across Maple Drive for its Mid-Del Technology Center, with complete programs in 11 different career fields from business and finance, to skilled trades and industry, to visual arts, and more.

For those of us who knew MCHS in the 1960s, however, we knew a school campus with fewer upgrades and programs than today but with absolutely no shortage of school spirit and pride. Our Bomber fight song was a takeoff (no pun intended) on *When the Saints Go Marching In* that was translated to *When the Bombers Go Flying In*. And our school spirit song may have seemed to others like a corny anachronism from the 1940s – Glenn Miller's *In the Mood* – nothing got us to our feet and clapping faster than hearing the award-winning Bomber Band or Orchestra launch into it at school events.

And speaking of the instrumental music programs, ours was second to none in the state. The marching band won many statewide competitions, and musicians were on full display

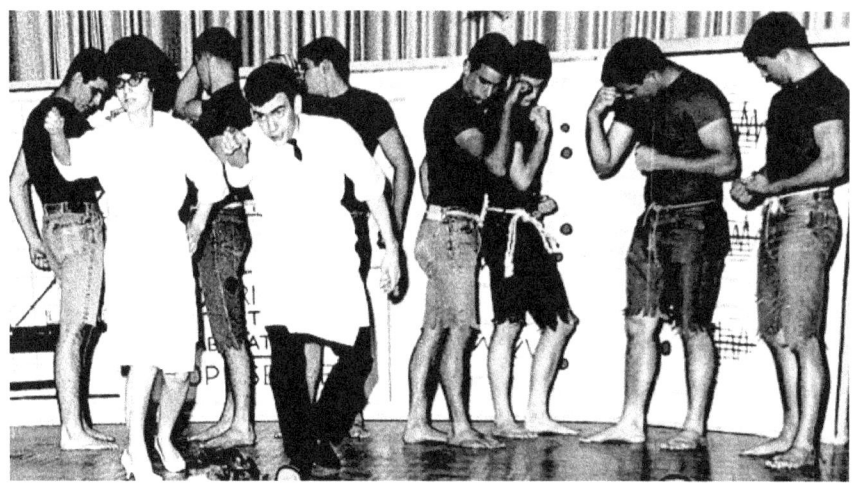

We were trying hard to look like muscle men in Li'l Abner while the scientists tried to figure us out.
Photo by Bomber Beam

for the entire score for our senior musical of Li'L Abner in the spring of 1964. Our QB1,

Roger Brady took the lead as Li'L Abner, while red-haired Ann Kelley was Daisy Mae. They led a cast of more than 90 of us in several performances of what is probably the largest stage production MCHS has ever produced. With accompaniment by multi-talented friends Charles Jordan (my future OU roommate) on the drums and Alexandria Rose on the piano, it seemed like a generational high school show. I was on-stage for only one song, but it was a fun one. I was in a group of about 10 athletes who were drafted the directors Jay Smith and Patricia McQueen to be the men of Dogpatch who volunteered to drink the "Kickapoo Joy Juice" concocted to turn the weak and lazy men into robust mounds of muscles.

The full cast of Li'l Abner during the show's dress rehearsal
Photo by the Bomber Beam

Our group included Mike Whitwell, Richard Bragg, Richard Harrison, Chuck Clayton, Tim Price, Mike Flannery, and me. Some of us went down to the C.R. Anthony Clothing Store in Atkinson Plaza, bought muscle tees that were a size or two too small for us to make us seem more muscular than we were, and then took the stage while scientists, played by Bob Switzer, Jeanie VanDusen, Keith Robinson, and Jim Smith, danced around us, feeling our muscles and making notes, all while the chorus sang the song, *Put 'em Back the Way They Was.*" It sounds ridiculous, and it was, but it all worked and was a highlight of our senior year.

The full cast of The Man who Came to Dinner. Jim Sanderson (in wheelchair) starred. The drunken reporter Bert standing behind him (with dangling shirt tail) is me. I did become a reporter in real life, but managed to retain my sobriety.
Photo by The Bomber Beam

The fact I was involved with the theater at all was a legacy my sister C.J. passed on to me when she graduated in 1962. She had been heavily involved with the Speech and Drama Department all three of her high school years, and I came to know that crowd through her. The only other play I had been in, however, was our junior class play, *The Man Who Came to Dinner*, directed by Patricia McQueen. Jim Sanderson starred in the role of Sheridan Whiteside. Others in the cast included Patti Singleton, Jay Waldrich, Margaret (Maggie) Palmer, Lisa Burchardt, and Arthur Watson. I played a drunken reporter, named Bert Jefferson who staggered out on stage after being spun around several times backstage by crew members. I was lucky to even remember my lines when I wobbled on stage. Both Roger Brady and Ann Kelley (who would be the leads in Li'l Abner) were also in the cast, along with about 30 other students that included Steve Coker, Grady McCorkle, David and Richard Guthrie, Mike Venator, Larry Burchart, et al. We had a blast.

Sometimes I'm asked what it was like going to high school in a military town, and I've given thought to that over the years and heard from other classmates about it, too. One thing that was different from a lot of other school districts, was the constant immigration and emigration of classmates, friends, and girls I dated. There was a large military presence at Tinker, although the majority of employees were civilians. That meant every two or three years military families would get new orders that would either bring them to Tinker or take them to another base assignment elsewhere.

Jim Ross said, "Somewhere around my senior year, I realized that kids I knew in grade school and junior high were no longer there." Brandi Bolding-Williams agreed. "I have so many memories of friends in junior high and high school that got transferred," she said. Memories of going to dances on base and getting to learn about military life was really fun, but it was always sad when friends would leave. I am really blessed that I was raised in such a diverse area." And Michael Hawk laughed, "Yes, I lost two girlfriends that way. Both of them had dads that got transferred to new airbases.

Ronald Carter lived the situation from the viewpoint of a military son.

"I was raised in a military family. Had friends, and then we'd get transferred two or three years later, maybe run into them again. It was great to talk about where we have been and other friends we met. Father retired, and we lived in Glenwood school area. All the kids would gather and play basketball and street football. Most of us are kind of in touch with the help of Facebook and other social media. My father was in the Marines. I joined after during my senior year at MCHS and after graduation left for boot camp in Parris Island 3 days later." Like the other former students, he made his comments on the well-trafficked Facebook pages for Midwest City Memories and the Midwest City High School History Center.

David Hutcheson noted that the transfer situation at Tinker was better than at many other military bases. "For the most part, folks that do a PCS (permanent change of station) to Tinker stay longer there than at other bases. I worked at the AWACS (Airborne Warning and Control System) unit, as a civilian, for 14 years. The GIs assigned there would be around for a long time."

Roger Brady told me he felt Midwest City residents felt comfortable with having Tinker there because of similar traditional values and patriotism shared, and because of the working-class nature of both the city and the base.

One thing that struck me as I was asking MCHS graduates about their memories on the Midwest City High School Memories Facebook page, which was where many of the memories in this chapter came from, is how a single physical object in town could cause people to remember so much. In this case, it was the railroad tracks that ran east and west just north of the high school's practice fields.

Steve Sears commented in 2023 when he mentioned, "It's interesting when you see something that you've missed for a lifetime. These are the railroad tracks that run behind the high school where I graduated 41 years ago. I've driven over them probably a thousand times, yet I've never seen a train travel on them. I stopped to take a good look at them today, and I couldn't help but wonder, when was the last time a train traveled on those tracks? Who was the engineer? How long have these tracks been here? How old were the trees used for the lumber to build this small bridge? It's really just a picture of evolution. In the background you see a modern high school filled with state-of-the-art technical equipment, to teach the young minds of our future. And in the foreground, you see a symbol of the past and one of the oldest forms of transportation which transports products from one place to another. And it's all in one place."

Other former student responses included the following:

- "I lived on S.E. 4th Street when I attended MCHS, and I would often take the railroad tracks as it was a straight shot to the high school," said 1964 graduate Ralph Woodrum, whose dad was transferred to Tinker from Georgia in 1961. "The train ran the years I lived in Midwest City. Every night the 9:35 would run like clockwork."

- "The tracks have a special meaning for us," said Richard Cheek, a 1963 MCHS graduate. "In the spring of '63 my good friend Jene [and future wife] and I used to go out there just to walk and talk when we got a break from [school] play practice. Sixty years later, we are still together. In 1986 we moved back to Midwest City and bought a house close to the tracks on S.E. 5th Street. Trains would occasionally run on the tracks in those days, usually going to Tinker. The last train we ever saw was a night train with no lights on the night of August 1, 1990. That was the night before [Operation] Desert Shield began."

- Chuck Moon, as well as others, had memories regarding pennies on the tracks. "I know those tracks all too well, having crossed them many times going back and forth to MCHS. The train used to run those tracks in my day. We would put pennies on the track when it was coming, and they would be smashed flat. I kept one that was a rarity. I had smashed a penny on top of a nickel. Usually, one would slide off the other but not this one. I've had this in my possession ever since I was a youngster playing neighborhood football in those fields. A penny smashed into a nickel. It used to be worth 6 cents. Now I wouldn't sell it for less than one million."

Several other Midwest Cityans responded they had tried Moon's experiment as well, but it had never worked for them. The penny always turned up missing.

Almost everyone who goes to high school has a prom story to tell, and mine involves our senior prom in 1964. I was undecided about going because I was still a dancer in training, thanks to my mom who gallantly tried to teach me at least the basic four-step waltz. As for the current dances of the day like the twist and the mashed potatoes, I was never really convinced there was a correct way to dance them. I just knew my body didn't always move that way. Today I would compare it to Elaine's erratic dance moves in an episode of *Seinfeld*.

But I did want to date a sweet and popular senior named Gloria Stoeckl, so I risked the embarrassment and asked her to the prom. The dance was held 20 minutes south of town on the campus of the University of Oklahoma, and it went fine. Either because she was a Southern Baptist (which then frowned on dancing) or because she sensed a reluctance on my part to tear up the dance floor, she seemed fine with not dancing much.

She was a great date, and that's the reason I regret what happened on our way home on this dark and stormy night. It had been raining hard – and still was – and my car got stuck in a low dip in the road out in the middle of a wheatfield. I asked Gloria to scoot over behind the wheel while I got out and pushed the car forward enough to get it going again. In the process, though, I ruined the rented tux I was wearing, as I was pretty sure it would shrink two sizes after all the waterlogging it took in that rainy dip where the water was up to my knees. Still, I dd get Gloria home safe and sound, but since I looked like a wet and wrinkled wash rag, I didn't think taking her to dinner was a good idea. On my own way home, I stopped at a burger drive-thru and lamented my ill-fated try to impress Gloria. She is such a great person, however, she never held that night against me, and we are still friends today.

Our high school years came to an end with our commencement the night of May 29, 1964. It was held in Oklahoma City's Municipal Auditorium, and some 550 of us graduated. Compare that to 14 who graduated in the first class only 20 years earlier, and you get an idea of how fast this city and school district grew.

A rainy graduation night changed party plans for many grads, and
more wound up than our house than expected. We celebrated
completing high school by partying in the same room that several us
when to preschool in at Jack & Jill. Fun night!

My parents hosted a graduation party after the commencement, and
it was originally scheduled to be at our Desert Oaks Country Club,
with swimming and dancing until midnight. Alas, the weather wasn't
with us, and we hosted it at our house. All 1200 square feet of it,
including the den. I don't think anyone minded, and it went on past
the midnight hour.

Many of my friends and classmates at Midwest City High School
went on to college and stellar careers in various professions. Others

found success without college. Many, like Jane Vickers Bogan, went on to earn graduate degrees and gave back to future generations with careers in teaching and school counseling. Some became coaches. However our lives went, most of us credited the educational experience and the community support we received for giving us a good launching pad in higher education and careers.

Some of us (and I include myself here) would be so-so students who waited a few years to wake up and show they could handle academics pretty well.

**Charles Jordan and Alexandria Rose Miller
were the top academic stars in our 1964 class.
Perfect GPAs throughout high school.**
Photo by the Bomber Beam

Others (we had several at MCHS) were producing terrific work in school and had the grades to show it. For example, our two valedictorians in 1964 – Alexandria Rose Miller and Charles Jordan – achieved perfect 4.0 GPAs every semester they were in high school. That was something that very few of us could even fathom. In fact, I still don't know how students do that, and I've spent a career in college teaching. It always amazes me when I see it.

I know Carl Albert High School and Del City High produced their share of illustrious grads, but those schools were out of my frame of reference, so I'll stick to the ones I knew at MCHS.

There were so many of our classmates who became successful that I fear singling out just a few. However, the following are just some that

I kept track of over the years, so I'll use them as examples of Bomber grads from the 1960s who excelled in their careers. A full listing of the hundreds of grads officially honored by MCHS over the years can be found on the school's Wall of Fame in the lobby of the high school's performing arts center. A photo of that Wall is found on the opening page of this chapter.

Several of us grads belonged to the First Christian Church in town and lined up one Sunday for a group photo.

The first example is one man I just mentioned: Roger Brady, who transferred to Midwest City from Sapulpa, Oklahoma, the summer before his junior year and graduated in 1964. Brady was starting quarterback for the Bomber football team. He became enamored with being part of a team, and that was a key motivation that took him into the Air Force after graduating from OU in international relations and getting a master's degree from Colorado State University. He married his high school sweetheart, Litha Keator, and the couple are still together today, more than a half-century later. Brady served in Vietnam and eventually worked his way up from second lieutenant to the highest rank possible of four-star general over the course of his 41-year Air Force career.

At the pinnacle of his career, Gen. Brady served as commander of all U.S. Air Forces in Europe and, concurrently, as commander of NATO Allied Air Command, based in Ramstein, Germany. In retirement, Brady wrote two books and completed an M.A. in Biblical Studies at Southeastern Theological Seminary.

Another 1964 graduate who went on to distinguish herself was Barbara Winn Sessions who, like Brady, was my classmate at MCHS. I worked with Barbara on the staff of the high school paper, *The Bomber Beam*. We then both went to OU where she became editor-in-chief of the *Oklahoma Daily* in 1967-68 during her senior year. That was a tumultuous year in America as the country was knee-deep in the Vietnam War and the '68 Tet Offensive. But it was also the year that both Dr. Martin Luther King and Sen. Robert F. Kennedy were assassinated. King's slaying happened during April of the spring semester, and it hit Barbara hard.

"I think the most seminal event during my career, and certainly as the time I was editor, was being there in the newsroom by myself when the wire machine started ringing uncontrollably, and I walked over and read the news that Dr. Martin Luther King had been shot," she recalled. "That was a very difficult time. The next day, people were going to learn about that death because we told them. That's a profound responsibility for students, and it does get you ready for the life events of writing and doing journalism." (3)

Sessions graduated later that spring, went back to MCHS to teach journalism, and then moved on to New York with her husband and became a communications consultant and writer. Her mission was to explain difficult subjects in plain language, and she did that for clients as diverse as the federal government to the United States Golfing Association. Barbara and her husband returned to Oklahoma where she began a long, long volunteer career in Love County near the Texas border, halfway between Oklahoma City and Dallas. She was asked to start a task force on childhood prevention in her community. She did, and that grew into a larger and more all-encompassing Love County Community Coalition organization that, among other things, helped young people find scholarships to go to college. She steered and expanded the work of that coalition for more than two decades.

Her work has drawn statewide praise and, Richard Barker, the administrator of Mercy Health in Love County said of her, "You know, there are 9,000 residents in Love County, and each and every one of them has been served by Barbara." (4) In recognition of her lifetime of

Grads like Tony Callaway, Chaniece Harkey, Barbara Sessions, Marty Thompson, Shirley Nicholson (left to right) and Bob Osmond (not pictured) helped to make the MCHS History Center a success.

service, the Gaylord College of Journalism and Mass Communication named Barbara Sessions a 2012 recipient of its JayMac Distinguished Alumni Award.

A third example of the successful graduates of this high school that grew with its city out of a wheatfield in 1942 Is Tony Callaway, yet another 1964 graduate. Tony had grown up in Midwest City's Original Mile, and was friends with my best friend, Mark Dehart, who lived just across my street. He loved football and distinguished himself on the Bomber team. Tony also served in Vietnam and was a graduate of Oklahoma State University. He became a highly successful Dallas architect, eventually becoming president and CEO of his own firm, Callaway Architecture LLC.

Marty Thompson and Bob Osmond hold the Energizer Bunny, designed and created by 1947 MCHS graduate Bud McMurray.

Late in Tony's career, he volunteered his services back to Midwest City High School by designing its Vietnam Memorial, which former graduates – led by a tireless and dedicated Bob Osmond of the 1964 class – constructed in front of the old entrance to MCHS. It commemorates the lives of the 22 Bombers who lost their lives fighting in Vietnam. A successful architect, Tony has designed many buildings and structures around the country, including the sixth-floor John F. Kennedy Museum in Dallas. He been a partner in three successful architect firms and has said of them, "Each one has grown substantially as we continued to provide economically successful projects. For me, it's about providing great service and developing an attractive and functional building that is economically successful for the owner. (5)

In reflecting on her MCHS experience, 1968 grad Pam Olson Boettcher who would become a CNN White House reporter, said she owes a lot to Midwest City. As I chatted with her in Norman, Oklahoma, on September 7, 2023, she told me, "The school district benefitted greatly from the federal impact funds and was able to provide us a high-quality education. Midwest City also had a great can-do spirit," she said. "We felt we can overcome everything, and we can succeed at just about anything. Midwest City was also a very cosmopolitan place, because people were coming in to Tinker from all over the world." Boettcher graduated from the University of Oklahoma, won the Miss Oklahoma competition in the Miss USA Pageant, became the first prime-time television female news anchor at the CBS affiliate in Oklahoma City and then went on to CNN. While there, she covered events in Russia, Poland, the former East and West Germany, as well as China and even the South Pole.

Another high achiever was Steve Vargo, class of 1963, who was outstanding both in academics and in football at MCHS, but whose personal life could have gone a different way without the support of people at the high school and in Midwest City. "I always felt the community was very welcoming to me and gave me a safe space to become a good student and athlete," Steve told me. "I came out of difficult circumstances and left home at 16. A friend and his family took me in, and I lived with them until I finished high school, and continued to be part of the family until this day. I'll always be grateful to them."

Vargo went on to the University of Oklahoma, graduated with a BA and MS in social psychology, started businesses in Midwest City and Oklahoma City, became president of the city's chamber of commerce, went back to OU, got a Ph.D. in Marketing and had a sterling academic career as an endowed professor at the University of Hawaii and later a major endowed chair at his alma mater, OU, typically logging 150,000 miles annually for international lecturing, authored or edited five books, and published over 140 book chapters and journal articles.

Not to be forgotten is my own sister C.J., who graduated MCHS in 1962. She has been my true north star throughout life since my toddler days in Columbus, Ohio, when she was chasing me around the yard. Her life's work, dedication, and caring spirit speak for themselves, and she has always been a great adviser to me in life. C.J. was a high school senior when I was a sophomore, and she was much more popular than I was in school.

For the first year, I seemed to walk in her shadow and didn't mind a bit. In her senior year, she was voted a runner-up in the annual Miss MCHS Pageant. When she graduated in 1962, she went on to OU and became a dorm counselor (now called resident advisor) in Cate Center, the then-women's dorm complex. Had it not been for C.J., my life would have taken a different trajectory. I was planning on joining the Navy right after high school, then considered going to Oklahoma State University. I even applied and was accepted. It looked like the Navy was going to win out over college, though as I entered my last semester.

That's when C.J. took me out to dinner one night, reminded me she was a girls dorm counselor at OU, and convinced me I could meet a lot more *coeds* at OU, especially those living in her dorm. She knew of my interest in the opposite sex, felt that might be the button to punch, and it was. So, in many ways, I went to college because of my big sister and having an inside track to meet OU coeds.

As my mom would later comment, "Hey, great. Whatever works!"

But C.J.'s professional contribution to the world was much greater than getting her brother into college. In her own right, she returned to Midwest City to teach speech, drama, and English at Jarman and later at Choctaw High School. She also served several churches as a pastor's wife and musical accompanist over a half-century. She wound up the last 15 years of her career co-founding a highly successful Midwest City home school, called ECHO, and serving as its chief administrator for many years. When I think of her doing that, I am reminded of our mother, who did a similar thing back in 1950 when she began Jack & Jill Preschool. Both these school programs benefitted Midwest City school children, and they did so 50 years apart.

These are just six of the many graduates who made the most of their Midwest City High School opportunities. Others included graduates who would become doctors, lawyers, nurses, educators, mayors, state senators, football and basketball coaches, professional athletes, and successful entrepreneurs. I often wish I could trace the seeds of my own career back to a vision I had as a student who then mapped out a careful plan to enter and succeed in that career. Alas, for me it was a much more haphazard launch; a series of serendipitous events, some of which seemed at the time like personal setbacks.

One of those came in October 1963, when I was a high school senior in Mrs. Householder's journalism class. She was a vibrant woman and teacher and was one of my inspirations to pursue journalism as a career.

On this particular day, however, I was leaning my desk backwards and daydreaming about being the next H.L. Mencken when, suddenly, the tilt proved too much, and the rear legs of my desk shot forward across the tile floor. My body went in the opposite direction, and I reached out frantically to grab the adjacent door frame on my way down, hoping to soften my fall.

It was a bad idea. I nearly lost my right ring finger just as my backside slammed into the unforgiving floor. My class ring had snagged on the doorway's metal lock plate and sliced through skin, tissue, sinew, and bone. The visual of my hand still caught on the door jamb, the finger dangling by skin and remaining tissue, is a hard one to forget. Today, several decades later, that finger still stings if I rap it against anything hard.

As the pain shot through my hand, a question shot through my head: could I learn to write left-handed and salvage a writing career? Or would it end right then and there as a staffer on the school's newspaper, *The Bomber Beam*? The worst-case scenario didn't happen, mostly because 17-year-old bodies are resilient. My hand healed, though the scar remains today, and six weeks later my future was looking brighter.

However, the hand didn't heal enough to swim in a scheduled meet with Putnam City High, so I instead went on a field trip to the then-McMahon School of Journalism at the University of Oklahoma. Fate was kind, and I wound up winning that day's reporting contest on campus, and my story about OU parking woes was featured in the *Oklahoma Daily* newspaper.

If I'd had any doubts before about journalism as a career, this first big-time byline erased them. And it might never have happened if I hadn't carved up that hand in Mrs. Householder's class. After graduating from MCHS, I enrolled at OU, got my B.A. in Journalism four years later and started a career that would begin in Edmond, Oklahoma, and wind up in Los Angeles, California, five decades later. In between was my coverage of the Oklahoma City bombing, a milestone I'll return to later in the final chapter.

One last important subject needs covering before leaving these high school years, and that is the world situation during the early to mid-1960s and the direct effect it had on us as seniors about to graduate. President John F. Kennedy decided in 1961 to make more of a commitment to advising South Vietnam in its fight against communist North Vietnam. To that end, he upped the presence of U.S. "military advisors" to 1,500 troops. Over the next four years, to 1965, that number would increase to 25,000 advisors. Presidents Lyndon B. Johnson and Richard Nixon would continue to increase those numbers in the years following Kennedy.

In 1965– the first year after my class graduated from Midwest City High School – 3,500 U.S. Marines went ashore as the first official combat ground troops to fight in Vietnam. That was only the tip of what would be a very long spear. In one year alone, 1969, there were 543,000 U.S. troops serving in Vietnam. By the time the U.S. ended its involvement there in 1973, more than 3.1 million Americans had been stationed in Vietnam during this decade-long war fought by young military draftees and enlistees eligible for call-up when they turned 18.

A total of 58, 220 of them were killed in-theater, according to the Defense Casualty Analysis System of the federal government. (6) Twenty-two of them were Midwest City High School graduates.

Vietnam was the cloud that arose and drifted over our high school years of 1961-64 and, for our graduates, until 1973. Today, the original Elm Street entrance to Midwest City High School is the site of the beautiful Bomber Vietnam Memorial, with the names of the 22 MCHS graduates who died fighting in that war and one who died years later, fighting in Operation Iraqi Freedom.

I knew some of those killed in Vietnam personally as classmates (four were from my graduating class). Another nine veterans from the Midwest City/Del City area lost their lives in that war.

The one whose name was best known beyond Oklahoma was Robert Kalsu, who was an All-State football player at Del City High School who became an All-American at OU and played for a season with the Buffalo Bills before taking a leave to honor his commitment to become an Army officer. He was sent to Vietnam and was killed in action there, making him the only active NFL player to die in Vietnam combat. Today, the Del City High School football stadium is named for him and unveiled a statue of him there in early 2024.

The National Archives in Washington, D.C. lists the following men who died in combat whose hometown was listed as Midwest City or Del City. Those names in italics are MCHS graduates are they are honored in the Bomber Vietnam Memorial, just outside the MCHS History Center on the school campus.

They are: *Edward Glen Baker, Donald Lee Bernard, Benjamin Forest Bolding, Randell Heathe Burnsed,* George Ralph Castillo, *Stephen Randall Costello,* Gailen Cheek Crosslin, *Stephen Scott Donohue, James Larkin Eatmon, Michael Roy Finerty, Rex Bradford Freeman, James Dale Guffey, Ronald Clyde High, John Kirby Johnson,* Harold Leslie Jones, Vernon Joe Johnson, James Robert (Bob) Kalsu, *Albin Lee Kendall,* Carl John Keahey III, *Jerry Allen Kiser, Randall Lee McElreath, Allen Perda Miller, James Delton Moffett,* Ronald Wade Patton, *Larry Lloyd Riley, Lawrence Stephen Robbins,* Hal Jones Rowlett, *Jimmy Doyle Sanders,* Ricky Lee Shackelford, *Kenneth W. Skinner III,* and Sammy Ray Smith.

My fellow graduates and I will always be grateful to the class of 1964 for spearheading the Vietnam Memorial project, unveiled on that class's 50th reunion in 2014. Bob Osmond led the fundraising for that memorial. Several years earlier, the Midwest City High School History Center had been created and put under the direction of 1953 alum

Shirley Nicholson. Osmond and Marty Thompson are the current cura-tors. Tony Callaway (MCHS '64) volunteered as architect of the Bomber Memorial, and alumni leaders like Alexandria Rose Miller, Chaniece

The Bomber Vietnam Memorial Plaza serves as an appropriate entrance to the MCHS History Center on the high school's south side.
Photo by Jim Willis

Kennedy Harkey, Linda Stell Smith, Barbara Sessions, and others helped make both projects a success. The Bomber memorial also carries the name of one MCHS graduate killed in Operation Iraqi Freedom, *Lance Michael Chase,* as well as four MCHS graduates, *Saundra G. Avery, Kimberly Kay Clark, Kathy Davis Side, and Paul Douglas Ice,* who were all killed in the Murrah Building Federal Building terrorist bombing in Oklahoma City on April 19, 1995. (7)

The Memorial Plaza stands just outside the school's History Center (which was originally called the Midwest City High School Museum) that was created in 1998 to remember the past people, achievements, and events of MCHS. Its exhibits go all the way back to the first year of MCHS operation in 1943 and to the first diploma, conferred upon

Van Buren Appleman, Jr. on June 2, 1944. Among the many artifacts, yearbooks, pictures, and documents in the center are old copies of the school newspaper, *The Bomber Beam,* which is where I got my career start in journalism.

Also on display is the football jersey worn by 1967 graduate Randy Burnsed, who was one of the 22 graduates killed in Vietnam combat.

The renovation of the school entrance into the museum/center was finished in the year 2000, and all 20,000 MCHS graduates were invited to attend a ribbon-cutting ceremony, said Damon Wingfield, then-president of the Midwest City High School Alumni Association who was also one of the group of alums that helped establish the museum.

It was Wingfield who first approached school superintendent Dr. Cheryl Steele about the project. She greeted the proposal enthusiastically and made space available for it in the original Elm Street entrance to the high school. Wingfield told Steele that the alumni association would organize and operate the museum.

The first monetary donation came from founding principal (and later superintendent) J.E. Sutton, who wrote a check for $100. The alumni leadership sent out a call to all MCHS grads to scour their homes, attics, and garaged for old yearbooks and other memorabilia from their high school days, and before long there was more material than could be displayed all at once in the museum.

Organizing the museum's collection and putting up display cases and panels became a labor of love for alumni, according to Shirley Nicholson. She was joined in that effort by Lois Lane Batey, class of 1951, and Jennie Hiel Maynard, class of 1950. Other alums began volunteering their time to work at the History Center and that is still happening 26 years later in 2024. Nicholson served as curator of the museum for over two decades before fellow graduates Bob Osmond and Marty Thompson took over as volunteer leaders and have reorganized it into what it is today.

Of the three high schools in the Mid-Del District, Midwest City High is the only one that has created and maintained a working history center that is used frequently by the school's many alums.

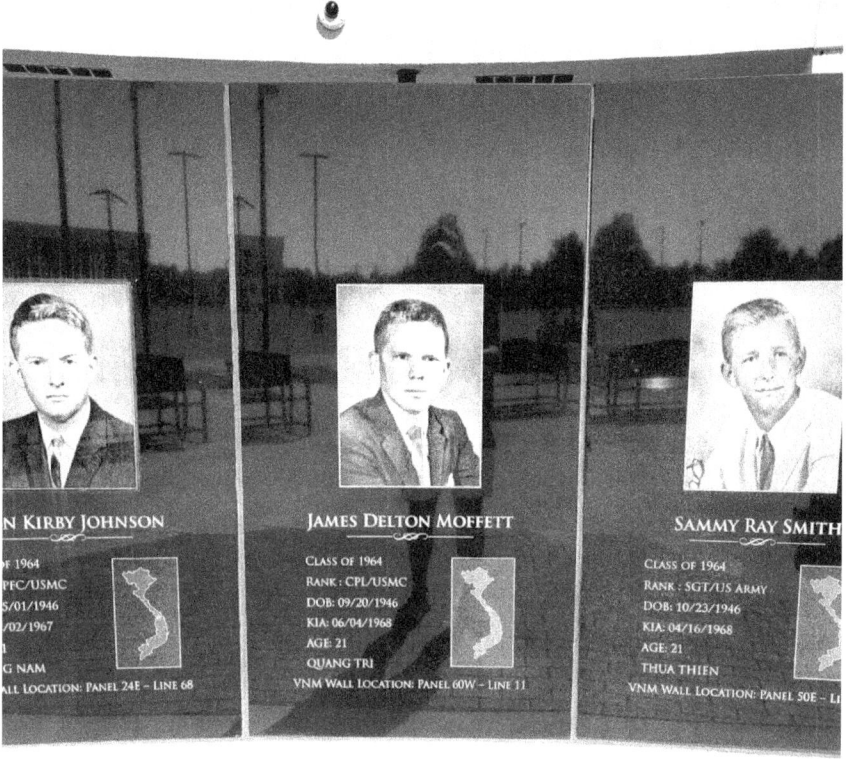

A close-up of three fellow 1964 MCHS graduates I knew who died in
Vietnam. They are only a few of the the the 22 MCHS grads who died in
that war, one other who was killed fighting in Iraq and four who died
in the Oklahoma City Murrah Building bombing in 1995.

Photo by Jim Willis

A Monochrome Town Finds Diversity

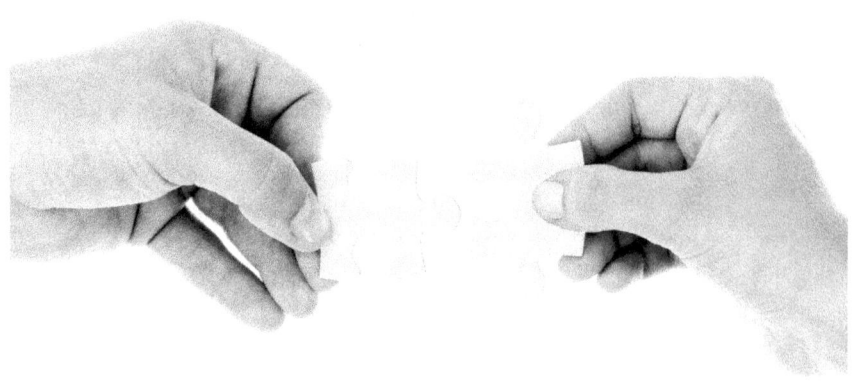

By the time my family moved to Midwest City in 1949, this town had mushroomed in population from its very first residents just seven years before to 10,166, according to the 1950 U.S. Census. It was the fastest-growing city in Oklahoma, if not the entire country, and this was only the beginning phase.

Depending on how the term is defined, we were all *newcomers* here, and we would see in a short time how homogeneous this town was in many striking ways.

Midwest City homes were well built, but they were built to go up fast because Tinker was going up fast. Entire streets of homes were constructed at once, even before many of the streets were paved, and many home designs were meant to be similar – in some cases identical – to help the quick construction time.

The homes of the Original Mile (OM) were all one-level, working-class family homes of only 900 square feet, with 2 to 3 bedrooms, kitchen, living room, one bath and a one-car garage. Standardized floor plans and some prefabricated sections were used, but these were not flimsy homes. All the homes on my street were brick homes, and most of the "OM" homes are still standing eight decades later, except those demolished for a new shopping Center in the early 21ˢᵗ Century.

Because of the similarity of the size and style of the early homes, and because they were priced below $4,000 and all residents were working-class homebuyers, there was an egalitarian feel about Midwest City.

The man who quickly became the first mayor of Midwest City, Royal Brust, bought the very first home sold at the corner of East Turnbull and Curtis Drive. He and his wife had two sons and one daughter and one of those sons, Ken Brust, described his feeling of equality among town residents: "One thing I think about now is we were all about the same in terms of socioeconomic class," Brust said. "We were all in the same boat. No one felt above anyone else. Usually both husband and wife worked, we all lived in similar houses. I'm not sure I thought about that at the time, but I felt it. There were a lot of kids in town, and it was just a great place to grow up." (1)

I had the same feeling growing up in Midwest City in the 1950s and 1960s. Ken's comment about the town having a lot of kids was true. In fact, one-third of all Midwest City residents were under the age of 10. (2) So, youthfulness and the *feeling of it* even among the middle-aged parents in town was another common trait among its residents.

As one who grew up in one of these early houses on East Lockheed

Drive, I knew the houses on my side of the street were nearly identical and you could look down the street and see that no one's home jutted out in front of the others. Each home was set back exactly 25 feet from the street.

Yet I always felt there was an individual, independent spirit among the *homeowners,* each of whom gave imbued their own home and yard with distinct characteristics. I recently discovered my observation about this yin-and-yang nature of the neighborhoods had been part of the town's design when I read architect Craig Whitaker's comments in Architecture *and the American Dream.*

In it, he notes, "Individualism and regard for community are equally important values to Americans, and we want both to be expressed simultaneously ... We may each be king of our own castle, but we all agree to line up our castles at the same distance from the road." (3)

Interestingly the spirit of patriotism, which ran so high during the war and postwar years, found a connection with homeownership. Home architects were not shy about stressing it, either. One ad in the 1942 edition of *Architectural Record* was headlined, "A Home Worth FIGHTING for is Worth PLANNING for NOW!" Underneath was the image of a soldier standing in front of a house. (4).

Lily Boettcher, whose parents grew up in Midwest City, drew that parallel in an excellent paper she wrote years later as a student at Yale University. She said, "In effect, the advertisement establishes that the war is more than a political fight; it's a challenge to American values. Not only are soldiers fighting for victory and American independence, but also for the right to construct a home and an environment in which to live happily and raise a family. *After the war, Midwest City's unique proximity to the military base only intensified this relationship between nationalism and community.* Atkinson developed Midwest City in conjunction with the Midwest Air Depot for the purpose of providing housing to the thousands of workers and military officials working at the base, thoroughly connecting the two spheres.

Atkinson would not just provide housing, however, but recognized that he also had to sell a *lifestyle* and included community facilities such as schools, churches, and commercial establishments. As much as housing reflects family values and newfound independence, community activities and services reveal social structures and encourage a particular set of values." (5)

New residents came not only from across the state of Oklahoma but from out of state as well, as evidenced like my own family that moved from Ohio. Tinker Air Force Base also introduced a *global* element to the city because war veterans assigned to Tinker had just come from battlefields in Europe and Asia. Some of them had fallen in love and married spouses from those countries and a few of these new internationals were starting their families in this new Midwest City. The reason most of them came was the abundance of jobs available at Tinker, a wonderful blessing for a state that had known mostly poverty and joblessness during the Dust Bowl years.

But of the 10,166 people who called this town home by 1950, all but 75 were listed in that year's census as *"Native Whites."* The remaining few were listed as "Other Races," with only 3 of them listed as "Negroes." Therein lies even further evidence of the city's racial homogeneity. Midwest City began as a town populated entirely by white families, and it would stay that way for a couple of decades. Those non-white families living in base housing at Tinker or living off-base just outside the city limits, were not listed as city residents, and most whites seldom laid eyes on them.

As one native Midwest Cityan, Mary Clem Good Morris recalled, "Other than the lady who cleaned our house, I never knew any black people. My parents were very liberal, but it wasn't something that was discussed. When I taught there later, I became friends with a black woman whose husband had moved there with the military. They were told Midwest City had a Sundown Law and that's why there are no black people in the schools. So, they bought a house just east of Midwest City. I started teaching in 1972, and I did have three black students in my classroom. I was not offended, but I was very curious. I remember being at the Uptown Cafeteria one day having lunch, and a group of black people were coming from Oklahoma City to have a sit-in. But they were served, and there was no commotion."

Then she added an important observation when thinking about the cultural influence of Tinker on Midwest City: "Tinker probably made people more aware of being around blacks. It was an influence that Tinker had." (6)

White and Tribal Relations

As I've thought about the lack of diversity in Midwest City during those growing-up years, it has occurred to me that, while the city did *seem* all white, that wasn't true if the *Native American* population was factored in. The thing is, Oklahomans feel comfortable in the presence of tribal members in the state with whom they have blended in over the decades.

Indeed, at least two realities made it easier for the white people of Midwest City to feel more at ease living with Native Americans than they might in living with African Americans. *First* was the knowledge that at least half of their own state had once been given to the five tribes of Cherokee, Creek, Choctaw, Chickasha, and Seminole tribes and officially called *Indian Territory*. And *second* was the fact that so many white Oklahomans themselves carried the blood of those tribes in them via intermarriage and childbirth over the passing decades. Among these were some of the earliest civic leaders in Midwest City.

So, for a long time, there has been a respect for Native Americans in Oklahoma that may not have existed in other states to such a degree. Interviews with some of these showed only occasional prejudice surfacing in town. And it was my own observation, knowing at least four student-athlete classmates at MCHS with Native American ancestry, that all were highly respected and successful in school and in their careers afterwards.

I became good friends with one full-blooded member of the Ojibwe Tribe, Robert Fairbanks, who lived just west on 29th Street toward Oklahoma City. I also dated one of his sisters, Tawana. Robert went on to OU and then to law school, graduating from both with honors. He became an officer in the Air Force, rising to the level of colonel as part of the JAG Corps, then entered private practice when he retired from the service. Before he was through, he had accumulated five other master's degrees in various fields. Robert was married to his wife Linda for 52 years, and the couple had six children. He passed away in 2019.

Native Americans, of course, were always a key part of Oklahoma's history until the state was opened to white settlers. In fact, the Oklahoma state flag pays homage to its Native American ancestry.

Against a sky-blue background is set an Osage tribal shield with a calumet (peace pipe). An olive branch, crosses, and eagle feathers. Its artist, Louise Funk Fluke, designed the flag to symbolize a people who are united by peace. And, as explained earlier, the Air Force base to which all of Midwest City owes its existence – Tinker Field – was named for a general who himself was raised as part of the Osage Tribe.

Nevertheless, there was no place to respond on a census form about tribal affiliation until 1970, and it wasn't until the 2000 census before the category of "Native American" was even included, when it was combined with "Alaska Native." The first time the Native American population was included at all in the total census count nationally was 1940, and then it was up to the census takers themselves to choose the race of the respondents. (7)

So, if respondents didn't *look* black or Asian in Oklahoma, they were probably counted by enumerators as white or – as the 1950 category listed it – "Native White," which would itself seem an oxymoron in modern times. After all, it certainly wasn't that there were no Native Americans in Midwest City, because a large percentage of Oklahomans either are full-blooded or mixed-blooded Native Americans.

As a previous chapter noted, before Oklahoma became a state in 1907, the eastern half of it was declared Indian Territory and it was owned and inhabited primarily by what are called the Five Civilized

Tribes, although others were present, too. The word "civilized" was applied to these tribes because, overall, they had assimilated into American settler culture more than members of other tribes.

They developed economic ties with the settlers, adopted their dress, spoke English, practiced Christianity, and even owned slaves. And every student of Oklahoma history knows the names of each of those tribes from elementary school quizzes forward: Choctaw, Cherokee, Creek, Seminole, and Chickasha.

If you live in Oklahoma, you generally assume many of your friends and neighbors carry Indian blood, and you probably do yourself. There is a respect attached to that, and I know it personally because I always regretted not having some of that blood in me, since I was not born in Oklahoma. In fact, as a child growing up on Lockheed Drive, I remember pretending I was part-Cherokee, because several guys in our neighborhood gang were (unless they were pretending, too!)

This being the case, neither I nor several other former classmates I've talked with in Midwest City – including Bob Osmond and Marty Thompson who both run the Midwest City High School History Center – can remember ever witnessing any prejudice toward Native Americans in town. And there were several students we knew who came from tribal ancestries who were among the most popular boys and girls in high school and who went on to highly successful careers.

Native Americans became eligible for educational assistance through the federally funded Jonson-O'Malley Act in 1934. This program was meant for school children of the Choctaw Nation, and it offered them any needed supplemental educational services that their school district offered. That act changed and was buttressed by others over the years and, today, the Department of Education's Title 6, or Indian Education Grant, is available to children who are members of nearly 40 different tribal nations.

Students seeking help under Title 6 must fill out – or have their parents fill out – Form 506 and submit it along with their proof of tribal membership. The different tribal nations set their own blood percentage for official membership, and it can be as small as 1/256th, according to Sheril Thompson, district coordinator for Indian education in the Mid-Del School District. (8)

Thompson said the Mid-Del District served 1,001 Native American students through the Title 6 program in 2022, and graduated 86 high school seniors, although those numbers vary from year to year. "The Covid years really hurt us," she said. "Before Covid, we served 1,500 students, but a lot of students went back to rural districts to be with family, and some didn't come back. Plus, the government is making it tougher now in insisting on proof that a student is a tribal member. At one point, it used to be you could just swear you were a member. Now you need that I.D. card." (9)

Supplemental services the Thompson's school district offer member Native Americans include the following:

- Basic School Supplies for PreK-12 (JOM)
- Indian Career Day for JOM Students
- College and Scholarship Counseling
- Career Counseling
- Cultural Presentations
- Tutoring
- Test Preparation Workshops and Online Tutorials for ACT and ACT testing
- Liaison for School/Student/Parent Communication

Black and white relations

When it comes to the assimilation of African Americans, however, none of us Midwest Cityans knew how that might fare for the simple reason that few of us *knew* any black individuals or families living in Midwest City while we were growing up. There were no blacks we knew of in the entire school system until the 1960s.

John Martin, who taught English and Journalism and coached at Monroney Junior High for many years, said his first black student, whose father was a colonel at Tinker, appeared in class in 1961 and played basketball for the school's Thunderbirds. But it was a couple years after that before he saw other blacks at Monroney. (10)

The first African American students that Osmond and Thompson found at MCHS don't appear until the 1969 *Bomber Yearbook*. There were three of them. Two were brothers, Derrick and Cedric Williams, and the third was Melvin McKenzie. The Williams' were juniors, they both played football, and they sang in the Vocal Music Choir. McKenzie was a sophomore and ran track. Former teacher Barbara Winn Sessions said she had blacks in her MCHS classes between 1972-75, when her stint in Midwest City ended. (11) That coincides with Mary Clem Good Morris' memory of students in her classes in the same years.

Official records are spotty, but it is generally agreed that the city and school district began becoming more heterogeneous starting in the late 1960s. One of the targeted groups of buyers for the Ridgecrest housing addition, which continued to grow and expand in the 1960s, were officers at Tinker and, by then, several of them were black.

In 1990, sociologist William Graebner wrote that, nationally, adults in primarily white communities attempted to steer their children away from associating with children of other subcultures and races. The idea was to create a social uniformity that would ward off juvenile delinquency, which was a growing problem in the nation's cities. Graebner called this practice "social engineering." (12)

Although Midwest City High School did host events for international exchange students, many parents did not warm up to students from subcultures, according to Lee. "Adults frowned on the clothing styles and behavior found in Oklahoma City schools, and Midwest City students considered themselves better when compared to urban students. (13) If you were a student at MCHS, you were probably more interested in showing school spirit and strengthening the ties in your own group than in promoting social integration.

But this was not unique to Midwest City by any means. The town was like so many other American towns when it came to the slow pace that integration took in the 1950s and 1960s. The years before 1954 were the days before the Brown v. Board of Education Supreme Court decision that first pronounced desegregated schools unconstitutional. Then, for a decade after the Brown decision, many states and school districts were slow to desegregate until Congress passed the first national Civil Rights Act in 1964, and the Civil Rights Act of 1968.

In short, they were the days before the Constitution's 14th Amendment equal rights protections and benefits were legally applied to all U.S. citizens, regardless of race or ethnicity. The passage of these three laws answered the following question affirmatively: "Does the Constitution's prohibition of denying equal protection always ban the use of racial, ethnic, or gender criteria in an attempt to bring social justice and social benefits?" With the signing of these laws, the answer was a resounding yes: equal protection and benefits are meant to apply to all, regardless of race, color, religion, sex, or national origin.

Among the benefits of the laws were the desegregation of schools, and cities and towns like Midwest City awakened to a new era and the beginning of changing demographic profile of their population.

A look at the U.S. Census figures for Midwest City's racial breakdown between 1950 and 1960 tells the story. In 1950, only seven years after Midwest City's chartering, just over 10,000 people had moved to town, and it was a very homogeneous group. Male and female "Native Whites" were almost equal in number with 5,080 male and 5,086 female. All other races combined totaled only 75, while the "Negro" category consisted of only three people, 2 female and 1 male. Ten years later, by 1960, the city had grown threefold with the population at 36,058, and the number of "Nonwhites" (the only other category) at 890.

Oklahoma historian Susan Moeri Lee noted, "Midwest City may have welcomed children and families in its advertisements, but it did not welcome people of color." (14)

Statewide, Oklahoma census figures show "Nonwhites" made up 7 percent of the population in 1950, and 1960 figures showed an 8.6 percent "Negro" population. Blacks in the Midwest City area settled just north of the city in the area known as Crutcho. Of that village's 1,457 residents, blacks totaled 588 in 1960. Crutcho had a small school, which still teaches pre-K through 8th grade. But the immediate postwar years brought a lot of families of war veterans, who worked at Tinker, to Crutcho as well as the adjoining eastern towns of Star and Spencer, and the town of Jones.

To accommodate the growing population, Oklahoma County (with Midwest City joining in) funded a school district to serve them known as Star Spencer. It would accommodate non-white school children. By 1956, Star Spencer had built a stand-alone junior and senior high school (today Star Spencer Mid-High School). Its current website says of its history: "The whole of Star Spencer can be compared to the melting pot communities of large metropolitan cities: White, Black, Portuguese, Iranian, German, Indian, Hawaiian, Vietnamese, and French are just a few of the ethnic groups who have graced the halls of Star Spencer." (16). Today, Star Spencer is part of the Oklahoma City Public School District.

In addition. Some of the children of black families at Tinker chose to attend Douglass High School, a nearby Oklahoma City school which was the first African American school to open in Oklahoma City, having been founded in 1891. As were all other schools in Oklahoma, Douglass would be integrated following the official ending of nationwide segregation and the passage of the 1964 Civil Rights Act.

Although the Army Air Forces had been ordered by the War Department to integrate in 1940, with the intake to increase dramatically after the start of the Second World War in 1941, historian Lee notes that it was 1948 before Tinker started integrating African Americans into its ranks on base. "Tinker Air Force Base employed black workers as well as integrated the enlisted men after 1948," she wrote. (17)."

Although no statistics are available, articles in the *Tinker Take-Off* [the base newspaper] promoted black organizations, advertised Oklahoma City all-black dance clubs, and the *Black Dispatch* (an area newspaper geared to African Americans) contained photographs and articles on [black] airmen." Further, she notes that while blacks shopped and visited friends in Midwest City, they did not live there.

"The public schools did not enroll any African American children, [it was not until 1969 that photos depicting the first three black students appeared in the Bomber Yearbook] nor did the town employ any as city workers. The citizens of Midwest City at times showed compassion to the black race but looked at Negroes with curiosity and amusement. In observance of Brotherhood Week in March 1952, the Midwest City Leader reported that Sooner School held an all-black program for the first time. Featuring church choirs from Oklahoma City, a music teacher from Douglass High School, and a minister from Langston College. The paper encouraged Midwest Cityans to attend." (19) Five years later, a group at Tinker Field selected a black family of nine to help during the Christmas season.

John Martin, the longtime teacher who left Monroney to become an administrator at Mid-Del's technical and vocational school, remembered with pride the way Midwest City helped Vietnamese families relocate in Midwest City during the 1960s and early 1970s.

"At one time during the Vietnam relocation program, the city would bring in 15-20 Vietnamese children to our schools, and we teachers were instructed to help them assimilate but to treat them the same as our regular students," Martin said. "They had to learn English and achieve on their own. They were not to be treated differently. They were all bright, though, and they wanted to assimilate. And they were certainly smart enough to realize this was a good deal for them. They worked hard and they achieved and graduated." (20)

Morri Rose, who is the grandson of Midwest City schools founder Oscar Rose, taught in the Mid-Del School District for 31 years, many of which were spent as elementary school principals and assistant principal at Del City High School.

In his dozen years teaching government and coaching golf at MCHS in the early 2000s, Rose told me in a 2024 phone conversation, "We had a lot of blacks in school by then. They were really good kids. I remember one, in particular, who was kind of a 'king of the hill' with black students there. One day the students were getting too noisy in my classroom, and this guy stands right up and says loudly, 'Will you all be quiet, so we can hear this man teach?!'"

Rose believed the integration Midwest City High School went fairly smoothly, without any racial incidents he remembered. He came to realize most kids in school were pretty much the same, despite their different skin shades. "All kids care about, really, is that someone cares about *them,* he said. "I learned to see that in them, and I got much of that view from my mom and my grandparents."

Former student John Carpenter recalled his own time of enlightenment about race and how the death of Martin Luther King Jr. made him more aware of the need for racial diversity in town. Carpenter wrote on the Jan. 14, 2024, Facebook page for Friends of Midwest City, the following:

"My reluctance to attend church changed somewhat in April 1968. Ray Baker was the minister at Wickline (Methodist Church), and I was in the eighth grade attending Monroney Junior High. Martin Luther King Jr. was killed on April 4 in Memphis, Tennessee. I remember being in church the next Sunday, as it was Palm Sunday, and part of Reverend Baker's sermon was about Dr. King.

Wickline Methodist Church, the first church
completed in Midwest City.

"Midwest City was an all-white town at that time. Tinker Air Force

Base wasn't that far removed from the days when it had separate water fountains and restrooms for their Black employees. I would not attend school with a Black student until the Fall of 1968 when Ford Swan became the first Black student at Monroney Junior High. Looking back, I am not sure how well Reverend Baker's words were received by some of the congregation. However, his words touched me at the time and, from then on, I have been conscious of racism.

"I took Black History at Oklahoma State University in the '70s but my eyes were really first opened by Reverend Baker's sermon. Looking back on that era, I realize it was a very brave thing for him to preach that sermon that day. He could have played it safe and discussed anything but what had happened, but thankfully he chose to challenge our congregation and our way of thinking about others. It was a long time ago, but his words have stayed with me ever since."

Overall, however, African American families were either discouraged from living in Midwest City, and/or chose not to do so. Martin believes it was mostly a matter of choice for the black families not to live in town, although he said he had heard of housing covenants discouraging black ownership of homes. Lee's thesis notes the existence of such housing and neighborhood covenants, which were not illegal then, that restricted African Americans from buying homes in the new city. However, some blacks did rent apartments in the Fleetwood Apartments that were constructed just north of 29th Street, across from Tinker.

In short, just because many of us Midwest Cityans cannot recall racial incidents that rose to the level of memorable violence, it does not necessarily mean that racial prejudice didn't exist in town, and I do remember engaging in some conversations among whites that displayed such prejudice, whether consciously or subconsciously. I suppose, in that regard, we were no less enlightened at the time than were other towns and cities in the state. Mostly, we were simply a segregated, white town that did not see itself as racist; just uninformed, for the most part. At least until the 1960s.

We had at least advanced since the earliest decades of the state in its treatment of blacks. The Oklahoma History Center notes that the state legislature passed a number of Jim Crow Laws shortly after statehood in 1907, and these made many blacks -- who came into the state with the 1889 land run -- question their decisions to move here. Additionally, city and county laws – or at least agreements -- by white property owners not to sell or lease to blacks, had been a part of the state's history since the early 20th century. One example historians cite is Okfuskee County.

"As early as 1911, whites in Okfuskee County attempted to block further immigration and to force African Americans into mixed but racially segregated communities incapable of self-support," the center explains. "Several of these white farmers signed oaths pledging to 'never rent, lease, or sell land in Okfuskee County to any person of Negro blood, or agent of theirs; unless the land be located more than one mile from a white or Indian resident.' To further stem the black migration to eastern Oklahoma a similar oath was developed to prevent the hiring of 'Negro labor.'" (21)

To counter the prejudice, some black leaders established several all-black towns in Oklahoma where the African American settlers hoped to find safe haven, lack of prejudice, and live in community with other blacks. One example the Oklahoma History Center wrote about was the town of Langston, 42 miles north of Midwest City, where the all-black Langston University would be built.

"E. P. McCabe, a former state auditor of Kansas, helped found Langston and encouraged African Americans to settle in that All-Black town," according to the history center. "To further his cause, McCabe established the *Langston City Herald* and circulated it, often by means of traveling agents, throughout the South. McCabe hoped that his tactics would create an African American political power block in Oklahoma Territory. Other African American leaders had a vision of an All-Black state. Although this dream was never realized, many All-Black communities sprouted and flourished in the rich topsoil of the new territory and, after 1907, the new state." (22)

Many of these towns could not survive the entire 20th century, but some did, and Langston (pop. 1,700) is one of them. Langston University, founded in 1897, today enrolls more than 1,800 students and is the only historically black college or university (HBCU) in Oklahoma and the westernmost HBCU in America.

Langston University, 45 minutes north of Midwest City, is the only HBCU school west of the Mississippi.

In a 1986 interview, city founder Bill Atkinson discussed the absence of black families from Midwest City's early years: "Economics. It all depended on economics. Midwest City was a middle-class community, and Negroes could not afford to buy homes here. Tinker had few blacks at this time because the jobs at the base were specialized jobs that blacks did not have the education to do. It was years before blacks would work in large numbers at Tinker and be able to afford to buy a house in this city." (23)

It is important to note that the whiteness of the Mid-Del School District at this time reflected the same demographics as most other area school districts in Oklahoma. Numbers vary, but Oklahoma had more than 50 "sundown towns" from the time of its statehood in 1907. In the previous decades of the 1870s and 1880s, many African Americans fled the former Confederate states and sought to find more peace in Oklahoma Territory. Some did, although some became slaves of Native American tribes there. Then, by the time Oklahoma achieved statehood in 1907, many towns in Oklahoma adopted sundown policies, either formally or informally. (24) Nationwide, some 10,000 sundown towns were estimated to exist between 1890 and 1960.

"The means to announce and enforce racial restrictions varied across the country. In its most blatant form, signs were posted at the city limits. Many sundown towns used discriminatory housing covenants to ensure no white person would be allowed to purchase or rent a home.

In the 1940s, nearby Edmond, Oklahoma promoted itself on postcards with the slogan, 'A Good Place to Live ... No Negroes.' In other cases, the policy was enforced through less formal norms and sanctions. Businesses that served Black customers or hired Black employees would be boycotted by the white townspeople, ensuring that Blacks had few, if any, job opportunities in those communities." (25)

Among these sundown towns were the nearby Oklahoma City suburbs of Norman and Edmond, both college towns. In his book, *Race and the University,* Oklahoma University Professor Emeritus George Henderson Jr, the first African American faculty member at OU to live in Norman housing, wrote about those times.

"In the 1960s, Norman became a haven for white parents who lived in the Oklahoma City metropolitan area but did not want their children to attend racially desegregated public schools. It was common knowledge that most property owners in Norman would not even rent to blacks. In 1967, for example, John R. Sadberry, a black University of Oklahoma graduate student and a Vietnam veteran, was turned down three times by Norman landlords, and Willie Wilson, another black graduate student, was turned down twenty-eight times. Both of them finally moved into university housing. Their experiences were typical for black renters. Two years earlier, the citizens of Norman had defeated an open-housing ordinance. Notwithstanding being classified as a southwestern state, Oklahoma was in all other ways southern, especially in terms of its laws and racial customs." (26)

This mirrored Dr. Henderson's own experience when he was finally sold a Norman home, only to have the owner back out of the sale, telling him frankly that his neighbors didn't want blacks in the neighborhood.

"Now I was beyond being irritated," Henderson later wrote, saying the seller referred to him disingenuously as 'Brother Henry.'

"I was way beyond angry. I could feel blood rushing to my face as my body stiffened and I shouted, 'I'm *not* your brother! As for your house, you can keep it. I'll void the deposit payment check!'"

With the help of three university faculty friends who interceded for him, Dr. Henderson was later able to buy a house, although it was below the standard his family was seeking. Still, he praised the realtors who handled the sale, and he and his wife Barbara became the first African American homeowners in Norman. (27) And, again, this was as late as 1967, my own junior year at OU.

Like so many other whites who grew up in Midwest City, I was unaware of the reasons why our town was all-white and, embarrassingly, probably didn't care enough to even ask why. In interviewing other former Midwest Cityans, I heard the same comment, often couched in some embarrassment.

I don't believe I ever even heard of *The Negro Motorist Green Book* until the movie, *The Green Book*, about a white man serving as chauffeur for a black pianist who toured the South in the 1960s, premiered in 2018. For those who still aren't familiar with it, the book was a guide to accommodations that served Black travelers in America. It was published by its author Victor Hugo Green, a postal worker and travel writer from Harlem, New York. Green updated it and published it until 1966, and at its height of popularity, it was a companion for some 2 million African Americans who traveled America's highways. (28)

Researchers have learned over time that most sundown towns intentionally kept hidden the ways in which they became and remained all-white. Other than the oral memories of former townspeople, few towns recorded any archives of how they managed to dissuade blacks from moving in.

Here is what the Edmond History Museum wrote about this suburb's history: "One of the most common topics museum staff receive are questions regarding if Edmond was a sundown town. In our review of the City of Edmond ordinances in the 1920s and 1940s, as well as the early City Council meeting minutes, we were unable to find any specific ordinance or law prohibiting African Americans from living in Edmond.

In the book *A Route 66 Companion*, edited by David King Dunaway, an African American named Edmond Threatt recounts growing up in the nearby town of Luther, to the north of Midwest City. He states that Edmond was, in fact, a sundown town, complete with a sign reading, *Don't let the sun set on you in this town*. Recalling a visit to the Edmond train station to pick up his sister, Threatt attempted to order a sandwich at a café, but was told to go around back. Threatt opted to leave instead. The police stopped him on his way out of town and questioned him for 'stirring up a little peace' and told him to get out of town.

Threatt also stated that if African Americans had property in Edmond, 'They would burn 'em out and wouldn't let them rebuild' or they would put a sign there that said, 'We had the Health Department up to check your house, it's not livable, you can't live there no more' and then, they give him a few dollars for it.'" (29)

Nevertheless, from the late 1960s forward, racial demographics began changing in Midwest City and surrounding suburbs like Norman and Edmond, as the school districts began integrating and blacks began buying homes in town. In the 2020 census figures, Midwest City is shown to have about 25 percent African American residents in its population, and all schools are fully integrated and have been so for five decades.

I have returned to my hometown many times since leaving in 1968, working in nearby towns in three subsequent years, and I cannot recall any stories of racial incidents that occurred over that time span. In interviewing others, I get the same story. Both curators at the Midwest City High School History Museum have seen no such stories, and one of them, Osmond, served more than two decades as a Midwest City police officer. Nor does Monroney's Martin remember any trouble.

Martin, who still lives in the area after 57 years of service to the Mid-Del School District said, "When integration happened, it happened very peacefully. I don't remember one single racial incident in Midwest City." (30)

Keeping the Planes Flying

The sights and sounds become second nature when you grow up across the street from an Air Force base, even though much of what goes on there is classified information when it comes to the operations involving military aircraft. What we in Midwest City did know is that the main mission of Tinker is maintaining and repairing the aircraft needed to carry out the air defense needs of our country. We respected that mission and the men and women who worked there and carried it out.

What we didn't realize, in hindsight, is the degree of *stress* these maintainers were working under, and that most of that stress was due to the nature and consequences of their work. After all, it was the daily work of each engineer and aviation maintainer to make sure those aircraft were safe to fly and that in-flight breakdowns did not occur. Lives were at stake; both the aircraft crew members as well as any civilians on the ground where those planes might crash. And, since all aircraft are most vulnerable to crashes on takeoffs or landings, these maintainers had the lives of fellow Midwest Cityans in their hands since housing additions had encroached so closely to the Tinker runways.

Case in point were the families living in the 836 homes built in the Glenwood Subdivision on the east side of town, just south of 29th Street which was the divider between the city and the base's runways. Glenwood sat directly beneath the runways' final approach and take-off zone.

Quality control is immensely important on the flight line of Building 3001, formerly the Douglas Plant, on Tinker's east side. This is the huge facility that occupies 2.4 million square feet, runs three quarters of a mile long and 1,000 feet wide. It is akin to a small city, and it is the largest single-use building in the State of Oklahoma. Some 10,000 workers, both military and civilian, focus on the mission of repairing and maintaining aircraft.

It has been here from the beginning of Tinker when it was the Midwest Air Depot. It was built between 1941 and 1942 as the Douglas Assembly Building for the Douglas Cargo Aircraft Plant. It was built with steel columns and trusses for the superstructure and bricks for the exterior walls. It was also built without windows, for security reasons and in case of attack, and the entire facility is self-sustaining. Workers can eat and exercise there and even conduct bank transactions.

The Douglas Company vacated the building in 1945 as the war ended, and the U.S. Army Air Forces annexed it and its plant. During the war, half of all the C-47 transport planes used in WWII, were built here, and even the Enola Gay, the B-29 Superfortress bomber that dropped the first atomic bomb on Japan, was restored here before it moved onto its next mission in the Bikini Atoll. Then the aircraft used to carry out the Berlin Air Lift operation (the DC-4 and C-54) were serviced here, along with the T-6 Texan Trainer, the KC-97, the F-105, and A-7. (1)

Building 3001, Tinker's former Douglas Building, is the hub of aviation maintenance at the base.
(U.S. Air Force Photo)

It is in the massive Building 3001 that "aviation maintainers" – both military and civilian -- work on detecting and diagnosing potential problems with the planes and engines, repair or replace those parts or systems, and then run tests on their readiness before returning the aircraft to duty. This is the hub of the Air Logistics Complex (ALC), or commonly known as the Air Depot.

Today, the main mission of the ALC is aircraft maintenance, serving the KC135 Stratotanker, E3 Sentry, B-1, and B-52 bombers. Additionally, every single aircraft engine in the United States Air Force is serviced right here in this complex. (2) Also, plans call for the KC46 Pegasus, the Air Force's next-generation tanker, to be housed at Tinker, as well as the B-21 Raider, which will replace the B-2 Stealth Bomber. Both platforms and many others will be fixed and maintained here at the Air Logistics Complex, the largest depot in the Air Force.

What was the work like for these aircraft specialists of Tinker? One longtime maintainer, Debby Doughty Hedrick, put it this way to me in an online message: "I was an electrician on the B1 Bomber at Tinker for approximately 12 years and then an industrial engineering technician (planner) retiring as planning chief for the B52 Bomber for approximately 10 years," she said.

"What I found stressful was knowing how much of a *learning curve* there was. And it was always *hurry, hurry, hurry.* Launch days were also stressful because if there was a problem it had to be diagnosed and fixed quickly with the aircrew still onboard. Sometimes the aircrew just wasn't wanting to fly and would nitpick issues. The positive side was that I had my hands all over the airplane. I took great pride in my work and contribution to the Air Force. It was also exhilarating when the launch took place.

"The B1 Bomber is one of the most beautiful aircraft to watch, especially at night with its afterburners. The B52 Bomber is also an amazing aircraft with its wings so long. It can take a punch and come back for more. When I was working on the B1, a Boeing tech once told me that when he was in active duty, he came to Tinker to observe for an issue and when he went back to his base at Dyess he told the other airmen that there are a bunch of farmers working at Tinker wearing overalls. But the amazing thing, he said, is that they know the aircraft inside out and really know what they are doing. I always thought was a cool statement," Hedrick explained.

Yet even the tremendous resources available to maintainers at Tinker don't eliminate the daily (and nightly) stress of keeping planes airborne and crews safe. These maintainers are the *unsung heroes of aviation.* They are also vulnerable to similar kinds of work-related threats that can plague flight crews themselves. Among these are fatigue, inexperience, understaffing, lack of teamwork, distractions, communication breakdowns, procedural discipline, and documentation errors.

Here are just two examples of situations encountered by aviation maintainers throughout both military and civilian aviation when understaffing, faulty teamwork, and communication problems resulted in damage to two multi-million-dollar aircraft:

"I was trying to be helpful by staying on overtime to help the dayshift wing-walk the aircraft into the hangar because they didn't have enough people," said one maintenance technician.

"The plane arrived back from the gate to the hangar. We hooked up the towbar to the tug to start moving the aircraft inside. Person 2 and I were the only wing-walkers, and Person 3 was on the tug. Person 3 didn't have a tail-walker but started pulling the plane inside the hangar, nose in. Person 3 angled the plane to me, so he cleared Person 2's side because of the hangar doors were not opened all the way. After Person 3 cleared the wingtip on Person 2's side, he cut the wheel so the wingtip on my side would clear. But when he cut the wheel, he could no longer see me and, if I went into his line of sight, I would no longer be able to see if the wingtip cleared. Person 2 was walking to my side so he could tell how much clearance we had," he said.

"That's when I crossed my arms and said, 'Cut it. Stop!' because the wingtip was going to hit the hangar door. Person 3 kept moving with the tug and hit the hangar door with my right-hand wingtip, damaging both. Person 2 even saw me cross my arms and did not say anything to the tug driver. The tug driver should have had a tail-walker before tugging the aircraft, and the hangar doors should have been more open. But Person 3 said it was enough room. Person 2 should have told the tug driver that I had my arms crossed." (3)

Sometimes, small oversights can cause big problems. One maintainer recalled when he was in training to do an engine run test.

"We three mechanics removed and replaced three fan blades in the engine and three opposites for weight purposes," he said. "Other blades underwent Non-Destructive Testing (NDT) for damage. After the blade replacement, I was asked to train for engine run qualification. Two of us were being trained, and we did an engine run for vibration per the Airplane Maintenance Manual (AMM), test number six. Ground operations pushed us into location (outside the hangar), and they were out front with communications with us and Tower.

"The vibrations for the fan were out of limits high. We couldn't go above 76 percent. We then returned to the gate, and the trainer called Maintenance Control. The trainer said they instructed him to have our team of three remove the spinner and run the engine again. We pushed back for more engine-run training. The trainer was in the first observer's seat, and another mechanic was in the doorway. Ground Ops was in front of the aircraft in a car, and all were in communications with Tower. We ran both engines up, and the vibrations were lower than before and closer to within limits. We taxied back to the gate and shut down. When we got out, the mechanics on the ground informed us that, when we started to go to full power, they heard a noise. Neither Ground Ops nor Tower had informed us of this. We then looked at the engine and noticed the damage to the blades and cowling. We called Maintenance Control and informed them. The barrel nuts for holding the spinner on came out of their respective mounts and flew into the blades and engine acoustic liner, creating the damage." (4)

Aircraft maintenance is a 24/7 job at air depots like Tinker.

This second example noted the use of NDT, or non-destructive testing, on the engine fan blades. Such inspections are done routinely at Tinker. Possibly the single most important piece of equipment in Building 3001 is the huge, state-of-the-art scanning electron micro-scope, which is the largest one in the world. This scope scans parts as small as 60 inches side for signs of cracks or latent problems. It's a key feature of the ALC's Quality Verification Center, and it can enlarge an image 1 million times as it scans the part for any signs of breakdown. Aircraft like the KC-135 tanker and the B-52 bomber have been flying for as many as 70 years, so their parts must routinely be inspected and repaired if needed.

Proper maintenance of structural and engine components on these aircraft can allow them to fly for up to 100 years. The electron micro-scope can scan via non-destructive inspection (NDI) methods, seeing what's going on inside them without first taking them apart. Some of these parts no longer exist so it's important to know if when are malfunctioning so they can be fixed or replaced without breaking down completely. The scanning electron microscope allows this job to be done.

Another piece of modern, digital technology used is *virtual reality*. It comes into play when training new maintainers to work on aircraft components. Using sophisticated Oculus-like headsets, trainees work on virtual engine and structural components virtually in the training rooms instead of teaching them repair techniques out on the flight line on the actual planes being serviced by working maintainers. (5)

The flight line is where the final stages of aircraft restoration take place. When the Program Depot Maintenance (PDM) maintain-ers are finished, each plane goes out onto the ALC ramp for its test flights where the Final Functional Checkflights (FCFs) put the aircraft through its paces. If in-flight problems are detected, the plane goes back inside to PDM. (6)

All this work goes on 24/7 at Tinker's Air Logistics Complex in Building 3001. While most of us town folks were bedding down for the night across the street in Midwest City, hundreds of workers at the

ALC were just starting another shift every night. Operationally, Building 3001 is the home of the Air Force's 76th Maintenance Wing (MXW). When the normal workday is done around 4 p.m., the swing shift takes over, and then the graveyard shift works until the next morning.

"Each and every employee working on the swing and graveyard shift is a true professional, making a huge impact on our ability to deliver engines and aircraft back to the warfighter in a timely manner," said Steve Hampton, Tinker swing shift superintendent. "The work our employees provide is key to keeping our production schedules and the continued support of the Air Force mission." (7)

The aviation maintainers not only repair aircraft and engines, but they also repair any malfunctioning machinery that makes those repairs. That's the job of the 76th Maintenance Support Group, always on-call in Building 3001. Before his retirement from Tinker, swing-shift maintenance supervisor Benny Womble led a crew of 15 electricians, mechanics, and electronics specialists to repair any machinery that needed it. Like so many other workers at Tinker, Womble said it was a privilege to work in the ALC. "If we're not fixing aircraft and engines and sending them out of this building, we're all going to be out of a job," he said. "And that's the truth." (8)

An example of a repair procedure that challenged the aviation maintainers at Tinker several years ago was related by Tinker Public Affairs Officer Howdy Stout. (9)

That was the first time or two that an 800-pound pivot pin in a B-1 Bomber's "swing wings" was removed and replaced. The pivot pin is what allows the B-1's wings to move in-flight. "It's a very interesting project," explained mechanic Tate Valentine, who helped to write a manual on how to do it, realizing that would be a standard practice in years to come on this bomber. "It is impressive: the planning, the scheduling, mechanics, and everything involved. It's a major project and it's something Tinker should be proud of."

The B-1 was developed to be a nuclear strategic bomber in the 1970s. It began its service the next decade and today is still used as a conventional long-range bomber. It was used to strike against the Taliban in

Afghanistan. But, due to its age, the bomber needs special maintenance attention, and a critical part is that pivot pin.

"We've done it a couple of times," Valentine said, noting that the techniques were developed at Edwards Air Force Base, in California. "We're doing two aircraft a year for two years," said shop supervisor Roger Walker. If engineers find significant war, the pivot pin inspection will become mandatory through the B-1 fleet."

The process was fraught with complexities. To get to the pivot pins in the first place, aircraft mechanics had to revote the aircraft's four engines and housings. That first necessitated emptying and disconnecting the fuel and hydraulic lines, as well as fire extinguishers. It takes a lot of time and, said Valentine, leave the sleek B-1 "looking like a lawn dart." And mechanic Randy Orr, the only other one who knew the pin-pulling technique said, "We probably have more trouble disassembling it than pulling the pin."

Once the engines and housings are removed, mechanics must brace the wings themselves to keep them still when the pivot pin is removed. Then a crane is rolled into place, its cable is attached to the 800-pound pin. Mechanics wrap the pin in a thermal blanket and heat it to 120 degrees Fahrenheit for at least four hours. Then they freeze it. Liquid nitrogen is pumped inside the hollow pin. The extreme cold causes it to shrink in diameter. "We have full gear on," Orr said. "Aprons, gloves, and face shields." As the pin shrinks, it dislodges from the heated structure and then it pops out.

"A little heat, a little cold, a little pressure, and a little time," said Valentine.

Then the pin is inspected and, if found to be okay, the mechanics must put it all back together again. That process becomes even trickier than getting it out, and timing becomes very important. "You have to have it sitting in there right or else," mechanic Clifton Chenevert said. "Work on this needs to be done properly. Because if it breaks, you can't just pull over to the side of the road."

Said Orr, "It's a responsibility."

Said Chenevert, "You have somebody else's life in your hands. It's not for everyone. It's not putting bicycles together at Christmas." If there is any doubt the fix was done wrong, the crew will pull the pins out again and start all over even after it is reassembled.

Morally, you don't have any choice," Chenevert said. "There's no guessing game. It's either good, or it isn't."

Orr said that keeping what he calls the "Corvette of the bomber fleet" in flying condition is stressful on all maintainers who work on it. The same is true for all other aircraft that come through Building 3001.

"It's an intensely difficult plane to work on," Valentine said. "There are so many areas of the structure hard to access. And the pace of the work is relentless as new planes keep coming in for these and other repairs. Most of these maintainers work overtime, six days a week, to keep the planes airborne."

Orr and Valentine both joined Tinker at the same time and became used to working long hours. "We hired on together and worked E-3s and B-52s and it's been that way at every weapons system we've been on," Valentine said. Work for the first shift starts at 4:30 a.m. All three shifts are busy 24/7.

"They've done a heck of a job," said shop supervisor Roger Walker, as he watched the mechanics reinstall the ejection seat on one of the bare metal B-1s. "Today they night work on one aircraft, the next day another. The work doesn't stop. They've gone way and above. We have a mission to help protect our country and these guys have done a heck of a job."

"The whole thing is stressful," said mechanic Chenevert, who noted this was on-the-job training for himself and some of the crew. (10)

A 2024 updated snapshot survey of 35 Tinker workers, both current and past, shows some similarities in their feelings about their jobs and working conditions there. Overall, most enjoyed their jobs, and one of the most mentioned reasons was the people they worked with and the excellent benefits of working for the government. These positives were balanced with some negatives, however, including the mixed quality of supervision in the ALC and relatively low pay, compared to what the private sector pays. Here are some sample comments: (11)

- One longtime software engineer from Midwest City described his experience working at Tinker as terrific. "Great people, great benefits, and a laid-back pace," he said. "The pay was good, but not amazing."
- An electronics engineer from Oklahoma City praised the "friendly people with a strong drive for improvement. That makes it easier to come to work." However, he added, "A negative, I would say, is pay. Most people who leave Tinker do so because of pay."
- A program manager listed work-life balance, flextime, great benefits, and excellent retirement as positives. On the downside, he said, "The environment is dependent upon where you are physically working. There are a lot of moving parts and slow processes. The upper management competency varies greatly."
- An aircraft mechanic from Midwest City praised the "excellent benefits, steady pay, and frequent raises." On the downside, he called his workplace "unorganized, with lots of down time, and hard to get training."
- Another engineer called the work "tolerable," but also said, "It's the government, so everything moves at a glacial pace."
- A former mechanical engineer from Oklahoma City presented a detailed evaluation of the work at Tinker. Reflecting from 2024, he called it, "A decent job for a new engineer. You get to learn with some of the best technology that is out there. There is a lot of formal training available, and PMXG (Propulsion Maintenance Group) management does a good job at letting engineers move between positions to find what they enjoy. It's a great place to become a subject-matter expert in a specialized area like engine test cell, plating, engine assembly, etc., then a couple years later do a complete switch and master a different area.

"The work-life balance is pretty good. No shade if you leave at 4 p.m. and don't want to work weekends. If you work extra hours, you get paid extra money. Currently, the environment is set up where you work at 76 PMX Group for three to four years to get some valuable experience, then either become a manager or jump ship to the private sector of to the "East Wall: (administrative side of B3001 for a less-stressful job.

"The pay is lower than the private sector. I ended up leaving for a 30K pay bump. That means there are very few senior engineers of 10 years or more experience. During my eight years, there was a shortage of engineering leadership. There are always manager positions they need to fill. If you handle yourself professionally and want to be a first-line engineering manager, you can get there in three years. Most engineers don't want these jobs because of the nonsense you have to deal with. This organization has way too many meetings. The environment at 76 PMX Group is reactionary. A lot of knee-jerk reactions and, in some departments, there seems to be an "emergency" every single day. There is also an incredible amount of red tape to get used to."

- And a current aircraft electrical and environmental worker gave his job five stars and said he enjoys the fact you can do so many different things on any given day. "A typical day at work includes checking out tools, pulling up jobs that need to be completed, checking the operational capability of parts, fixing and/or replacing parts that no longer function, and reinstalling parts onto the aircraft."

Some Midwest Cityans provided other glimpses of life in Building 301, posting on the Facebook page of Midwest City Oklahoma Memories and Histories in 2024. For Example, some female workers from the administrative side of Building 301 spoke of what it was like for a woman to work among so many men that they walked past daily on the maintenance lines. Betsy Bray Baustert recalled, "As a high school worker, walking back and forth throughout the building, I never cared much for the catcalls and whistles coming from the mechanics working on top of the planes. It made me nervous." Her co-worker, Celia Armstrong, agreed. "Walking down the long collection of large planes being worked on by all those whistlers was both educational and uncomfortable," she said. "But it was a great place to work and learn." And Suzi Kaiser Byrne said, "I worked in Personnel and had to cross the aircraft moving line several times a day. I was followed several times back to my office. Fortunately, there were some pretty protective men who worked in the same office. It was humiliating and intimidating."

And one humorous post came from Chris Caram who remembered his parents fondly when speaking of Tinker's aviation maintainers: "My mom and dad actually met each other there during the war. Rumor had it that she dropped a wrench and it hit him in the head. He came up cussing and yelling, and the woman happened to be my mom. Kismet? My dad retired from Tinker."

In sum, most workers at Tinker seem to like their jobs and the people they work with, although they have had to put up with work-place frustrations found in most industrial settings. Tinker workers know they could probably make more money taking their skills into private aviation, but the ones who stay are proud of the fact they are in the front lines of insuring that the air power needs of America's defense systems are supplied and that those aircraft and engines are in good working order. When their shift is over, many of them return to their homes in Midwest City to assist in raising their families. Many become involved in civic, church, and sports activities in town. These aviation maintainers find various ways of relieving their work stress, and all are hoping for safe travels for the pilots and crews who fly the planes they have repaired.

Regina Southern is the daughter of a longtime aviation maintainer at Tinker. She reflected in 2024, "I have my dad's Tinker yearbook from his years working on the planes through two wars, 1948-1978. Lots of memories or air shows. Building 3001 was where Dad did his machinery work. He told us after the plane was serviced, he went on test flights with the pilot. My dad was the best of the best, and pilots never worried when Big John, as he was called, was the maintainer. He worked the graveyard shift. I never heard him complain. I'm his 70-year-old daughter now who likes to reflect on sweet memories. Dad passed at

63 in 1983. He was a POW in Germany in WWII and returned by the grace of God." (12)

Every time I hear a story like Regina's I think of what the legendary NBC newscaster Tom Brokaw called her father's contemporaries: *The Greatest Generation*. In his book of that name he wrote, "...it is, I believe, the greatest generation any society has ever produced." He said these men and women fought not for fame and recognition, but because it was the "right thing to do." (13)

Throughout my growing-up years in Midwest City, across the street from Tinker AFB, I was proud to be surrounded by these members of Brokaw's Greatest Generation. Subconsciously, I was probably inspired to try my best when faced with difficult challenges in life.

Fighting to Save Tinker

A call to action urges Midwest City area residents to come and protest the potential shutdown of Tinker in 1993. A similar threat occurred in 1995.

Tinker Air Force Base is a major player in the country's elaborate defense system.

It is one of the largest and most important military installations in America. The base is spread over more than 5,000 acres, has two 10,000-foot runways, 7,000 military personnel, and 15,000 civilian employees. It is home to several major military units including the Oklahoma City Air Logistics Center, 76th Aircraft Maintenance Group, 552d Air Control Wing, 507th Air Refueling Wing, 513th Air Control Group, 72nd Air Base Wing, 72nd Medical Group, Navy Strategic Communications Wing One, Defense Logistics Agency's Defense Distribution Depot Oklahoma City, Third Combat Communications Group, Air Force Sustainment Center, 38th Cyberspace Engineering Installation Group, and Defense Megacenter Oklahoma City. (1)

The first of these, the Oklahoma City Air Logistics Complex, is the single largest unit at Tinker. It is also the biggest facility in the entire Air Force Material Command. About half of all employees – military and civilian – who work at Tinker, work for this complex.

On a year-round basis, they deliver ongoing, state-of-the-art combat power for the nation. These specialists perform programmed depot maintenance and modifications on aircraft such as the KC-46, KC-135, B-1B, B-52, E-3, and Navy E-6 airplanes. They conduct repairs and overhauls for the F100, F101, F108, F110, F117, F118, F119, F135, TF 33 engines, and provide auxiliary combat support services for the Air Force, Navy, and Marine Corps. The complex develops and sustains a wide-ranging portfolio and mission-critical software for the Air Force and other customers, as well as providing global aircraft battle damage repair capability for multiple weapon systems. (2)

Overall, some 27,000 military and civilians serve and work at Tinker Air Force Base, and the economic imprint on the State of Oklahoma is over $3 billion annually. It is the state's largest single-site employer and second largest employer overall. Only the state government itself has a bigger payroll.

Even with all this, however, Tinker has confronted times when its future has been in doubt and, at least twice in the 1990s, when it was a candidate for complete closure by the federal government's Base Realignment and Closure Commission (BRAC). It has managed to escape such fate each time, but it hasn't been easy, and the base needed the help of metro-Oklahoma City to keep the gates open. First and foremost, that included Midwest City, its host town whose sole reason for creation back in 1942 was to service the needs of the new base's workers. It was the people of Midwest City who most clearly understood the gravity of losing Tinker: Shuttering it might well mean shuttering much of the town itself.

The federal government isn't in the business of closing down towns, and that's what makes it hard when the Congress and the Department of Defense try to manage an effective economy of scale between the country's defense needs and the size of its current inventory and capacity of its military bases.

Like many such installations, Tinker was established to meet the county's air defense needs as it headed into World War II. Bases like Tinker completed their wartime missions admirably, but when the war ended, defense leaders asked, "Do we still need all these bases? Can some be downsized or consolidated?"

Those questions were raised about Tinker, and Midwest City feared the answer might be to close the base sometime during the immediate postwar years. After all, it was never a given that an air depot built to service warplanes would need to be a *permanent* base after the war. That was the risk Bill Atkinson took when investing so much of his life into starting the town. It was a bet that some other investors would not take when Atkinson tried to lure them into starting businesses there. The thought of sinking money into a retail business or professional practice in a boom town that could wind up a ghost town after the war, well, that was too much for some to take on.

Happily, for both the base and Midwest City, Tinker survived the shutdown scares. It did, however, lose some of its workforce temporarily as its mission changed to fit a time of peace. Here is how a Tinker writer described it:

"After the war Tinker Field continued in a reduced capacity and contributed maintenance to the aircraft of the Berlin Airlift. The Douglas assembly plant was acquired by the War Department for Tinker's use and the Field was upgraded to Base status. Through the Cold War, Tinker continued maintaining and revising aircraft of all types, notably the B-29 Superfortress, B-47 Stratojet, and C-97 Stratofreighter, and their replacements, and their replacements' replacements." (3)

This would be only the *first* time the base faced such a threat, however, although it would be almost 50 years later before two others came. And when they came, they were only two years apart.

The history of base closures and realignments has been a complex one for both the federal government and the cities and towns affected by potential loss of their bases. In the 1980s, the Department of Defense faced serious challenges in trying to close bases they felt weren't essential, especially in a time of military downsizing and evolving technology. But procedural requirements put in place by Congress were so challenging that no base closings occurred at all. (4)

The deadlock in Congress finally ended when lawmakers established a new process for closing military bases on October 24, 1988. The procedure was called P.L. 100-526, and it established a bipartisan commission, appointed by the Secretary of Defense, to assess defense needs and existing resources and to recommend closures or realignments to Congress. Legislators would either accept these recommendations as a whole or reject them.

That new procedure was begun but quickly resulted in complaints of partisanship regarding which bases would stay open or close. In response, yet another procedure was passed (P.L. 101-510) that created a new authority for additional base closure recommendations by a series of independent, presidentially appointed commissions. The Senate would have to give their advice and consent to these appointments, and these new commissions would be called the Base Realignment and Closure (BRAC) commissions. They would operate in 1991, 1993, and 1995. After that, their authority would end. Altogether, 98 major military bases and hundreds of smaller installations were recommended for closure, while many other facilities were recommended for realignment. (5)

Tinker is the largest of three air depots in the Air Force.
(U.S. Air Force photo)

Tinker Air Force Base was included on the BRAC's list of potential base closures in 1993 and 1995, prompting great consternation among central Oklahoma residents and, especially, Midwest City. That concern turned to quick action on the part of the citizenry who appointed a task force to keep Tinker open and functioning at its current level. The head of that task force was Air Force Lt. Gen. Richard Burpee (Ret.) who was himself a former base commander at Tinker.

The BRAC recommendations were to begin soon and were to end by the year 2001. The estimated savings of these actions was determined to be about $57 billion over 20 years. Congress would approve several amendments to help local communities recover from the loss of their bases. Many of these communities managed to reinvent themselves by developing new economic bases and jobs to replace those lost. They also found other use of the base facilities left behind. But not *all* the towns did, and some struggled to survive the loss of their bases.

After the BRAC authorizing legislation expired, a new commission on base closures was established. Political and budgetary pressure against more base closings rose to a higher level, so new authorizing legislation by Congress was required to continue the process of base closure and realignment. (6)

From 1988 to 1995, however, a lion's share of attention from Oklahoma civic and governmental leaders turned to saving Tinker Air Force Base and other military bases in the state like Vance AFB in Enid. A story from the December 30, 1988, edition of *The Daily Oklahoma* announced the news to eagerly awaiting readers and shows the type of reaction typical of towns when they hear their base *won't* be shut down.

"ENID -- Residents here got an early jump on celebrating the New Year when it was announced Thursday Vance Air Force Base would remain open. Church bells rang and civic officials shook hands after it was announced Vance was not on a list of military bases recommended for closing by the Defense Secretary's Commission on Base Realignment and Closure."

Written by Michael McNutt, the story continued like this:

"This is a good way to start the new year," said Sen. David Boren, D-Seminole. Many in this city of 50,000 braced for bad news after a national magazine included Vance in its list of bases that could be targeted for closure. Christmas greetings last week were exchanged half-heartedly, with knowledge that Vance's closing could prove devastating to the area ... Rumors circulated as late as Wednesday that Vance would close, when talk spread that newspapers in Dallas and Des Moines, Iowa, had reported the base-closing commission had included Vance on its list." (7)

Although Vance AFB employed only a fraction (about 10 percent) of the workforce at Tinker, those 2,400 employees and their payroll meant – and still mean – a lot to the Enid area. When it was discovered that the base didn't make it on to the final list of bases to be closed, area residents were clearly elated.

The angst of Midwest City – indeed all metro-Oklahoma City – would surface and be tested five years later. On May 21, 1993, the base closure commission voted to consider closing the (then-named) Air Logistics Center at Tinker Air Force Base. As noted earlier, this command is the largest single operating unit at Tinker, employing more than 12,000 civilian and military workers. Without this huge command, the future of the rest of Tinker would look grim. As for the impact on Midwest City itself, estimates were that half of the town's workforce would lose their jobs, as some 7,000 residents worked at Tinker. Then, if those jobs were lost and those people moved elsewhere for work, the fallout on the city's businesses would mean more job losses for those restaurants, stores, and service industries.

Oklahoma City mobilized its task force, led by Lt. Gen. Burpee, and went to work meeting with Pentagon officials and base closing commissioners. Burpee was not only concerned with the 1993 decision but also knew there would be another round of closure recommendations coming two years later, in 1995. That's how the commission's agenda had been set up. Meanwhile, the Midwest City Chamber of Commerce pitched in to help with the Save Tinker effort.

The highest-profile event to save Tinker took place on Saturday, June 5, 1993, when 5,000 people from the Midwest City and Oklahoma City areas answered a call to come to the base on the day when the base closure commission was there to review the Oklahoma City Air Logistics Center. Tinker had recently been added to the list of possible closures.

The thousands of volunteers came to form a human chain around Tinker, although there were only enough to stretch around half of the massive base. Organizers hoped the show of support would draw 15,000, but the 5,000 supporters who showed up were impressive enough as they stood around the base perimeter, arms spread out and hands clasped, for a distance of almost 6 miles. Often, in places where gaps in the line occurred, people would use American flags as extensions to reach the next person in line. One Oklahoma City television station even paid the $2,000 fee to have Metro Transit buses shuttle people to different positions around Tinker. (8)

Some political leaders in the state shared an optimism that Tinker would survive but felt efforts should be put into attracting more personnel from other military bases that would be closed. They also urged

Tinker leadership to shore up any production problem areas existing at the base. In a real way, the fight to save Tinker from the 1993 round of closures was connected, then, to the second round of closures that lie ahead. They were prepared for a busy two-year campaign.

The congressional delegation from Oklahoma hoped the Pentagon would convert to an *"interservice" approach* to maintaining fixed-wing aircraft and other systems. That would mean air logistics centers like Tinker could compete for more repairs of Navy aircraft and other jobs. Tinker supporters felt the best-case scenario would be the Pentagon would decide to keep open all the air logistics centers and shut down more depots in *other* service branches. That is what the Pentagon decided to do, closing a large number of Naval air facilities, and transferring those operations to other bases. Tinker benefitted from that, and now is home to **Navy Strategic Communications Wing One.**

On June 6, 1993, Oklahoma's Gov. David Walters, Oklahoma City Mayor Ron Norick, and Maj. Gen. Burpee (Ret.) pled Tinker's case before a hearing by the base closure commission in Corpus Christi, Texas.

"If Tinker Air Force Base closes, it will make the '80s oil bust look like a cake walk," Norick told the commission. After the meeting, the Oklahoma delegates said they felt more confident than they had the day before, when the commission did their on-site visit at Tinker. "Yesterday, some of their questions were less friendly, somewhat more pointed, but today we were able to address them directly," said Rep. David McCurdy, D-Norman. "We started talking about issues of capacity and flexibility and unique capability as strengths as opposed to weaknesses. This was an important meeting." (9) The commission had expressed concern that the Air Logistics Center at Tinker was too large for the work it was handling. But the Air Force presented data showing that was not the case.

Ultimately, on June 25, 1993, the base closure commission voted to leave open all the air logistics centers (Tinker being the largest) that they had been considering closing. That included even the lowest-rated center – and the cheapest to close – McClellan Air Force Base in

Sacramento, California. As *The Daily Oklahoman* reported on June 27, "The decision to keep McClellan open could wind up enhancing Tinker's survival chances in 1995, since the Sacramento base would likely still be the one the Air Force would recommend for closure [then]." (10)

As it turned out, the vote to keep Tinker open was unanimous by the seven base closure commissioners, and it ended a month-long state of anxiety for so many who depended on Tinker for their livelihood. In the open session of the commission meeting, none of the commissioners even suggested Tinker be closed, partly on the endorsement of Secretary of Defense Les Aspin and Air Force commanders who had recommended Tinker's air depot stay open.

One commissioner, James Courter, said Tinker and two other air logistics centers were added to the panel's review list on May 21 simply to compare them to McClellan Air Force Base, which was already on the possible closure list.

"Tinker obviously has great military value to the Department of Defense and to the Air Force in general," said Rep. Dave McCurdy, D-Norman, after the vote. (11) Had the vote gone the other way and had Tinker lost, not only would the air logistics center be shut down but also the base's defense distribution center and the regional processing center. Some 14,000 jobs were at stake. But all were saved by the board's action, and subsequent approval by Congress and President Bill Clinton.

Said Sen. David Boren, "If we would have lost Tinker, we would have lost one of the nation's most important national defense assets. This is a very, very happy day." (12) He added a note of caution, however, saying another round of closures would be coming in 1995.

One of the commissioners, Harry C. McPherson Jr. said, "Tinker has performed for the nation in a great way when the nation needed Tinker. The nation is in its debt. Tinker has public and elected support that is second to none." (13)

Some saw this 1993 decision as a wake-up call to Tinker, Oklahoma City, and Midwest City. They believed it to be a sort of veiled blessing because it gave them time to – in their opinion – set the record straight about how the base was more than able to take on *new* projects and mission such as fighter training. Everyone understood that the air crashes into the Glenwood Subdivision years ago had put the spotlight on residential encroachment and made such training missions at Tinker too dangerous for these neighborhood residents. But Glenwood and its 800+ homes had been razed after Oklahoma County condemned the neighborhood, bought it, auctioned off the homes and cleared the land.

Still, there were Air Force concerns about what would happen to other adjacent available lands. The county needed to address that issue, perhaps to the point of buying up that land and leasing or giving it to Tinker to quell the fears. The Oklahoma City Chamber of Commerce had already led efforts to do that four decades earlier when they purchased and donated 638 acres west of Tinker to the Air Force, and then prevented some 4,270 acres of land south and west of Tinker from being used as residential land by buying it to develop an industrial area. Later, in the 1970s, Oklahoma County leased almost 250 acres north of 29th Street (the razed Glenwood neighborhood it had bought) to Tinker for $1 a year.

Knowing that they had one more bullet to dodge, Tinker and city leaders turned their attention to defending the air base from 1995 closure recommendations when the commission would meet for its third scheduled round of base reviews. For its part, the Air Force had already proposed a plan of downsizing the country's five Air Logistics Centers rather than closing any of them. They felt that would accomplish the same readiness and budget goals while having less of a negative impact on communities near the bases.

But in April 1995, the federal General Accounting Office (GAO) criticized that plan and felt it did not appear to be well thought out or adequately supported. The accounting arm of Congress issued its report saying the base closure commission should wait to approve the proposal until the Air Force was able to back it up with more conclusive data about how it would reduce excess capacity in its air depot system, which included Tinker.

The GAO wrote that the proposal does not "fully address the

problem of significant excess capacity in the depot system, and it is not clear that the realignments will achieve indicated savings. Moreover, they [the Air Force] appear to be adding work to depots that are being downsized outside the (base closing) process." But the Air Force argued it "is actively addressing those concerns.

It is important to note that nowhere in the report did the GAO question the basic reliability of the Air Force process. We are confident that our process of comparing bases is fair, accurate, and impartial." Still the GAO called the supporting data subjective and hard to verify. (14)

The next month, in May 1995, both Tinker and Vance AFB were added to the list of possible base closures. They weren't on the Pentagon's original list in April but were two centers that were added later by the BRAC. The commission announced it would visit Tinker on June 7 for its on-site review, and the next day it would go to Vance, an hour away in Enid for a review of that facility. A regional hearing would then take place in Dallas on June 10 where the base closure commission would listen to different views about the fate of each base.

That prompted another call for supporters of Tinker to show up on June 7 as a symbol of the community's pride of Tinker. But whereas the 1993 "Hands around Tinker" crowd numbered 5,000 when the commission visited on a Saturday, this time the BRAC would visit Tinker on a *Wednesday*, when most people were at work and couldn't attend so easily. Therefore, the turnout was only 50 supporters, a tiny fraction of before.

Nevertheless, the small group stood near the gate when the commission members pulled up, waving American flags, several homemade signs saying, "Save Tinker," and a large banner. Said Steve Siebenaller, one of the supporters from Midwest City, "I want to show my support for Tinker and jobs Tinker provides." Another supporter, Linda Blevins, stopped canning beets at home when she heard of the rally and drove over to join the supporters. Her husband was in his 30th year as a Tinker employee. "For every person here, there are thousands who wish they could have been here," said organizer John Conner, citing the mid-week timing as the reason for the small crowd. (15)

Despite that small turnout, both Tinker and Vance survive this second shutdown threat. On Thursday, June 22, the base closure commission voted in Washington to instead close down air logistics centers at McClellan AFB in Sacramento, California, and Kelly AFB in San Antonio, Texas, setting those closing dates for 2001, giving the cities time to adjust. Not only would Tinker remain open, but it would pick up almost 90 percent of the work from Kelly and 25 percent from McClellan, according to Pentagon estimates. (16) All that added work would translate into thousands more jobs for Tinker.

"I'd say we dodged a nuclear warhead," said Oklahoma University economics professor Bob Dauffenbach. The director of the Center for Economic and Management Research at OU said. "I'd always heard that if they only closed one base, we were in good shape. But if they closed two, well ... You're [now] looking at an effect that could be double the Micron gain," referring to the unrealized hope that Micron Technology Inc. would build a plant near Tinker that could have added 3,500 new jobs to the area. (17)

However, Gen. Burpee tempered that good news with the sobering fact that some 4,000 existing jobs at Tinker would be eliminated because of an Air Force order to cut 26,000 jobs from its air logistics centers by 2001. Still, Tinker was looking at a net gain in jobs by 2001, according to Burpee.

So, as 1995 began drawing to a close, Tinker Air Force Base and Midwest City found themselves resting much easier about their joint future. The threats of Tinker's closure were now just a bad memory. I was in Oklahoma City at the time, on leave from my teaching post at Boston College, and I remember the sense of relief that flooded over the metro area and, especially, Midwest City. At the same time, however, we had all been distracted by another breaking event in downtown Oklahoma City and we were feeling relief after hearing this news, with a deep feeling of grief ever since dawn broke on the day of April 19.

That was the morning the Alfred P. Murrah Federal Building was blown up by domestic terrorists, killing 168 Oklahomans in or near the building. Thirteen of those were from Midwest City and Tinker Air Force Base.

Tinkertown Today

The modern entrance to Midwest City from
the south, off 29th Street. Gone is Atkinson
Plaza Shopping Center and, sadly, our
Skytrain theater.
(Photo by Jim Willis)

    I left Midwest City in 1968 when I graduated with my degree in
journalism from the University of Oklahoma in nearby Norman.

    Like most college students, I had been back and forth between
campus and home over the four college years, living at home over
Christmas break and in the summers. I lifeguarded at Desert Oaks
Country Club and the NCO swimming pool at Tinker. But my feelings

were that this town represented my past and not my future. I was ready to launch an adulthood of looking over the next hill, then the next, and then several more. The wanderlust that I attribute, in part, to watching those Columbus, Ohio trains and then all the Tinker Air Force Base planes arrive and depart to places unknown, well, that wanderlust was now embedded in my soul, and it told me it was time to start my own journey.

It would be a long trip with many stops, adventures, and misadventures over the decades. After ear surgery failed to clear me for further Navy duty, I headed to seminary to train for the ministry, then changed direction into a career in journalism, along the way pursuing graduate degrees, and finally into a career of college teaching and writing non-fiction books.

I worked for newspapers in Oklahoma, Texas, and Missouri, before getting a Ph.D. in Journalism from the University of Missouri and launching into college teaching and writing in 1980. Then it was off to campuses in Indiana, Boston, Memphis, Oklahoma, and California. Starting in 1995, I was asked to lecture many times in Europe either on behalf of the U.S. State Department or as a guest professor invited for semesters by two German universities.

That Oklahoma teenager who seemed at war with school during his junior high years had not only made peace with it but also made a career of teaching. And it was a career that didn't end until I was 74, retiring from California's Azusa Pacific University in 2020, humbled by being awarded both the liberal arts college and university-wide researcher of the year awards. Somewhere along the way, I guess I'd grown up. If so, I have my upbringing in Midwest City to thank for setting me on the right track.

The original downtown shopping center in the early 1960s.

I returned home many times over those years to see Mom, Dad, and C.J. My sister had spent the latter decades of her career teaching in Midwest City area schools before co-founding a successful private homeschooling program and directing it for several years. In doing so, she was following in our mother's footsteps as the founder of Jack & Jill Preschool in 1950. To me personally, though, C.J. has been a lifelong confidant, advisor, and true big sister in the best sense of that term.

I watched as the city grew and changed from visit to visit. America's Model City of 1951 had grown large and very diverse. The city that was once all contained within its original mile along Southeast 29th Street now had spread north to Northeast 23rd Street and east into the country to Hiwassee Road. In effect, Midwest City now encompasses an area of 25 square miles with a population of nearly 60,000 people. It is the eighth largest city in the state of Oklahoma. In 2023, it had a median household income of more than $52,000 and an unemployment rate of 4.1 percent. (1)

If you're a native of this city, or if you lived here during its first few decades, you would not recognize the town if you were to enter from what has traditionally been its

main entrance in the Atkinson Plaza Shopping Center on 29th Street and Mid-America Boulevard. The reason is that original shopping center is no longer there. For that matter, neither are the first few residential streets just north of 29th, nor the original city hall complex and – sadly – the original library where I was inspired in grade school to become a voracious reader and writer.

All of this – all of what had anchored Midwest City's original mile – was razed in the early 2000s and replaced with a huge, sprawling, modern outdoor shopping mall called the Town Center Mall, which opened in 2005. What had been a hometown shopping center unique to this city was replaced with a sparkling new cookie-cutter corporate mall full of the latest franchise stores and restaurants found in cities coast to coast in America. It was all anchored by big-box stores like Lowes, Best Buy, and J.C. Penney.

Looking south through the "hangar" entrance to the Town Center Plaza.
(Photo by Jim Willis)

The new shopping district replacing Atkinson Plaza. Looking south through the entrance built to resemble an airplane hangar.

Now Midwest City has all the modern retail outlets at its disposal, but it has lost its unique hometown, commercial personality.

The city today faces some major challenges. A lot has changed in the Original Mile. While the Town Center Mall is seen by latecomers as a positive change, the residential neighborhoods have fallen victims to some 80 years of age, and many either need repair and/or updating. What was a relatively stable population has become more of a transient one in these older parts of town, and whereas all neighborhoods were filled with homeowners, today many are filled with renters. In fact, the 2023 U.S. Census updates show only 56 percent of the housing units in Midwest City are owner-occupied. The rest are rentals, and the median rent in 2023 for all sizes of homes and apartments was $1,150.

The former mostly white Midwest City has morphed into becoming a very diverse community, where whites-only now number only 61 percent of the population, while blacks-only are 23 percent. Hispanics/Latinos make up 11 percent of the profile, Native Americans are 2.6 percent, Asians are 1.5 percent, and those of two or more blended races are 10.6 percent. (2)

Although Mid-Del School District statistics show whites making up only 34.5 percent of the student population, that percentage may be lower than Midwest City's census percentage because of at least three reasons: First, 17 percent of the city's population is age 65 and over (3), whereas it was a much younger town in its first thirty years. So, a fewer percentage of households are occupied by school-age childrenSecond, private schools are becoming schools of choice for many white families nationwide. Third, the Mid-Del School District spreads beyond the limits of Midwest City, encompassing Del City and some adjacent areas on the north and east side of Midwest City.

The "OM" obelisk in the new town plaza, remembering the Original Mile.The town's siren tower is behind it.

(Photo by Jim Willis)much younger town in its first decade or two. So, a fewer percentage of households are occupied by school-age children.

Nevertheless, to pay homage to the former distinctiveness of the Original Mile, the city hall complex has been replaced with a small circular park with statuary proclaiming this was the "OM". And there is also a statue of the city's founder, W.P. Bill Atkinson. And next to him? His Shetland pony, of course.

As for the city's Mid-Del School District, it has grown to include three high schools (Midwest City, Del City, and Carl Albert), and 18 elementary and middle schools, all with a total 12,436 students, with a student-teacher ratio of 16-1. The district's revenue is $133,507,000 (of which 9.1 percent still comes from federal aid), and its graduation rate is 91.6 percent.

The most obvious difference, seen in walking onto any of the campuses, is demographic diversity. This is no longer a monochrome community with whites-only schools. The district's minority enrollment now outnumbers its white enrollment, a dramatic turnaround from the years I spent in schools there in the 1950s and 1960s. As the district reported to the *U.S. News and World Report Educational Survey* in 2022, the student body was 34.5 percent white, 30.4 percent black, 16.3 percent Latino, 1 percent Asian or Pacific Islander, 3.5 percent American Indian or Alaska Native, .4 percent native Hawaiian. A total of 13.9 percent are listed as two or more races. (4)

As for Tinker Air Force Base, it has continued to thrive through the ups and downs of past years and has adjusted to the needs of the country's defense mission and of the Air Force itself. Tinker now employs more than 26,000 military and civilian workers and is the largest single-site employer in Oklahoma. It has an annual statewide economic impact of $3.51 billion, creating an estimated 33,000 secondary jobs. Tinker owns 4,048 acres, leases 810 acres and has 642 acres of easements. The total number of buildings is 458. (5)

In 2011 the Air Force announced it would restructure Air Force Materiel Command from its 12-center configuration to a new five-center model. When this took place, Tinker became the host site for the Air Force Sustainment Center (AFSC), which provides "war-winning expeditionary capabilities to the warfighter through world-class depot maintenance, supply chain management and installation support." (6) The AFSC brought together the oversight of the aircraft maintenance missions at Tinker's Oklahoma City Air Logistic Complex, Warner Robins ALC at Robins AFB, and Ogden ALC at Hill AFB. Tinker was also given responsibility for supply chain management wings here and at Scott AFB.

Tinker's largest organizational unit is the Oklahoma City Air Logistics Complex, which is the biggest of three air depot repair complexes in the Air Force Materiel Command. The Air Force explains, "It provides depot maintenance on the C/KC-135, B-1B and E-3 aircraft, expanded phase maintenance on the Navy E-6 aircraft, and maintenance, repair and overhaul of F100, F101, F108, F110, F118, F119, and TF33 engines for the Air Force, Air Force Reserve, Air National Guard, Navy and foreign military sales."

More than 10,300 military and civilian employees work at the OC-ALC, as per Tinker's main website. The complex is headquartered in the historic Building 3001, which covers 62 acres and stretches for three-fourths of a mile. Inside this building, employees work on maintaining aircraft, engines, components, and accessories and carry out the administration of all these duties. (7)

The 72nd Air Base Wing provides base installation and support services for the headquarters, Air Force Sustainment Center, the Oklahoma City Air Logistics Complex, and 45 associate units assigned to six major commands, including the largest flying wing in Air Combat Command, the Navy's Strategic Communications Wing One, and several defense agencies. More than 1,600 personnel and 1,343 contractors work within the 72nd Air Base Wing. Tinker is also home to eight major Department of Defense, Air Force and Navy activities with critical national defense missions.

Tinker has also been extremely helpful to Midwest City and other towns adjacent to it like Del City and Moore during times of severe weather and ubiquitous tornados that touch down so frequently in the area. In 2013, for example, a massive tornado struck the area just south of Tinker in the city of Moore, costing 23 lives and the loss or heavy damage of thousands of homes. Tinker AFB personnel swung into action and assisted residents of Moore in rescue, recovery, and cleanup, just as they had done in the 1995 F5 twister that struck Moore, Tinker itself, and the east side of Midwest City. More about that storm in a moment. In fact, Tinker has had a history of helping storm victims since April tornadoes in 1943 and 1947 ripped apart adjacent areas and towns.

The base itself was hit with a devastating tornado on March 20, 1948, and then again five days later. Several military and civilian workers were injured in those storms that together caused $16 million in damage to aircraft and buildings. A total of 85 airplanes were damaged beyond repair and another 99 were damaged. Tinker developed a plan from that point on to get as many airplanes into the air as possible when imminent tornados were forecast.

Although tornado warnings are routine spring and summer occurrences for the Midwest City and Tinker areas, the region is well-served with sophisticated early warning systems, thanks to the presence of the National Weather Service's Severe Storm Center in nearby Norman and to the 72nd Operations Support Squadron Weather Flight at Tinker. At that unit, base weather forecasters assess the atmosphere and keep in touch with the National Weather Service and local media and storm chaser reports to determine when the storm alarms should sound for Tinker and Midwest City. (8)

I had kept track of a lot of these developments in Midwest City and Tinker in my years living elsewhere around the country. I knew of the threats that the Base Closure and Realignment Commission had posed for the livelihood of my hometown, and I was glad to see Midwest City and Oklahoma City come together to help save the air base. I couldn't imagine Midwest City without it.

I was also pleased when I heard of a new community college being established in town. The year was 1970 when Oscar Rose Junior College (now Rose State College) opened its doors. As a career academic, I know the added value that a college can bring to a town.

The welcome addition of Rose State has turned Midwest City into a college town.
(Photo by Rose State College Foundation)

This school was aptly named for the man who built and supervised the Midwest City school system for so many years, and its mission was to provide higher education to the community and surrounding area. This new college began with only a handful of students and one building. Since then, however, Rose State has welcomed more than 270,000 students from 66 Oklahoma counties, 34 states, and 25 countries. Its attractive and sprawling campus, located on the north side of Midwest City's Original Mile between Air Depot and Sooner Road, has grown to 22 buildings, and the college has awarded more than 23,000 degrees. Today it welcomes more than 13,000 students and patrons each year to campus, according to its website. (7) Among those are nearly 8,000 traditional students.

Additionally, Rose State offers many continuing education courses to area adult residents and showcases many live stage products and performing arts entertainers each year.

The creation and development of this college has produced probably the single most significant change for Midwest City. It has turned the former prairie town, built to service Tinker Air Force Base, into a college town. It has added higher education and continuing education for adults to the cultural and economic profiles of Midwest City, Oklahoma. It is fittingly named for the founder of the city's educational system.

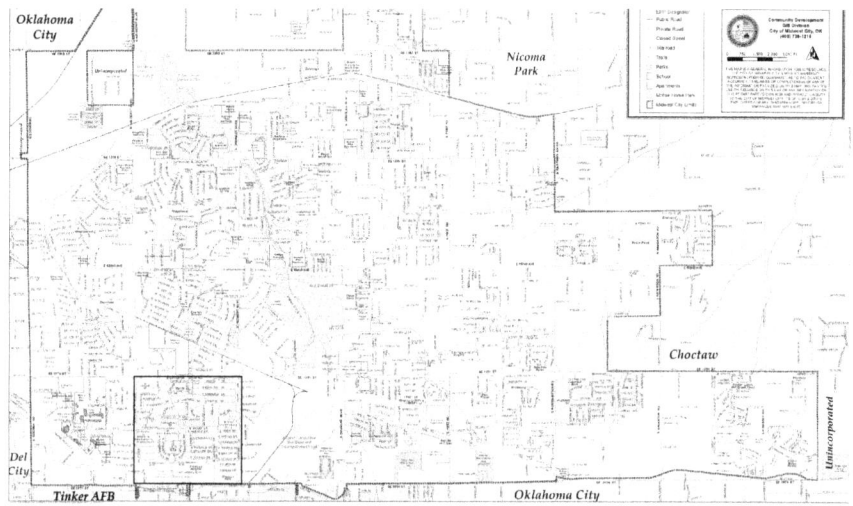

The map of Midwest City as of 2018. The "Original Mile" is in the lower left boxed section north of Southeast 29th Street. Tinker AFB is across that street to the south.

Map by Community Development Division, Midwest City

13

Bittersweet Homecomings

*Fair
winds
and
following
seas*

I enjoyed coming home to see my family, but I had lost track of most of my high school friends along the way, so a big part of the life I knew then was missing, and that was sad. There were other reasons for the bittersweet feelings I had with my homecomings, and some are summed up by a writer Erica Allaby who, in 2018, published a provocative essay on *"The 3 Stages of Returning to Your Hometown."* When I read it, I realized

I now have been through all those stages. I realize I left a great place to go find what I'm made of, maybe to find it in even a better place.

Allaby writes, in part:

The first time you return home, you feel trapped and confined to the bubble that you had once managed to break out of. Nothing has changed...except for you. All the feelings that had long since been buried make their way to the surface again ... Did you just dream up all of the progress you made? You count down the minutes until the next jail break.

The second time you return home, you are more confident in your transformation. You feel out of place in the only place you used to feel at home, as if everyone in the town has moved on without you. ... You look at things that once blended into the background differently ... You get past high school stereotypes. You realize that people change.

The third time you return home, you find the old comfort of driving on familiar streets. You learn to accept to breathe in the new details of an old place. Sweet little things remind you of your past but don't transport your heart there. You realize that people don't change.

Hometowns are where it all began. Where the best and the worst of your childhood happened. Where you loved and you learned. Where you realized that it sometimes takes leaving something great to find something better. Your hometown is your living history. (1)

Of all the times I've gone home, four stand out as most impactful, and one of them was life-changing and forced me to see my home state and its people in a deeper, passionate light.

It was this homecoming that came first.

The earth shakes

I was visiting my parents in March 1995, taking a leave of absence from my teaching post at Boston College for the spring and trying to put the wheels back on my life's *Radio Flyer* wagon of emotions. I had just lost my wife of 15 years to divorce, and this shattering experience had left that wagon in pieces, scattered across a thousand miles of grieving. I was searching for a way to forget. Or at least to deal with the pain.

I was questioning who I was and where to go from there. I felt the need to *re-center* myself, reconnect with my past, parents and sister. Home was where it all started, so home was obviously the place to do all that. Then, on Wednesday morning, April 19, 1995, my personal pain collided with a far greater collective pain that emerged from the dust, debris, and devastation that was the bombing of the Alfred P. Mur-

Suddenly, I was a reporter again.

rah Federal Building in downtown Oklahoma City, about 10 miles from my Midwest City home.

Hearing a distant, undefinable sound from a diner where I was eating breakfast, I didn't realize at first how this event would affect me personally. By the end of the day, that reality was streaming in like a door to a dark room opens slowly, in this case, it filled it with sadness.

It was the start of a time of deep grieving for everyone in Oklahoma, but especially for those in the Oklahoma City area. A total of 168 people, ranging from 3 months old to 73 years old, were killed in this bombing, and more than 650 were injured. An estimated 646 people were in the federal building when the bomb went off. Five of the dead were outside the building and even in adjacent buildings.

Thirteen of the dead were from Midwest City (2), four of whom graduated from Midwest City High School and two of them were stationed with the Air force at Tinker. Of the 19 children who died in the Murrah Building (17 of them in the America's Kids Day Care Center), three of them were from Midwest City, and all were infants and toddlers ranging from 6 months to 16 months.

The bomb gutted all nine floors of the Murrah Building, which was imploded three weeks
later after search-and-rescue crews found and removed the dead and injured.
Photo by Jim Willis

One of the victims who typified the heroism displayed at the
bombing g site was a Midwest City woman killed trying to help others
get out of the collapsed Murrah Building. She was Rebecca Needham
Anderson, a nurse who saw the breaking news bulleting on TV in her
home and drove immediately to the bomb site, 10 miles east, to help
rescue victims. She was especially concerned for the children who were
trapped in the day care nursery, located on the building's second floor.

Arriving at the site and identifying herself as a nurse to the police,
she rushed into the building's remains and began digging through its
rubble, pulling out victim after victim, taking each outside to safety,
and returning for more. On one of her return trips into the building, a
slab of debris fell from the jagged edge of a hole above her head in the
ceiling. The piece hit her in the back of the head, but she managed to
stagger outside to tell her fellow first responders she had been hit.

Refusing to take a moment to rest, she turned and went back into
the building to rescue more victims, but she collapsed from a sudden
seizure. A fellow rescuer saw her fall, picked her up and carried her out
where she was rushed to the hospital. There she regained consciousness
two times. Her husband was at her side, and she told him when she

awoke the second time that she had no memory of what had happened. She then blacked out again, this time for the last time. She was pronounced dead four days later April 23. She was 37 years old.

Skip Fernandez and his trained Golden retriever Aspen rest just moments after their shift on the Murrah Building rubble pile where they searched for signs of life and pulled bodies of bombing victims buried beneath the debris.. (Photo by Jim Willis)

Even though Anderson did not die in the blast *itself,* she was nevertheless listed as the 168th and final victim of the bombing. She was honored posthumously with several awards for heroism, and a *Time Life*

Special Edition of the bombing referred to Rebecca Anderson as the "Fallen Angel of Mercy." (3)

The two Airmen 1st Class females from Tinker, Lakesha Richardson Levy, 21, and Cartney McRaven, 19, were typical of many of the fatal victims who were in the building taking care of personal business. Levy was there to get a new Social Security card, while McRaven was there to have her name changed on her card.

The most famous face of all the bombing victims was that of 1-year-old Baylee Almon, whose family lived on the eastern edge of Midwest City in the Choctaw area. Young Baylee was one of the children killed in the America's Kids Day Care Center, on the second floor of the Murrah Building. The iconic photo of her being carried away by Oklahoma City Fire Capt. Chris Fields from the building, with her head bloodied and life already drained away, was featured in the news media around the world.

Shot by amateur photographer Charles Porter IV on his lunch break, who submitted his photo to the Associated Press, became the worldwide face of the Oklahoma City tragedy. The next year it won the 1996 Pulitzer Prize in spot photography. As was the case with so many other families of victims, as well as first-responders themselves, life would never be the same for Baylee's surviving family and for fireman Fields again who struggled with emotions of that day for years, while rising to the fire department rank of Major and getting some good professional counseling along the way. (4)

One of the Midwest Cityans who saw first-hand the lifesaving work at downtown hospitals on April 19 was Carol Bolding Sykes, a graduate of MCHS and the University of Central Oklahoma. A registered nurse in Oklahoma City at the time of the bombing, Sykes recalled, "I was on duty at Integris Southwest Medical Center. I had a patient in the room at the end of the hall nearest to the bombing site. She had a miscarriage and then a D&C. She was bleeding too much, and I went to call her doctor at the desk which is in the center building. After I talked to the doctor, I went back to check her, and her husband told me they felt the building shake and it was on TV that a bomb had gone off downtown.

"I hadn't felt anything at the desk. My patient's blood pressure dropped some more and bleeding somewhat increased. I knew she needed a D&C. I went to call her doctor and couldn't get through. All their phones were not working. I called his office and told them what was going on and so they could get the doctor to come in if he called them. Meanwhile I looked for any of our doctors, but none were there. Finally, one came up because he had a patient in labor. He prepared to take my patient to surgery. A few minutes later her doctor came rushing in. We got her to surgery, and she did fine." (5)

As it routinely does, when surrounding cities need emergency help, Tinker assigned personnel from across the base to provide search and rescue efforts at the bombing site and helped in other ways. Units pitching in were the 552nd Control Wing, Tinker Fire and Emergency Services, the 38th Engineering Installation Wing, the Navy, and the then-Oklahoma City Air Logistics Center. One of the many at Tinker volunteering his service was Air National Guardsman Ronald Brazer, who was a training manager with the 137th Security Forces Squadron.

Shortly after the bomb went off, Brazer reported to the site to help by transporting first responders to and from ground zero on a 48-passenger bus and helped in securing the perimeter of the bomb site. "When the explosion happened, it reverberated even though we were like 16 miles from ground zero," Brazer said. "Because we were at the [Will Rogers World] airport, we actually all were thinking that an airplane must have crashed at the airfield because that was the strength of the shockwave." (6)

Yet another connection that Tinker had with the bombing tragedy was that it served as the makeshift federal courtroom (in Building 460) to which Timothy McVeigh, then the suspected bomber and later convicted of it, was brought for arraignment the day after he was captured. That arraignment would have happened in the Murrah Federal Building but, because he had blown it up, Tinker served in its place as the only other federal installation nearby.

"It was interesting to see his demeanor," said Henderson Ray, a sheet metal mechanic at Tinker and an Oklahoma County reserve deputy who was one of the first responders and who was on base when McVeigh was brought in for arraignment. "Tinker is and was part of the Oklahoma City community," Ray said. "It's unique in the way that Tinker has developed within the community and the amount of investment that the community has in Tinker. But this event showed that Tinker did and does step up for the community." (7)

As I would later reflect on this day, I had been in the news business for three decades and had seen many faces of tragedy during that time. There was the sweet innocence of a 5-year-old girl who was killed by a falling beam as she sat in church one Sunday morning in Garland, Texas. Ten years later, in Boston, Charles Stuart turned a gun on his pregnant wife in his car, moments after emerging from a class on childbirth. Blaming it first on a black attacker, Stuart later took his own life after Stuart's brother Matthew told police it was Charles himself who had been the shooter. Charles Stuart's plan was to get the life insurance payout from his wife Carol's death. (8)

Then, just a few weeks before this morning's encounter, there was the tragedy of four children and their teacher gunned down in a Jonesboro, Arkansas middle school. In between, there have been so many other stories of pain that they have faded, for me, into a collective blur over the years. All except the Oklahoma City bombing.

As a journalist who transitioned into teaching college students to become future reporters and editors, I have trained myself to put distance between me and the pain of others. I have coached my students to do the same. Remember what you are, I say. Do your job first. Remain objective. Yes, there are times when that pain invades you personally. But it usually in the quiet, reflective moments after the tragedy – if, in fact, there is time for such moments.

Always, though, there are the exceptions. Thankfully, for me, Oklahoma City was that exception in the spring of 1995. It may sound macabre to say I found a renewed energy and life force in the midst of such a tragedy. But I did. I needed a way to express my own pain, and I found it in joining with others who were grieving over something much more painful. What a privilege it was to have the chance to articulate their pain. What a catharsis it was to be able to release my own in the process.

I will always be grateful to the *Edmond Evening Sun* – the newspaper at which I began my career many years covering the aftermath of that bombing. That northern suburb of Oklahoma City lost 26 residents in the bombing. In my journalist's role, I was able to search for an provide answers to questions about the bombing, who were killed and injured, and how the recovery was going. It is safe to say that everyone in the state was wondering about all of this, and many would find they had a legitimate reason for it when they discovered someone they knew – possibly loved – was a victim in that explosion.

Reporting on this tragedy began to distract me from my own personal loss of my wife, and I knew I was in a community of other grievers who were hurting. As I told their own stories of grief and recovery, I was also telling my own. I fell in love with the people of Oklahoma again, after so many years of trying to put distance between me and the state. I would stay on for a couple of months to write about the aftermath, then decided to move on with my life and career elsewhere. But that going-home experience helped considerably in putting me on a personal path to healing, even as I mourned the loss of fellow Sooners.

Over the years since the bombing, I have spoken to many groups, both in the United States and in Europe, about covering this tragedy. Always the thought is within me that I grew personally and learned how to move beyond my personal grief as I watched survivors and families of the victims do the same.

On a professional level, I had been confronting burnout with this business of journalism going into Oklahoma City three years ago. I wondered if there was any real reason for us journalists to go around exposing the pain, problems, and perils of others. At the end of my first day of bombing coverage, I found a new meaning to journalism. I am sure the same has happened to reporters covering such tragedies as the assassinations of John F. Kennedy and Martin Luther King. Such journalism puts all humanity on the same page in the hymnal of brotherhood, understanding, and support.

Such journalism is washed clean of the manipulation and sensationalism of pseudo-news and trash reporting. Such journalism deals openly with the gut questions that friends and families of the dead and suffering are desperately seeking answers to: What happened? Why? And what can I learn from it?

Most of these questions are beyond the purview of journalism. The answers – or at least some clues – are found in discussions with loved ones, or in reading thoughts of those writers gifted at expressing consoling thoughts. But journalism can help. It can open the doors to the mind and heart as it shows all of us, we are not alone in our grief. It can show us there are others who can help. And it can make even the most objective of us feel the emotions that make us real people.

That was certainly my experience. This was a visit to my hometown to recenter myself after my own personal tragedy; a chance to be close with a family who loved me and to roam around familiar surroundings. I figured all of that could help me deal with my pain, and it did. But what neither I nor anyone else had envisioned was the Oklahoma City bombing.and it was this event and the coming-together of other fellow Sooners that put my own pain in perspective and gave me a renewed purpose in life at a point when I was considering leaving my profession entirely.

Weary workers in a building adjacent to the Federal Building pause to
absorb the blown-out Murrah Building across the street in Oklahoma
City..
Photo by Jim Willis

Standing near the site of the razed federal building, with all ten
fingers laced through the chain-link fence still separating mourners
from the insanity of that bombing, with my eye fixed on the hallowed
ground before me, and with the vivid memory of what that killing
ground looked like three years ago, the feelings of love and pride for
my hometown and state returned.

I no longer wanted to put distance between myself and Oklahoma
as I once did as a younger man. This is my state; these are my people.

I knew that in feeling for them and helping to articulate their grief, I was becoming whole again.

The twister

Four years later, in May 1999, I made another significant visit home and, once again, found myself thrust into the role of reporter when I encountered the most devastating tornado Midwest City – if not the entire state of Oklahoma – has ever recorded. It happened on the evening that I was home to receive an honor that I would have never dreamed of receiving as a struggling high school student back in the 1960s. I would write about that night years later in 2023 on a writers' site called *Retrospect*. This is what I said: (9)

Two signal events provided the drama in my hometown on Monday night, May 3, 1999. One was an awards ceremony at Midwest City High School were six of us alums were being honored as new inductees on the school's Wall of Fame.

The other was the tornado.

The first ceremony would have been one to remember — if it had actually occurred. But it did not; it was blown away by this other event: the one that still raises goosebumps when I recall it. Left in the wake of this massive twister was a city devoid of electrical power but loaded lot of shaken residents and a lot of storm debris. Some of it landed very close to where the 300 of us were huddled at good ole MCHS.

Although located in the center of a geographical strip known as Tornado Alley, Midwest City had not suffered a seriously damaging tornado in 50 years until this night. Although we were often visited fleetingly by twisters touching down, none had done the widespread damage that tonight's would.

For those of us gathered at Midwest City High School, the school's jazz band was just finding its groove, old friends were embracing, and the fun was just beginning when Principal Rick Bachman took to the lectern in the cafeteria. His calm voice belied his concern when he made what seemed a strange announcement.

Bachman walked to the podium and said something close to, "Our great band reminds us of the music played by the ensemble aboard the Titanic, but we don't want to be like the passengers on that ship, so let's quietly and orderly leave this building and walk over to the fieldhouse."

At table after table, smiles dissolved into quizzical looks. Bachman went on. "We have just received word that a fierce tornado has been spotted near the city's southwest corner. It's moving our way so, just to be safe, let's move on over to the fieldhouse."

That athletic structure was located less that 100 yards south of the main school building, and most of us did exactly as Bachman asked. A few decided to risk it by going home and riding it out there. As we walked, I chatted with Mom and Dad about how this wasn't a total surprise. "This must be that same twister that started up down in Chickasha an hour ago, and was headed north," I said. "Remember how the weatherman said it was one of the biggest the state has seen? But Chickasha is about 35 miles south of here." Dad replied, "Right. Tornados usually stay on the ground only a few minutes at any one time. How could that funnel still be touching ground an hour later?"

In this case, it did. This was the same funnel.

Inside the fieldhouse, some guests mingled in the hallways; others took seats. A few moments later, the court was lit up with overhead lights, and a hundred or so spilled out into it. Some students found a basketball and began shooting hoops.

"This is pretty eerie," one teacher said. "It's like we're in a bomb shelter waiting for the blast." Many huddled around a television featuring a live account and video of the approaching tornado. Midwest City and the adjacent Tinker Air Force Base were in its sights.

"Oh my God," uttered one parent who had shown up to see a friend's daughter honored. The sentiment was repeated several times as you passed through the huddled masses.

"Fifty years and no real tornados; now this," another woman whispered to her husband.

My sister C.J., who came to see me be inducted in the ceremony, appeared in the locker room with a chunk of hail the size of a softball. "Just for your information," she said, "this is what it's doing outside."

At that moment, the television blurted out the news. "Residents of Midwest

City should take cover immediately! This tornado is headed straight for your downtown area."

Hearts sank. Out on the basketball court, school officials made the announcement. "Everyone must leave the court and move to the hallways or underground locker rooms. The twister will be here in a couple minutes."

There was no panic among the group. Only the dread of what was coming. You don't grow up in Oklahoma without getting used to this dance every spring. Nevertheless, we knew it was serious this time. Some embraced loved ones; others held hands; some prayed, and many just waited and stared upwards to ground level.

"Midwest City, take cover! Tinker Field, take cover!" the radio warned again. We listened from the locker room as the storm winds howled above us. We waited for what seemed the inevitable, and I drew a map in my head of where we were in relation to the funnel. I realized my parents' home was between us and the twister. I was glad they were with me at the school because their home would be hit before the monster swept over us.

Our eyes were glued to the TV, watching the tornado approach us, creating electric sparks, pops, and flashes as it took down power transformers on telephone pools in its track toward Midwest City. Then suddenly, the TV screen went dark and, a second later, the locker room was plunged into blackness, too. The storm had taken out the power lines. A couple people had transistor radios and turned them on.

Over those radios came another message.

"Wait a minute," the reporter said, "the funnel seems to be making a slight left turn, going north toward Oklahoma City. It is missing most of Tinker." In the darkness, hearts were buoyed. "It now seems headed north, up the west side of Midwest City between Air Depot and Sooner Road," the radio voice continued. If that was true, it would miss us at the high school by at least a couple blocks.

"Pray for Del City," one voice said in the dark, referencing the adjacent town to the west that began at Sooner Road.

Although the twister would miss our street, it did wind up venting its fury on Midwest City's west side, as well as Del City. As word of the storm's new path filtered through the crowd, a new worry began. A strong odor of natural gas began to fill the field house so, once again, we were all evacuated to the main school building. But once outside, the early evening May sun shone again, the air was still, and the feeling of relief spread through the crowd as the danger seemed over for us. Most headed not back to the school but to their cars for a drive home to see if it was still there and, if so, what damages it had sustained.

Once I knew my parents' home on Lockheed Drive was unscathed, I turned my car toward Oklahoma City and the building housing the city's newspaper, *The Oklahoman.* "Here I go again," I remember thinking," I come home for one reason, all hell breaks loose, and I wind up being a reporter again."

When I got to the newspaper office, I looked for my old editor friends Joe Hight and Ed Kelley and told them I'd just been with a group that had escaped the twister in Midwest City. "Start writing," Joe said. "Just find an empty workstation in the newsroom and pound out a story for us."

Later that evening, in an afterthought I suppose Ed Kelley had been pondering, he came over to me and said, "Jim, it's always good to see you. But the last time I saw you in town was when McVeigh blew up the federal building." Then, with a wink, he added, "Would you mind waiting awhile before you come home again? Disasters seem to come along with you!"

My drive back to Midwest City late that night took me through the city's traffic-congested west side covered with downed power lines, especially along Air Depot. Many residents and businesses had lost power across most of the city and had limited or no phone service. Debris, probably blown from the west and the funnel track, littered the city's west side. Street signs and billboards were twisted into pretzels. Many cars were showing the hailstone damage, and at least three cars had been blown across I-35 from the Hudiburg Chevrolet dealership into the swimming pool of the La Quinta hotel on the other side of the highway we called the Tinker Diagonal.

The next day we all realized how lucky we had been at that high school ceremony. The twister was officially labeled the Bridge Creek/

Moore Tornado, measured as an F5 tornado, the most powerful grade a twister is given by the National Weather Service. In fact, meteorologists said it registered the highest wind speeds ever measured globally, with winds recorded at 301 mph. It was the strongest tornado ever recorded in the Oklahoma City metro area. It had covered a path of 38 miles from its point of touchdown, staying on the ground for 85 minutes. That, in itself, was record-breaking.

The death toll from the tornado was 41, with many others injured. More than 8,000 area homes were destroyed, as was much of the city of Moore located just south of Midwest City, and loss damages topped $1 billion. Even so, it could have been worse, had it not been for the sophisticated tornado spotting and tracking system developed by world-class meteorologists and storm chasers from the National Severe Weather Center in nearby Norman and by the same kind of weather sophistication exhibited by units at Tinker Air Force Base.

In fact, it was the first storm to ever use the tornado emergency tracking system of the National Weather Service. In short, this was one of those homecomings I will never forget. That I'd had two such momentous ones in a four-year period still seems unbelievable. I headed back to my home in Tennessee a few days later. Oh, and that ceremony I had come home for? I received my gold watch in the mail a week later, back in Memphis. That was fine with me.

Dad says goodbye ...

Two other hard-hitting homecomings. came later, separated by seven years, but they both produced the same heavy sadness, for the same reasons. I was teaching at Azusa Pacific University in Southern California when I got a call on an October day in 2006..

Ltjg. W.J. Willis

"Dad just passed away, Jim," she said solemnly and with a catch in her throat. My heart seemed to stop for a few seconds, as life around me on campus that day dialed down into slow motion. The man who brought me and our family to Midwest City back in 1949 was suddenly gone, a couple weeks after his 97th birthday. I called my wife Anne, who was teaching at another university, and we began planning to fly to Oklahoma for Dad's funeral, to be held a few days later.

I spent much of the rest of that day in reflection, remembering some fond moments with Dad as a child. He would take me with him on Saturday mornings to Sears where he would inspect table saws and eventually buy one to remodel our home, often asking me to help. Afterwards we would do regular hamburger lunches together at John Kerlin's diner at 15th and Midwest Boulevard, sitting at the counter on those round spinning bar stools as Dad and John chatted away while the latter flipped hamburgers on his open grill.

Other memories flooded in. There were the family camping trips, one to Pike's Peak, Colorado, when Dad would grow so frustrated wrapped in yard of the canvas umbrella tent whose main pole refused to extend upwards without a fight.

Then there was the moment I was so proud of Dad for buying that new ice cream cone for a little kid he didn't know who had just spilled his on the hot summer pavement at the Dairy Queen in Midwest City.

Dad and I didn't have the deepest conversations or verbally express our feelings of love too much until his final years. Now, suddenly, I regretted that. I was glad I was able to be with him just 12 days before his passing, on his birthday.

Dad had made his professional mark in Oklahoma by rising in management at the state's oldest and best television station, the legendary WKY-TV (now KFOR). He became the president of the Oklahoma City Advertising Club, director of public relations for the city's first United Way drive and retired at 65 to become a well-known oil and pastel artist in the state, winning some 250 awards and co-founding the Artisans 9 art galleries, spread across Oklahoma City and Norman shopping malls.

More than that, however, he had made his mark on me. As I was growing up, he was my first editor when I would bring him my childhood stories. I got into journalism because of him. Dad's was a good and lasting mark, and I still talk to his spirit in private, asking his advice and – at times – going to him in grief or in times when I feel in need of forgiveness for mistakes I've made. I signed on to Naval officers training because that's what he had done in his younger years. I realized I've become a lot like him in many ways, and I understood him now better than I ever did before.

... and then Mom

The fourth sad homecoming came seven years later when Anne and I were still in California, and my sister called again, this time to tell me our mom had passed away.

She was 103, three weeks away from 104 – and we believe she was the oldest living woman in Midwest City at the time. C.J. and I have joked since that we always knew Mom was stubborn; we Just didn't know she was that stubborn! As I had done with Dad, I spent time reflecting on

Mom in her Washington D.C. days where she met Dad.

what this woman – whom I considered a pioneer in many ways – had meant in my life, and how her persistence and determination had flowed into me and imbued me with the ability to see my way tough challenges in life. This strong woman who had followed her husband to a state removed only a few years from the Dust Bowl Era,

giving up the somewhat privileged life she'd had in Pennsylvania, was now gone from our lives. I hoped I could continue to feel her presence as I had with Dad. No problem, I've discovered in the years since; she was too dominant an influence in my life, and I still feel her spirit close by. In my memory, I will always see her most clearly as that 40-something entrepreneur who began and ran Midwest

City's first curricular-driven preschool, Jack & Jill that serviced so many young Midwest City families. It was the first rung on what would be my own tall ladder of education.

After her funeral had ended, three Midwest Cityans in their late 60s came up to me to say they had been Mom's students, and a couple still had their old Jack & Jill pink or blue scrapbooks. So, the folks are gone but I still go home to see C.J., and we reminisce a lot about Mom and Dad and our life at 301 E. Lockheed Drive. I usually go by the Arlington Memorial Gardens, where both are buried in the same grave, to talk to them and try to feel their closeness. Occasionally, I get to see my cousins Sarah Hannah and Bill Willis, and I always wish my cousin Bob, Bill's younger brother, were still alive to see. We became close friends in our adult years.

But I also go back to see former classmates with whom I've re-established contact over the years and to meet some I didn't know well in school but who I now do. Among them are Jane Vickers Bogan, Chaniece Kennedy, Bob Osmond, Marty Thompson, Mary Kay Haven, Mike Pickens, and Kay Hughes, who lived right across Lockheed Drive from me in our growing-up years. Many others, like Mike Maddox, Ralph Lantz, Steve Vargo, Mary Clem Good Morris, Barbara Sessions, Garnett Haubelt, Ken Brust, and Jim McKee, I've stayed in touch with over Facebook but have not been able to see since most – like me – have moved away from Midwest City.

Roger Brady has become a good friend over the years and, although he lives in North Carolina, he has graciously come to California several times to guest-lecture at my university and hosted Anne and me in his and Litha's Raleigh home.

I recently met up with Dr. Steve Vargo who, like me, became an academic and who is now an endowed professor of marketing at the University of Oklahoma. Jane Vickers Bogan and her husband Joe live in Norman and have become good friends, and my wife and I always visit with them in their Norman home when we come to Oklahoma. And then, of course, there is the lure of OU football in the fall, and I've made the long drive from Kentucky twice in recent years to watch the Sooners play.

In sum, when I think back on my years with my family and friends in Midwest City – especially between 1949 and 1968 -- I realize we all learned a lot about ourselves and life from that town and from the presence of Tinker Air Force Base. Does that mean we all came out of this town with similar worldviews, political ideologies, and opinions on how to change the world, or who we should elect to do it? Of course not. Midwest City was the place we started from, but many of us *grew in different directions* whether we left town or stayed put.

Still, I like to think we all retained some very good, positive values. If so, it came partly from living in a *town* with traditional values. But it was also one in which – because of Tinker -- families were coming and going from and to different parts of the country and world.

Whatever individual worldviews we have come to embrace, I think we've all realized over the years we will always have the shared of Midwest City to keep us friendly with each other. As an example of this, when one former Midwest Cityan posted on one of the several Midwest City Facebook Pages that are currently active, she asked if she could hear from others who lived in the city's "Original Mile." She got 87 responses within 24 hours. Two of them were the following:

"I grew up at 195 E. Fairchild and my husband grew up on Lockheed. We now live at 206 E. Fairchild. I have lived on this street most of my life, and I love being here. A lot of people have come and gone, but's still home. I went to Eastside, Jarman, and I'm proud to be a Bomber."

And this one:

"I lived at 1316 Givens Drive and spent my whole childhood here. Eastside, Jarman, MCHS, all over that original mile. We walked it, rode it, lived it, and loved it."

These are just two of the many former Midwest Cityans who like staying in touch with each other and reminiscing about their youthful adventures there. How many of them do it? Well, the *Midwest City High School History Center* Page alone has 2,300 members, while the *Midwest City Oklahoma History and Memories* Page has 10,100, and the Friends of Midwest City Page has 9,500. Another 5,400 are members of the *Midwest City Bomber Alumni Memorial Page*, and the *Midwest City Memories Page* has 3,600 members. Even the page belonging to my own 1964 MCHS Class Page has 181 members, or one-third of all of us who walked commencement 60 years ago.

Many still get together at least twice a year for fall and spring lunches, usually at the decades-old Pelicans Restaurant on Air Depot, just north of Reno.

Writing this book has caused me to spend a lot of time examining the question of how much of Jim Willis was shaped and molded by this adopted hometown of Midwest City. The answer is a lot. I've grown in my appreciation of a town I used to take for granted, knowing it was a fine launching pad. I think most of us who grew up there have given something of ourselves back to the community and its people. Who knows: maybe we've left our mark on it, just as the city and Tinker have left their mark on us?

Besides the wanderlust that I've discussed before, a commitment to traditional values and a penchant toward trying to see the best in people were instilled here. Ironically, the monochrome Midwest City had also been my launching pad into the celebration of diversity as I went to college, where I discovered a multicultural world and realized I'd been living in a racial bubble, safe and friendly though it was. Later, in my adult years, I became a father to two Asian sons and the grandfather to three grandchildren who identify primarily as black.

As I've said more than once, there was the inspiration that the town's *library* gave me to become a career writer and that my schools gave me to become an educator.

I've even wondered what effect those *Shetland ponies* have had on my life since Midwest City. Well, they turned me into a lover of horses and, over the years, I've shared my life with four of them in Oklahoma, Texas, Missouri, and Tennessee.

Now, all these decades later, I have a chance to give something tangible back to Midwest City by sharing this personal history of the blended civilian/military community of *Tinkertown* that has formed the characters and career aspirations

for so many of us who grew up there. Perhaps longtime Midwest City resident Cindy Jo Lopez, captured the magic many felt in the first couple decades of the town when she wrote this:

Cindy and Buddy
Courtesy of Cindy

"I lived at 426 Ercoupe. Looking west, there was nothing but pasture and trees at the end of our street, with horses and cows ... My dog Buddy was wanting to go down there and chase every living thing. He knew the boundaries of our yard, but if we let him get just over it, he was gone. He became deaf once he stepped over the line! I would catch crawdads, lizards, see snakes, and rabbits, horned toads, turtles, and feed the cows and horses. Midwest City was a wonderful place to grow up!" (17)

I agree.

Appendix: Chronology of Selected Key Events

October 16, 1940

A dozen civic leaders in Oklahoma City meet to create the Industries Foundation so the Chamber of Commerce can purchase land and facilities for a rumored military aircraft factory. Two months later, the foundation decides to seek an air depot for the Oklahoma City area.

December 7, 1941

Japan attacks Pearl Harbor, and America goes to war.

April 8, 1941

The WarDepartment announces the new air materiel depot will be built in or near Oklahoma City. It will cost $14 million, cover 1,500 acres, and employ 3,500 people.

April 29, 1941

Oklahoma City voters pass a $982,000 bond issue to purchase land for the air depot.

May 21, 1941

The air depot is designated "Midwest Air Depot."

1941-1942

W.P. "Bill" Atkinson determines the depot's exact site and buys first 160+ acres of Oklahoma farmland about 10 miles southeast of downtown Oklahoma City; the genesis of Midwest City.

July 18, 1941

Construction starts on Midwest Air Depot. Formal groundbreaking ceremonies are 12 days later.

December 11, 1941

The U.S. Senate approves nearly $7 million more for construction of the Midwest Air Depot, increasing the total to just over $21 million.

January 15, 1942

Lt. Col. William Turnbull arrives in Oklahoma City and assumes command of the Midwest Air Depot.

January 23, 1942

The Army Air Forces awards the Douglas assembly plant to Oklahoma City. The plant, adjacent to the Midwest Air Depot, will employ 24,000 people, cost $20 million, and will build C-47 "Skytrain" cargo planes.

March 1, 1942

Midwest City Depot renamed Oklahoma City Air Depot.

April 1942

Atkinson builds first home in Midwest City at E. Turnbull and E. Boeing
within the "Original Mile."

June 7, 1942

Major General Clarence L. Tinker (of Pawhuska, Oklahoma,) killed in fighting near Wake Island.

October 14, 1942

Oklahoma City Air Depot is renamed Tinker Field.

March 11, 1943

Midwest City is incorporated

April 1943

Oscar Rose is hired by the Sooner School Board. (Sooner School District No. 52). Sooner School only goes to 8th grade. Students above 8th grade go to OKC Schools

June 1943

Oscar Rose hires J.E. Sutton as first principal of the new Midwest City High School

September 1, 1943

Midwest City School is organized and ready but without a building.

The Polio Epidemic delays the start of school, and prefabricated "hutments" are brought in from Dallas and put together by teachers, students, parents, custodians, and administrators.

September 20, 1943

School starts: 17 teachers and 413 students.

Enrollment jumps to more than 1,000 by end of year.

April 6, 1944

The new brick building for Midwest City Public School (later known as Jarman Junior High and Middle School) is completed.

June 2, 1944

14 Seniors graduated from First Class of MCHS led by Van Buren Appelman, Jr.

April 30, 1945

Airplane crashes just north of MCHS in field where Rose Field is now,

just missing the school. Students & teachers help with rescue efforts.

November 1, 1945

Oklahoma City Air Technical Service Command assumes command and jurisdiction of Building 3001, the former Douglas plant, on base.

February, 1946

B-29s, including the "Enola Gay," are prepared for atomic bomb tests on Bikini atoll.

July 15, 1946

OCAMA receives its first jet engine at Tinker. It is a J33-11 used for experimental work. Eight months later, jet engine overhauls begin at Tinker.

1947

The United States Army Air Corps is renamed the Air Force.

Nicholas "Nick" Harroz opens Nick's Brett Drive Grocery which later becomes the giant Crest Foods.

January 13, 1948

Tinker Air Depot is renamed Tinker Air Force Base

March 20, 1948

Tornado hits Tinker AFB causing $10 million in damages (50 planes damaged, 50 destroyed) and injuring 8 people.

March 25, 1948

At Tinker AFB, Meteorologists Major Ernest J. Fawbush and Captain Robert C. Miller correctly predict that atmospheric conditions are ripe for tornadoes in the vicinity of Tinker AFB and issue the historic first tornado warning.

March 25, 1948

The second tornado within five days hits Tinker AFB causing another $6 million in damages (84 planes damaged, 35 destroyed) with one personal injury and no deaths. Fawbush and Miller became instant heroes.

October 12-December 21, 1948

General Fred S. Borum and a team go to England to oversee the Berlin Airlift maintenance support. The team involves the Oklahoma City Air Materiel Area (OCAMA) personnel from Tinker who help to establish maintenance and overhaul procedures for aircraft used in the Berlin Airlift.

1950

The population of eight-year-old Midwest City tops 10,000.

1951

Midwest City is named America's Model City by the National Association of Home Builders

Fall of 1952

The ill-fated Glenwood Housing Addition is annexed into Midwest City.

1952-53

Construction begins on Atkinson's upscale Ridgecrest Country

Estates, north of Reno Avenue, and Shetland ponies are given to the first 100 homebuyers.

1953
Del City High School opens and will become the second of three public high schools in the Mid-Del School District.

January 1, 1953
OCAMA's production line becomes a 100 percent jet engine production line.

June 17, 1954
The Air Force accepts the first production model of the B-52 Bomber. Two mohts later, work begins on a 4,500-foot extension to the north/south runway in anticipation of B-52 management and modification.

November 10, 1955
First B-52 Stratofortress lands at Tinker Air Force Base

July 1, 1956
OCAMA becomes the B-52 and KC-135 support site. The Director of Suplies and Services becomes responsible for all supply management functions in support of the B-52 and KC-135.

October 24, 1957
C-119 Flying Boxcar crashes in the Holman Addition, killing four crew.

December 17, 1957
Air Materiel Command of the Air Force establishes OCAMA as a bomber-tanker command.

September 17, 1958
Douglas C-124 Globemaster II crashes a few miles short of the runway threshold. One crew member is killed and seven seriously injured.

1960
Population of Midwest City more than triples from 1950 to more than 36,000 residents.

August 25, 1961
F-100 Super Sabre fighter jet crashes on take off (1,800 gal. fuel)

into a Glenwood Subdivision house at 325 Ferguson Drive killing 2 sisters) and injuring several others. Fire sweeps the block, engulfing seven other houses.

The pilot parachutes to safety two blocks away.

October 6, 1962

Midwest Regional Hospital is Dedicated

November 8, 1962

W.P. "Bill" Atkinson, founder of Midwest City, loses the Oklahoma Governor's election to Henry Bellmon, the state's first Republican governor. A stinging and prolonged editorial campaign by E.K. Gaylord's Oklahoman and Times newspapers contribute to Atkinson's loss.

January 10, 1963

Carl Albert High School opens in eastern Midwest City on Post Road and becomes the third public high school in the Mid-Del School District.

February 3-July 31, 1964

Sonic boom testing begins daily in the skies over Midwest City and Oklahoma City and run for 178 straight days.

1964

The Oklahoma Journal newspaper is founded in Midwest City by W.P. "Bill" Atkinson as "The paper that tells both sides of the story." It goes into a pitched battle against E.K. Gaylor'd Daily Oklahoman and Oklahoma City Times and will last 16 years.

Mid-1960s

Midwest City and the Mid-Del School Districts begin diversifying racially, white and black. The trend continues and both the city and its schools become very diverse permanently.

January 1, 1968

Tinker AFB employment reaches the highest point in history to date. Nearly 25,000 civilians and 4,404 military members are assigned to OCAMA and tenant units.

December 18, 1968

F-4C Phantom Jet Fighter aborts a landing and damages about 10 blocks of power lines and poles and trees while unknowingly dragging 300 feet of steel cable and 3,000 feet of runway barrier system used for emergency landings. The housing addition damaged is again Glenwood.

October 7, 1969
TF-100 Super Sabre training jet crashed into the Glenwood Addition (five blocks from the school) destroying three houses and damaging several others.

September 21, 1970
Oscar Rose Junior College opens. It is later named Rose State College.

February 5, 1973
Mid-Del Schools Board votes to close Glenwood Elementary at the end of the school year 1972 - 1973.

May 8, 1973
A County Wide Capital Improvement Bond issue to raze Glenwood Addition passes by 88.7% of voters in order to "Save Tinker" from closing.

May 1974
Northrop T-38 Talon crashes into a home on Del Casa Circle. Both pilots were killed.

March 23, 1977
First E-3A Airborne Warning And Control System (AWACS) arrive at TAFB. Twenty-seven such planes will call Tinker home and serve a huge part of the base's mission.

January 13, 1978
Glenwood Addition closes (835 houses & one elementary school) returning 283 acres to open space beneath Tinker glidepath.

1978
Heritage Park Mall Opens on Reno Avenue.

January 20, 1982
Star Elementary School Explosion kills six students, one teacher, and injures 42 others when a boiler explodes in the kitchen.

April 7, 1983

First Sam's Club store opens in Midwest City.

August 8, 1985

A-7D Attack Jet loses power, catches fire, and crashes into a house (on North Air Depot Blvd. north of N.E. 23rd Street) after the pilot safely ejected. Two are killed, one injured.

March 23, 1988

First B-1B "Lancer" landed at Tinker Air Force Base

1990

Population of Midwest City tops 52,000 residents.

1993 and 1995

With the help of Oklahoma City, Midwest City, and surrounding communities, Tinker AFB survives two base-closure threats by the government.

March 20, 1999

Midwest City founder W.P. "Bill" Atkinson dies at 92.

May 3, 1999

F-5 Tornado hits killing three people in Midwest City and destroys many homes and businesses.

May 8, 2003

Another major tornado hits Midwest City.

2003

Rose State College dedicates the Reed Center
(a 60,000 sq. ft. convention center).

2003-2005

The south side of the "Original Mile" is razed, and the new Town Center Shopping Plaza replaces the original Atkinson Plaza (later Lockheed) Shopping Center.

February 15, 2010

Heritage Park Shopping Mall closes for good.

September 10, 2020

First KC-46A Pegasus arrives at TAFB for maintenance.

July 10, 2012

AFMC activates the Air Force Sustainment Center (AFSC) at Tinker AFB. Also the Oklahoma City Air Logistics Center becomes the Oklahoma City Air Logistics Complex and the 72nd Air Base Wing, the 448th Supply Chain Management Wing, and 635th Supply Chain Operations Wing realign to AFSC. Lt. Gen. Bruce A. Litchfield becomes the first AFSC commander.

2023

The B-21 Raider stealth bomber, an upgrade from the B-1 and B-2, arrives at Tinker Air Force Base.

Colonel Abigail L.W. Ruscetta becomes base commander.

- *Lists compiled from Tinker and MCHS History Center data and author's research.*

Bombers Coda I

Class of '64 Bequests

Here is a memory test for my 1964 graduating class of Bombers: How many of these former classmates can you remember, and do you have any idea why they willed the things they did to those who came after them? This is from a document for our class that was called "Class History and Prophecy."

Charles Jordan and Alexandria Rose will Richard Harrison and Carolyn Eames next year's OU Honors 'Banquet.

Tim Price wills his Mexicar to anybody, and the senior boys will to next year's senior boys the road map to Mexico that was willed to them by last year's senior boys.

Donna Earnest, Sherry Duston, and Nancy Bowers will the Del City Dairy Queen to Cookie Lawhon and Trudy Stuart.

The seniors of the "Li'l Abner' cast will Mr. Jay Smith to anyone who wants him.

Linda Crisman, Vickie Thompson, Marilyn Nelson, Lisa Burchardt, and Alexandria Rose will Harold Newsom to the girls.

The Secret Six will Sam 68 to Dianne Nelson. (This should keep you guessing awhile.)

Mr. Harris' first hour class wills his lectures to anyone
with the willpower to stay awake, and his second hour wills to Hercules Harris a one-year subscription to Motor Trend Magazine.

Rick Markham wills the Senior Class Executive Board meetings to next year's president. Good luck.

Graduating members of the Key Club will various toothbrushes, rusty tubs, cans of paint, mud, cow manure, and other prizes, plus five pounds of wet spaghetti to next year's initiation committee.

Ann Kelley wills David Owens to any junior or sophomore girl who can break down his anti-girl campaign.

Charlene Buckley, Phyllis Heartsill, Litha Keator, and Gloria Stoeckl will their tennis shoes from the elephant of the senior Class Float to next year's seniors.

Mr. Winn's Trig-Solid classes will to next year's students, Mr. Winn. With the hope that his jokes will improve.

Barbara Winn wills all her dad's old tests and one slightly used Algebra answer book to any junior or sophomore with enough money to buy them from Jim Winn, who has made fine use of them all this year.

The "M" Club wills the entire junior and sophomore pep club all extra athletic equipment in hopes that they will be good athletic supporters.

Grady McCorkle wills Steve Vargo's smile, that he didn't want anyway, to Knox Busby.

Mike Venator wills the sophomores to Lincoln Park Zoo.

Larry Burchart wills a good right cross to the basketball team to be used at next year's Northwest game.

Jed Dixon wills all his wrestling holds to Carol McCray.

I, Walter Smith, the most immature senior, will to Joe Flowers, the most immature junior, my mommy.

We, the muscle men of Li'l Abner will our muscles to Mr. Harris.

Ashley Rutherford wills his strength and masculinity to John Ware.

Certain seniors will to the library all the magazines we didn't check out. They're in the lockers. Go get 'em.

Mrs. Carlisle's fourth hour class wills to her all the patience, fortitude, understandings, and nerves we drained from her.

Mrs. Looper's first hour wills her Sue Madewalls' chewing gum.

Pat Shea wills her parking place at the Neighborhood Dairy Queen to anyone who wants to take up permanent residence there.

Bombers Coda II

Predictions for 1974

Here were a few predictions for what some 1964 MCHS grads would be doing in 1974, based upon their school interests and actions. They are from the pages of the *Bomber Beam*.

Ralph Lantz will swim the Panama Canal.

Jim Sanderson will win the opener for his team, the New York Mets.

Ann Kelley will still be running around the MCHS track field.

Derryl Millican will still be debating somebody, somewhere, over something.

Walter Smith will still be arguing with his teachers over his grades.

Barbara Winn will be running her own newspaper called "The Tigger Times."

Doug Bevoni will win the Masters Golf Tournament. If his actions don't get him disqualified.

Roger Brady will be living in Dogpatch.

David Guthrie's experience as president of the MCHS Student Council will prove invaluable to him when he accepts the Presidency of the United States.

"Tom Jones" will still be showing in Oklahoma City.

The MCHS Speech Department will put on a drama entitled, "Tom Jones."

Bob Osmond will wrestle Antone Leone for the title.

Mike Flanery and Smokey McKinney will still be going to rush parties.

The Northwest Classen senior boys will form an organization with the MCHS senior boys to be known as The Big Brothers of America.

The senior chemistry students will be experimenting with something called, "Sonic booms."

Grady McCorkle will still be pumpin' gas.

Jim Willis' first record will become a million seller. It's title: "The Great Yawns."

Judy Mikeska will still be ditching journalism class.

The Bomber Beam will be $10,000 in the red.

The Senior Class will vote English Literature as its favorite subject.

Alexandria Rose will still be the smartest woman in Midwest City.

Jane Vickers will be president of the Oklahoma State Cheerleaders Association.

Jay Anthony will have Oklahoma in his rearview mirror and be doing a job nobody else understands.

Chaniece Kennedy will still be bragging about MCHS to anyone who will listen.

Chapter Notes

1. Crowder, James L., "Tinker Air Force Base," The Encyclopedia of Oklahoma History and Culture, The Oklahoma Historical Society, Oklahoma City, Oklahoma, as accessed on September 21, 2023, at https://www.okhistory.org/publications/enc/entry?entry=TI004

2. Team Mighty, "The namesake of Tinker Air Force Base was a total badass," We Are the Mighty, June 27, 2022, as accessed on September 24, 2023, at https://www.wearethemighty.com/articles/the-namesake-of-tinker-air-force-base-was-a-total-badass/

3. Ibid.

4. Ibid.

5. "The Nazi German Air Force 1935-1945," n.d., Feldgrau German Armed Forces Research, 1918-1945, as accessed on September 21, 2023, at https://www.feldgrau.com/ww2-german-luftwaffe-airforce/

6. "Hawker Hurricane," BAE Systems report, n.d., as accessed on September 21, 2023, https://www.baesystems.com/en/heritage/hurricane#:~:text=The%20Hawker%20Hurricane%20was%20a,in%20the%20Battle%20of%20Britain.

7. "Spitfire: British Aircraft," n.d., as accessed on September 20, 2023, at https://www.britannica.com/technology/Spitfire

8. "The Army Air Corps to World War II," Air Force Historical Support Division as accessed at https://www.afhistory.af.mil/FAQs/Fact-Sheets/Article/459020/the-army-air-corps-to-world-war-ii/

9. "Selective Training and Service Act of 1940," as accessed on September 21, 2023, athttps://en.wikipedia.org/wiki/Selective_Training_and_Service_Act_of_1940#:~:text=The%20first%20peacetime%20conscription%20in%20the%20United%20States%2C%20the%20act,determined%20by%20a%20national%20lottery.

10. "260,270 Oklahoma Men Drafted Since Statehood," The Oklahoman, 1A, as accessed on September 15, 2023, at (https://www.oklahoman.com/story/news/1987/11/27/260270-oklahoma-men-drafted-since-statehood/62669846007/)

11. "Selective Training and Service Act of 1940."

12. Crowder, James L., "More Valuable than Oil: The Establishment and Development of Tinker Air Force Base, 1940-1949," The chronicles of Oklahoma 70 (Fall 1992).

13. Ibid.

14. Ibid.

15. Ibid.

16. Ibid.

17. Ibid.

18. Ibid.

19. Ibid.

20. Wikle, Thomas A., "World War II and the Story of Douglas Aircraft Plants in Tulsa and Midwest City," The Chronicles of Oklahoma, p. 389, as accessed on December 21, 2023, at https://gateway.okhistory.org/ark:/67531/metadc2017427/m2/1/high_res_d/2017-v95-no4_COO_Wikle.pdf

21. "Midwest City Douglas Aircraft Company Plant," The Encyclopedia of Oklahoma History and Culture, Oklahoma Historical Society, Oklahoma City, Oklahoma, as accessed on September 20, 2023, at https://www.okhistory.org/publications/enc/entry.php?entry=MI010

22. Ibid.

23. Jagla, Irene, "The Gooney Bird: Unsung Hero of WWII, Museum of Flight, August 29, 2018).

24. Wikle, p. 392.

25. Crowder, "More Valuable than Oil."

26. Wikle, p. 398.

27. Tinker Air Force Base History: Rosie the Riveter, as accessed on December 18, 2023, at https://www.tinker.af.mil/About-Tinker/History/

28. Nunnery, Jack, The Tinker Takeoff, December 23, 1942, as accessed on December 21, 2023, at https://www.tinker.af.mil/Portals/106/Documents/History/Rosie%20the%20Riveter/TT%20122342%20-%20Hazel%20Vickers%20Voted%20Typical%20Woman%20War%20Worker.pdf?ver=IA8-TtpjomY4pQwqtoDHEA%3d%3d

29. Wikle, p. 399

30. Crowder, "Tinker Air Force Base."

31. Ibid.

32. Craven, Wesley Frank, and Cate, James Lea (eds), "The Army Air Forces in World War II, Vol. 6, as accessed on September 21, 2023, at https://www.ibiblio.org/hyperwar/AAF/VI/index.html

33. "The Civil Air Patrol: U.S. Air Force Auxiliary, as accessed on September 21, 2023, at http://okwg.cap.gov/squadrons/tinker-afb.

34. Crowder, James L. Jr, "Tinker Air Force Base."

Chapter 2

1. Cindy Mikeman interview with, at Atkinson Heritage Center and Museum, Midwest City, Oklahoma, September 6, 2023.

2. Ibid.

3. Ibid.

4. Meacham & Associates, "Final Report: Reconnaissance Level Architectural/ Historical Survey of the Original Mile of Midwest City, Oklahoma, "August 31, 1992, as accessed in the Midwest City High School History Center on September 7, 2023.

5. _____, "Hometown Psychology: The Importance of the City You Live In," Well Told, as accessed on September 26, 2023, at https://welltolddesign.com/ blogs/journal/hometown-psychology-the-importance-of-the-city-you-live-in#:~:text=They%20say%20that%20home%20is,the%20person%20you%20are%20today.

6. Ibid

7. Bowman, Scarlett J., "W.P. 'Bill' Atkinson: The Ma who Built a City, Lost a State, and Challenged a King." Thesis submitted for a Master of Arts in History, the University of Central Oklahoma, spring, 2015.

8. Mikeman interview.

9. Bowman, p. 30.

10. Ibid, p. 31.

11. "Modest Start, Atkinson becomes Leading Builder," Midwest City News, 26 October 1944, 1; Atkinson, "Living Historical Center," undated, 13, computer hard-drive, AHC.

12. Hunt, Kay, "Midwest City founder's legacy lives on," The Oklahoman, March 29, 2017. As accessed on September 17, 2023, at http://www.Oklahoman.com/story/news/military/2017/03/29/midwest-city-founders-legacy-lives-on/60609875007/

13. Crowder, James L. "More Valuable than Oil: The Establishment and Development of Tinker Air Force Base, p. 238. Autumn, 1992, as accessed on September 15, 2023, at https://gateway.okhistory.org/ark:/67531/metadc2031684/

14. Lee, Susan Moeri, "The Social and Cultural History of Midwest City, Oklahoma, 1941-1959," p. 12, A thesis submitted for the Master of Arts degree at the University of Oklahoma, 1996, as accessed at the Midwest City High School History Center, Midwest City, Oklahoma.

15. Meacham & Associates, p. 11.

16. Ibid, p. 12.

17. Ibid.
18. Ibid.
19. Ibid.
20. Sutton, J.E., "History of Mid-Del Schools," as accessed on YouTube on February, 2022, at https://www.youtube.com/watch?v=tZi-6LYyLZI
21. Meacham & Associates, p. 14.
22. Ibid.
23. "How Curious," podcast episode "Which Oklahoma Community was America's Model City in 1951," by Rachel Hopkins, KGOU Radio, airing on October 17, 2023, and streaming at www.kgou/show/how-curious.
24. Ibid.
25. Ibid.
26. Bowman, 20.
27. Pam Olson Boettcher, interview with author in Norman, Oklahoma, September 8, 2023.
28. Mary Clem Good Morris, interview with author via Zoom, on August 27, 2023.
29. Kathy Jorgensen Stepanaskie, comment on the Facebook page of Midwest City Oklahoma History and Memories, January 18, 2024, as accessed on January 27, 2004, at https://www.facebook.com/groups/115957895581
30. Lee, p. 13.
31. Lee, p. 66
32. Lee, p. 68
33. Ibid.
34. "Modest Start."
35. Hunt.
36. Mikeman interview.

Chapter 3

1. Rothman, Joshua, "Are You the Same Person You Used to Be?" New Yorker, October 3, 2023, as accessed on September 24, 2023, at https://www.newyorker.com/magazine/2022/10/10/are-you-the-same-person-you-used-to-be-life-is-hard-the-origins-of-you
2. Ibid.
3. "Wordsworth, William, "The Rainbow," The Reader, as accessed on September 24, 2023, at https://www.thereader.org.uk/featured-poem-the-rainbow-by-william-wordsworth/
4. _____, "Seven things you might be surprised to learn about Citizen Kane," BBC Arts, as accessed on September 24, 2023, at https://www.bbc.co.uk/programmes/articles/527gjFsdyND-

DQvJsgmdc53x/seven-things-you-might-be-surprised-to-learn-about-citizen-kane#:~:text=%22Rosebud%20is%20the%20trade%20name,%2C%20which%20Kane%20never%

5. Figures in Landon Y. Jones, "Swinging 60s?" in *Smithsonian Magazine*, January 2006, pp 102–107.

6. "The Baby Boom," Khan Academy, n.d., as accessed on September 21, 2023 at https://www.khanacademy.org/humanities/us-history/postwarera/postwar-era/a/the-baby-boom

7. Hoig, Stan, "Land Run of 1889," The Encyclopedia of Oklahoma History and Culture," n.d., Oklahoma Historical Society, accessed on September 21, 2023, at https://www.okhistory.org/publications/enc/entry.php?entry=LA014

8. Boettcher, Lily, "Midwest City: Planning a Community, Planning Values," a paper presented at Yale University for American Cultural Landscapes, November 20, 2009, p. 9.

9. Ibid.

10. _____, "Midwest City," The Encyclopedia of Oklahoma History and Culture, Oklahoma Historical Society, Oklahoma City, Oklahoma, as accessed on September 15, 2023, at https://www.okhistory.org/publications/enc/entry?entry=MI009

11. Lee, Susan Moeri, "The Social and Cultural History of Midwest City, Oklahoma, 1941-1959," p. 137, A thesis submitted for the Master of Arts degree at the University of Oklahoma, 1996, as accessed at the Midwest City High School History Center, Midwest City, Oklahoma.

12. Morris, Mary Clem Good, interview via Zoom with the author, September 3, 2023.

13. Ibid.

14. Pickens, Mike, interview via zoom with the author, September 22, 2023.

15. Hawk, Michael, comments on "Midwest City Memories II" Facebook page, posted August 23, 2023.

16. Morris interview.

17. Patterson, Anne, exchange, September 6, 2023.

18. Bob Ard, comment made to author on August 23, 2023.

19. H.B. Atkinson, obituary, The Oklahoman, January 30, 1998, as accessed on September 29, 2022, at https://www.oklahoman.com/story/news/1998/01/30/hb-atkinson/62293174007/

20. Henry Croak obituary, The Oklahoman, May 1, 1995, as accessed on September 29, 2023, at https://www.oklahoman.com/story/news/1995/05/01/henry-croak/62392187007/

21. Kelley, Ann, "Midwest City to demolish shopping plaza," The Oklahoman, June 9, 2003, as accessed on September 29, 2023, at https://www.oklahoman.com/story/news/2003/06/09/midwest-city-to-demolish-shopping-plaza/62040151007/

22. Meade Rutherford obituary, Find a Grave, April, 1997, as accessed

on September 29, 2023, at https://www.findagrave.com/memorial/30703405/meade-rutherford

23. Marion C. Reed obituary, Barnes & Friederich Funeral Home, n.d., as accessed on September 29, 2023, at https://www.bffuneralhome.com/obituaries/Marion-C-Reed?obId=1546854

24. James M. Gregory obituary, The Oklahoman, August 25, 1989, as accessed on October 2, 2023, at https://www.oklahoman.com/story/news/1989/08/27/james-m-gregory/62603327007/

25. "A look back at some notable Tinker's leaders," The Oklahoman, May 14, 2017, as accessed on October 1, 2023, at https://www.oklahoman.com/story/news/military/2017/05/14/a-look-back-at-some-notable-tinkers-leaders/60599798007/.

26. Ibid.

27. Sessions, Barbara Winn, "Honoree Worked Alongside Mid-Del Legends Rose & Sutton," article prepared for the 50th Reunion of the 1964 class of Midwest City, High School, May 2014, as accessed on September 7, 2023, at the Midwest City High School History Center, Midwest City, Oklahoma.

28. Ibid.

29. "About Crest Foods," as accessed on October 1, 2023, at https://www.crestfoodsok.com/about.

30. "Oklahoma's Largest Employers," Oklahoma Commerce, as accessed on October 1, 2023, at https://www.okcommerce.gov/doing-business/data-reports/reports/oklahomas-largest-employers/

31. Ibid.

32. Ken Brust telephone interview with author, October 12, 2023.

33. Royal A. Brust obituary, The Oklahoman, May 21, 2006, as accessed on October 1, 2023, at https://www.legacy.com/us/obituaries/oklahoman/name/royal-brust-obituary?id=6865206

34. Dollye Barton obituary, The Oklahoman, December 28, 1988, as accessed on October 2, 2023, at https://www.oklahoman.com/story/news/1988/12/28/dollye-mrs-r-lewis-barton/62628835007/.

35. "Skytrain Theater," Cinema Treasures, as accessed on October 2, 2023, at https://cinematreasures.org/theaters/25990

Chapter 4

1. Beck, Julie, "The Psychology of Home: Why Where You Live Means So Much," The Atlantic, December 30, 2011, as accessed on October 10, 2023 at https://www.theatlantic.com/health/archive/2011/12/the-psychology-of-home-why-where-you-live-means-so-much/249800/

2. Lee, Susan Moeri, "The Social and Cultural History of Midwest City, Oklahoma, 1941-1959," p. 45, A thesis submitted for the Master of Arts degree at the

University of Oklahoma, 1996, as accessed at the Midwest City High School History Center, Midwest City, Oklahoma.

3. "Junior Police Reorganize," Midwest City News Leader," April 8, 1949.

4. Robert K. Junior, comments made on Midwest City Memories II Facebook page on October 6, 2023, as accessed on October 10, 2023, at https://www.facebook.com/groups/3185527945057775

5. Judy Mikeska, comments made on Midwest City Memories II Facebook page on October 6, 2023, as accessed on October 10, 2023, at https://www.facebook.com/groups/3185527945057775

6. Ellerbee, Linda, "When Television Ate my Best Friend," Weebly.Com, as accessed on October 9, 2023, at https://mrmorris7m.weebly.com/uploads/2/1/7/1/21719406/whentvatmybestfriendss.pdf

7. DeFrange, Ann, "Circle 4 Ranch, Foreman Scotty, Lassoed TV Era," The Oklahoman, Nov. 20, 1994, as accessed on October 9, 2023, at https://www.oklahoman.com/story/news/1994/11/20/circle-4-ranch-foreman-scotty-lassoed-tv-era/62408121007/

8. Ibid.

9. Beutler, Mark, „Variety in Store," 405 *Magazine (formerly Slice Magazine)*, December 28, 2012. 28 December 2012, as accessed March 15, 2020.

10. Wilson, Linda D. "T.G.&Y. Stores." *Encyclopedia of Oklahoma History and Culture.* Accessed August 2, 2017.

11. "Tinker Air Force Base Fact Sheet," as accessed on October 11, 2023, at https://www.tinker.af.mil/About-Tinker/Fact-Sheets/Display/Article/384766/tinker-air-force-base-fact-sheet/#:~:text=Today%2C%20with%20more%20than%2026%2C000,has%20642%20acres%20o

12. "How Curious," podcast episode "Which Oklahoma Community was America's Model City in 1951," by Rachel Hopkins, KGOU Radio, airing on October 17, 2023, and streaming at www.kgou/show/how-curious.

13. "Galloping Popularity for the Pony," Life Magazine, August 13, 1956, as accessed on October 16, 2023, at https://books.google.com/books?id=ekgEAAAAM-BAJ&pg=PA84&source=gbs_toc_r&cad=2#v=onepage&q&f=false

14. "Ten Fascinating Facts about the Shetland Ponies," Northlink Ferries, as accessed on October 17, 2023, at https://www.northlinkferries.co.uk/shetland-blog/ten-fascinating-facts-about-shetland-ponies/#:~:text=They%20are%20unique%20creatures,are%20also%20amongst%20the%20hard est.

15. "How Curious" podcast.

16. Ibid.

17. Mary Clem Good Morris interview with author via Zoom, September 1, 2023.

18. "How Curious" podcast.

19. Mary Clem Good interview via Zoom with author, September 1, 2023.
20. Cindy Mikeman interview with, at Atkinson Heritage Center and Museum, Midwest City, Oklahoma, September 6, 2023.Ib
21. Lee, Susan Moeri, "The Social and Cultural History of Midwest City, Oklahoma, 1941-1959," p. 59. A thesis submitted for the Master of Arts degree at the University of Oklahoma, 1996, as accessed at the Midwest City High School History Center, Midwest City, Oklahoma.
22. Ibid.
23. Ibid.
24. Ibid.

Chapter 5

1. Philbrook, Herbert A., "What Can You Do About It? Threat of Communism," film by the National Education Program, Searcy, Arkansas, as accessed on December 4, 2023, at https://www.youtube.com/watch?v=z_pVsGbtbuw
2. Nikita Khrushchev on QuotationsPage.com
3. Lewin, Moshe, *The Soviet Century* (edited by Gregory Elliott), 2005, as accessed on December 4, 2023, at https://www.google.com/books/edition/The_Soviet_Century/ETQpY-32DysC?hl=en&gbpv=1&dq=moshe+lewin+the+soviet+century&printsec=frontcover
4. "Statement by the President Upon Signing the Federal Civil Defense Act of 1950," The National Archives, January 12, 1951, as accessed on December 4, 2023, at https://www.trumanlibrary.gov/library/public-papers/10/statement-president-upon-signing-federal-civil-defense-act-1950
5. Ibid.
6. Lee, Susan Moeri, "The Social and Cultural History of Midwest City, Oklahoma, 1941-1959," p. 126, A thesis submitted for the Master of Arts degree at the University of Oklahoma, 1996, as accessed at the Midwest City High School History Center, Midwest City, Oklahoma.
7. Lee, p. 127.
8. "Oklahoma County Tornadoes," National Weather Service, 2022, as accessed on December 5, 2023, at https://www.weather.gov/oun/tornadodata-county-ok-oklahomhttps://www.weather.gov/oun/tornadodata-county-ok-oklahoma
9. "Duck and Cover: Bert the Turtle," (1951) Raymond J. Mauer (writer) and Anthony Rizzo (director), as accessed on December 5, 2023, at https://www.youtube.com/watch?v=IKqXu-5jw6o
10. Ibid.
11. Ibid.
12. "Duck and Cover: Preparedness Measure," Encyclopedia Britannica, as accessed on December 5, 2023, at https://www.britannica.com/topic/duck-and-cover

13. Jane Bogan, text interview with author, December 5, 2023.

14. Lee, p. 126.

15. Deal, Brian M., Timlin, Diane M., and Goran, De. William, "Urban Encroachment of Military Lands: Military Installations at Risk," US Army Corps of Engineers, Engineer Research and Development Center, January 2002, as accessed on November 14, 2003, at https://apps.dtic.mil/sti/pdfs/ADA401147.pdf

16. Ibid.

17. Bob Osmond, curator of the Midwest City High School History Center, in an interview with author via phone on November 8, 2023.

18. Sutton, James Edgar, "History of Mid-Del Schools," May 1982, as accessed on October 15, 2023, at, https://youtu.be/tZi-6LYyLZI?si=Ybo8iTgUlXjcf7oD

19. Donna Elledge, Facebook comment on Midwest City Oklahoma History and

20. Memories Page, June 1, 2020, as accessed on November 20, 2023, at https://www.facebook.com/groups/11595789558i/posts/10163685991680582/?paipv=0&eav=Afa9huaxq8nJqy6NbEe5Sijxl-FDeA5Uukl8EsxBU357PE5xzYCDhdDgXQeLnkIOBUHs&_rdr

21. Mize, Richard, "Position at end of Tinker runway dooms one of Midwest City's earliest neighborhoods," The Oklahoman, May 14, 2017, as accessed on November 12, 2023, at https://www.newspapers.com/image/452642033/?terms=neighborhood%20position%20&match=1

22. Ibid.

23. Ibid.

24. Hatch, Katherine, "Doomed Pilot Dodges Houses," The Daily Oklahoman, September 2, 1962, as accessed on November 20, 2023, at https://www.newspapers.com/image/453379116/?terms=crash&match=1

25. Mize.

26. Bonnie Hill, comments on Wikimapia, "Former Tinker AFB Housing Area," as accessed on November 20, 2023, at http://wikimapia.org/11690176/Former-Tinker-AFB-base-housing-area

27. Comments from a retired senior Air Force command pilot, via email, on November 18, 2023.

28. Mize.

29. Brewer, Graham Lee, "You just never know," The Oklahoman, May 14, 2017, as accessed on November 12, 2023, at https://www.newspapers.com/image/452643851/?terms=Tinker&match=1

30. Ibid.

31. Ibid.

32. Ibid.

33. Ken_____, commenting on Wikimapia, "Former Tinker AFB Housing Area," as accessed on November 20, 2023, at http://wikimapia.org/11690176/Former-Tinker-AFB-base-housing-area

34. "Sonic Boom," USAF Fact Sheet 96-03, Armstrong Laboratory, 1996, as

accessed on November 21, 2023, at https://gulflink.health.mil/aljubayl/aj_ref/ n10en040/sonic.htm

35. Ibid.
36. Lackmeyer, Steve, "Lowering the Boom: Supersonic travel dreams came crashing down with testing in OKC," The Oklahoman, Sept. 8, 2021, as accessed November 21, 2023, at https://www.oklahoman.com/story/news/2021/09/08/oklahoma-city-supersonic-travel-sst-dreams-ended-testing-okc/5700739001/
37. Ibid.
38. Ibid.
39. Ibid.
40. Levy, Larry, "Test Counted at 5 Pounds? FAA Denies It," The Daily Oklahoman, July 18, 1964, as accessed on November 19, 2023, at https://oklahoman.newspapers.com/image/451962439/?terms=sonic%20boom%20tests&match=1
41. "Sonic Boom," USAF Fact Sheet 96-03.
42. Nwanevu, Osita, "Boom and Bust" Slate, July 29, 2014, as accessed on November 21, 2023, at https://slate.com/technology/2014/07/oklahoma-city-sonic-boom-tests-terrified-residents-in-1964.html
43. Ibid.
44. Lackameyer.
45. "Decision Made Before Council Calls for Halt," The Daily Oklahoman, July 29, 1964, as accessed on November 19, 2023, at https://oklahoman.newspapers.com/image/451982560/?terms=sonic%20booms&match=1
46. Ibid.
47. "The Home: Learning to Love the Boom," *Time*, May 7, 1965.
48. Lackameyer.
49. Borsky, Paul N., "Community Reactions to Sonic Booms in the Oklahoma City Area," National Opinion Research Poll, University of Chicago, February 1965, as accessed on November 21, 2023, at https://apps.dtic.mil/sti/pdfs/AD0613620.pdf
50. Ibid.
51. Nwanevu, Osita.
52. *Time*, "Learning to Love the Boom."
53. Lackameyer.

Chapter 6

1. Pam Olson Boettcher, interview with author in Norman, Oklahoma, September 8, 2023.
2. Lee, Susan Moeri, "The Social and Cultural History of Midwest City, Oklahoma, 1941-1959," p. 88. A thesis submitted for the Master of Arts degree

at the University of Oklahoma, 1996, as accessed at the Midwest City High School History Center, Midwest City, Oklahoma.

3. Cosby, Hugh E., and Dona Belle, "People of Midwest City," 1980, p. 28, Cosby Cameron Publishing, Inc., as accessed at the Midwest City History Center, Midwest City, Oklahoma.

4. Cosby, p. 30.

5. Tharp, Bill, "Early school days recalled," Midwest City Leader, n.d., as accessed on September 6, 2023, at the Midwest City High School History Center, Midwest City, Oklahoma.

6. Sessions, Barbara Winn, "Honoree Worked Alongside Mid-Del Legends Rose & Sutton," report prepared for 50th Reunion of the 1964 Class of Midwest City High School, p. 2, as accessed on September 6, 2023, at the Midwest City High School History Center, Midwest City, Oklahoma.

7. Sessions, p.p. 2-3.

8. Sutton, James Edgar, "History of Mid-Del Schools," May 1982, as accessed on October 15, 2023, at, https://youtu.be/tZi-6LYyLZI?si=Ybo8iTgUlXjcf7oD

9. Sessions, p. 3.

10. Lee, pp. 66-67.

11. Sessions, p. 4.

12. Ibid.

13. Sessions, p. 3.

14. Lee, p. 67

15. Sutton.

16. Lee, p. 87

17. Sutton.

18. Ibid.

Chapter 7

1. Clark, Katy, "Those Middle School Years Might be Awkward, but Here's What They're Teaching Our Kids," Raising Teens Today, n.d., as accessed On October 22, 2023, at https://raisingteenstoday.com/middle-school-might-suck-but-heres-what-its-teaching-our-kids/

Chapter 8

1. Willis, Jim, "Daily Life in the 1960s Counterculture," pp, 32-33, (Greenwood Press. Santa Barbara, CA), 2019.

2. Willis, p. 32.

3. "Barbara Sessions: 2012 JayMac Distinguished alumni recipient," accessed on YouTube on October 23, 2023, at https://www.google.com/search?q=bar-

bara+winn+sessions&rlz=1C5CHFA_enUS992US992&oq=barbara+winn+ses-
sions&aqs=chrome..69i57j0i546l3.6030j0j7&sourceid=chrome&ie=UTF-8#fp-
state=ive&vld=cid:601ec934,vid:pbMfVX4YW8A,st:0

4. Ibid.

5. Tony Callaway Profile, Linkedin, as accessed on October 25, 2023, at www.linkedin.com/in/TonyCallaway.

6. Defense Casualty Analysis System, Department of Defense, accessed on January 30, 2024, at https://dcas.dmdc.osd.mil/dcas/app/conflictCasualties/vietnam/vietnamSum

7. Panels of the Bomber Vietnam Memorial Plaza, located in front of the Midwest City High School History Center, in Midwest City, Oklahoma.

Chapter 9

1. Ken Brust, interview via phone with author, August 31, 2023.

2. Lee, Susan Moeri, "The Social and Cultural History of Midwest City, Oklahoma, 1941-1959," p. 20. A thesis submitted for the Master of Arts degree at the University of Oklahoma, 1996, as accessed at the Midwest City High School History Center, Midwest City, Oklahoma.

3. Boettcher, Lily, "Midwest City: Planning a Community, Planning Values," paper for AMST207, Yale University, November 20, 2009, p. 8.

4. Boettecher, p. 9.

5. Ibid.

6. Mary Clem Good Morris interview with author via Zoom, August 28, 2023.

7. Jacob Wallace, "The Census Hasn't Always Counted Native Americans; Now It Tries." The Journal. Accessed on November 1, 2023, at SShttps://www.the-journal.com/articles/census-hasnt-always-counted-native-americans-now-it-tries/#:~:text=1930%3A%20The%20census%20includes%20an,the%20race%20of%20census%20residents.

8. Sheril Thompson interview via phone with author, November 5, 2023.

9. Ibid.

10. John Martin interview with author via phone on October 25, 2023.

11. Barbara Winn Sessions in text to author on November 5, 2023.

12. Graebner, William, "The 'containment' of Juvenile Delinquency: Social Engineering and American Youth Culture in the Postwar Era," *American Studies Journal*, Vol. 27, March 1, 1986.

13. Lee, p. 132.

14. Lee, p, 130.

15. Ibid.

16. "History of Star Spencer," as accessed on November 3, 2023, at https://www.okcps.org/Page/1643

17. Lee, p. 130.
18. Lee, p. 131.
19. Ibid.
20. Martin interview.
21. "All-Black Towns," The Encyclopedia of Oklahoma History and Culture," Oklahoma History Center, as accessed on February 22, 2024, at https://www.okhistory.org/publications/enc/entry.php?entry=AL009#:~:text=Many%20African%20Americans%20migrated%20to,rushed%20to%20newly%20created%20Oklahoma.
22. Ibid.
23. Bill Atkinson interview, as accessed in "The Social and Cultural History of Midwest City, Oklahoma, 1941-1959," by Susan Moeri Lee, as accessed in the Midwest City High School History Center, September 8, 2023.
24. Coen, Ross, "Sundown Towns," as accessed on November 15, 2023, at black-past.org/African American-history/sundown-towns), August 23, 2020.
25. Ibid.
26. Henderson, George. *Race and the University: A Memoir* (Norman/University of Oklahoma Press, 2010), p. 10.
27. Henderson, p. 11.
28. Green, Victor Hugo, *The Negro Motorist Greenbook* (New York: Victor Hugo Green, 1936-1966).
29. "Was Edmond a Sundown Town?" Edmond Museum of History, as accessed on November 21, 2023, at https://www.edmondhistory.org/was-edmond-a-sundown-town/
30. Martin interview.

Chapter 10

1. Molly M. Fleming, "These Walls: Building 3001 at Tinker Air Force Base," *The Journal Record*, October 9, 2015, as accessed on January 18, 2023, at https://journalrecord.com/2015/10/these-walls-building-3001-at-tinker-air-force-base-real-estate/#:~:text=Building%203001%20at%20Tinker%20Air%20Force%20Base%20was%20constructed%20between,n
2. Sam Eckholm, "Inside the World's Largest Aircraft Maintenance Facility," as accessed on January 19, 2023, at https://www.youtube.com/watch?v=SXBdw1Ty38g
3. Susan Napier-Sewell, "What Happens When Aviation Maintainers are under Stress?" July 20, 2020, TapRoot, as accessed on January 20, 2023, at https://www.taproot.com/what-happens-when-aviation-maintainers-are-under-stress/#:~:text=Distraction%2C%20fatigue%2C%20confu-

sion%2C%20inexperience,that%20have%20become%20temporar-
ily%20grounded.

4. Eckholm.

5. Ibid.

6. Ibid.

7. Brandice Armstrong, "24-hour Tinkering: Maintenance around-the-clock, Tinker Public Affairs news release, October 9, 2008, as accessed on January 17, 2023, at https://www.tinker.af.mil/News/Article-Display/Article/387404/24-hour-tinkering-maintenance-around-the-clock/

8. Ibid.

9. Howdy Stout, "Pivotal success," Tinker Public Affairs news release, September 18, 2009, as accessed on January 20, 2023, at https://www.tinker.af.mil/News/Article-Display/Article/386608/pivotal-success/

10. Ibid.

11. "Tinker AFB Reviews," January 9, 2004, Glassdoor, as accessed on January 18, 2023, at https://www.glassdoor.com/Reviews/Tinker-AFB-people-Reviews-EI_IE254067.0,10_KH11,17_IP2.htm?filter.iso3Language=eng&filter.highlight-Section=PROS

12. Regina Southern, comment on Facebook page of Midwest City, Oklahoma History and Memories, January 28, 2024, as accessed on January 29, 2024, at https://www.facebook.com/groups/115957895581

13. Tom Brokaw, *The Greatest Generation*, (New York: Random House), 1998.

Chapter 11

1. "Tinker Air Force Base," Military Installations, Defense Department Website, as accessed on February 2, 2024, at https://installations.militaryonesource.mil/military-installation/tinker-afb/base-essentials/major-units

2. Oklahoma City Air Logistics Complex, Tinker Air Force Fact Sheet, as accessed on September 15, 2023, at https://www.tinker.af.mil/About-Tinker/Fact-Sheets/Display/Article/384764/oklahoma-city-air-logistics-complex/

3. Tinker AFB History, as accessed on November 1, 2023, at https://www.tinker-afbhousing.com/history

4. Lockwood, David E., and Siehl, George, "Military Base Closures: A Historical Review from 1988 to 1995," CRS Report for Congress, as accessed on November 25, 2023, at https://apps.dtic.mil/sti/pdfs/ADA463013.pdf

5. Ibid.

6. Ibid.

7. McNutt, Michael, "Enid Rejoices; Vance Air Force Base Escapes Ax," *The Daily Oklahoman*, December 30, 1988, as accessed on November 28, 2023, at https://www.newspapers.com/image/452052625/?terms=

8. Brus, Brian, "Spirit Encircles Air Force Base," The Daily Oklahoman, June 6, 1993, as accessed on November 29, 2023, at https://www.newspapers.com/image/454558319/?terms=tinker&match=1

9. Godfrey, Ed, "Closing at Base Could Be Dire, Officials Told," The Daily Oklahoman, June 7, 1993, as accessed on November 29, 2023, at https://www.newspapers.com/image/454560473/?terms=tinker%20base%20closure&match=1

10. Casteel, Chris, To Community, Tinker Threat Wake-up Call, The Daily Oklahoman, June 27, 1993, as accessed November 29, 2023, at https://www.newspapers.com/image/454623306/

11. Casteel, Chris, "Tinker Survives Base Closing Ax," The Daily Oklahoman, June 6, 1993, as accessed on November 29, 2023, at https://www.oklahoman.com/story/news/1993/06/26/tinker-survives-base-closing-ax-unanimous-panel-vote-ends-anxiety-about-14000-jobs/62455462007/

12. Ibid.

13. Killackey, Jim, "Panel Warns Tinker to Face Realities," The Daily Oklahoman, June 6, 1993, as accessed on November 29, 2023, at https://www.newspapers.com/image/454558319/?terms=tinker&match=1

14. Casteel, Chris, "Logistics Center Plans Fall Short, GAO Says," The Daily Oklahoman, April 15, 1995, as accessed on November 27, 2023, at https://www.newspapers.com/image/454173308/?terms=tinker%20base%20closure&match=1

15. Beckloff, Lisa, "Middle-of-Week Visit Hinders Tinker Turnout," The Daily Oklahoman, June 9, 1995, as accessed on November 30, 2023, at https://www.newspapers.com/image/454489681/?terms=tinker%20base%20closure&match=1

16. Casteel, Chris, "Base Closure Panel Spares Tinker," The Daily Oklahoman, June 23, 1995, as accessed on November 22, 2023 at https://www.newspapers.com/image/454538985/?terms=tinker%20base%20closure&match=1

17. Hogan, Gypsy, "City's Economy Dodges 'Nuclear Warhead,'" The Daily Oklahoman, June 23, 1995, as accessed on November 20, 2023, at https://www.newspapers.com/image/454538985/?terms=tinker%20base%20closure&match=1

Chapter 12

1. U.S. Census Data for Midwest City, as accessed on December 10, 2023, at www.census.gov.

2. "Mid-Del School District," as accessed on December 9, 2023, at https://www.usnews.com/education/k12/oklahoma/districts/midwest-city-del-city-100599

3. "Tinker AFB Today," as accessed on December 10, 2023, at www.tinker.af.mil.

4. Ibid.

5. "Oklahoma City Air Logistics Complex," as accessed on December

9, 2023, at https://www.tinker.af.mil/About-Tinker/Fact-Sheets/Display/Article/384764/oklahoma-city-air-logistics-complex/

6. Kimberly Woodruff, "Tinker Weather Flight Aways on Alert; Severe Weather Taken Seriously," as accessed on December 10, 2023, at "https://www.tinker.af.mil/News/Features/Display/Article/846513/tinker-weather-flight-always-on-alert-severe-weather-taken-seriously/

7. "About Us," Rose State College Website, as accessed on January 27, 2024, at https://www.rose.edu/content/about-us/

Chapter 13

1. Erica Allaby, "The Three Stages of Returning to Your Hometown," as accessed on December 20, 2023, at https://www.talesofexploration.com/being-human/2018/2/5/the-3-stages-of-returning-to-your-hometown

2. "Quick Facts about Midwest City, Oklahoma: 2023 Population Estimates," U.S. Census profile, accessed on February 22, 2024, at https://www.census.gov/quickfacts/fact/table/midwestcitycityoklahoma/PST045223

3. Ibid.

4. "List of Dead in Oklahoma City Bombing," New York Times on the Web, as accessed on January 8, 2024, at https://archive.nytimes.com/www.nytimes.com/library/national/061497okla-list.html

5. "Rebecca Needham Anderson," obituary in Find a Grave, as accessed on December 20, 2023, at https://www.findagrave.com/memorial/8935187/rebecca-anderson

6. Melanie Eversley, "Iconic Oklahoma City photo caused twists and turns," USA Today, April 19, 2015, as accessed on December 19, 2023, at https://www.usatoday.com/story/news/2015/04/18/oklahoma-city-photo/25957831/

7. Carol Bolding Sykes, Midwest City High School Facebook Page, April 19, 2023, as accessed on December 8, 2023, at https://www.facebook.com/groups/337065601696470

8. Christian Tabak, "Tinker recalls the OKC bombing 25 years later," 72nd Air Base Wing Public Affairs, April 10, 2020, as accessed on January 2, 2023, at https://www.tinker.af.mil/News/Article-Display/Article/2145214/tinker-recalls-the-okc-bombing-25-years-later/

9. Ibid.

10. Adrian Walker, Evan Allen, et al, "Nightmare in Mission Hill," The Boston Globe Archives, as accessed on February 2, 2024, at https://apps.bostonglobe.com/metro/investigations/2023/12/charles-stuart/

11. Jim Willis, "The Ceremony that Wasn't," Retrospect, March 4, 2003, as accessed on January 3, 2023, at https://www.myretrospect.com/stories/the-ceremony-that-wasnt/

12. Cindy Jo Lopez, comment on Facebook page of Midwest City, Oklahoma Memories and History, August 26, 2015.

Selected Index by Chapters

(Main References of Each Entry)

About the Author

Anne and Jim
(Photo by Litha Brady)

Jim Willis is a veteran journalist, college professor, and author. He is Professor Emeritus of Journalism at California's Azusa Pacific University and has held tenured faculty posts at Boston College, the University of Oklahoma, Oklahoma State University, the University of Memphis, and Ball State University. He has written 18 books and holds the Ph.D. from the University of Missouri School of Journalism, but he an ardent sports fan of the University of Oklahoma, where he received his B.A.

He now lives in Winchester, Kentucky, with his lovely and talented wife, Annie. The couple have five grown children and six grandchildren. The Willis pair share their home with their beloved family zoo of four dogs and three cats.

Although Jim is now a Kentuckian, he continues to feel, *"Deep in my heart, Oklahoma will always be home ... even if my folks couldn't get me a Shetland pony. I made up for it later with four horses."*